T0120218

BOYS' BOOK OF

FRONTIER FIGHTERS

True Stories of Bravery from the Men and Women of the Plains and Prairies

BY

EDWIN L. SABIN

Author of
Boys' Book of Border Battles
and
Boys' Book of Indian Warriors and Heroic Indian Women

Skyhorse Publishing

Copyright © 2013 by Skyhorse Publishing
Originally published in 1918 by George W. Jacobs & Company

The stories included in this book reflect the attitudes of their times
and do not necessarily represent the views or opinions of Skyhorse
Publishing, Inc.

All Rights Reserved. No part of this book may be reproduced in any
manner without the express written consent of the publisher, except
in the case of brief excerpts in critical reviews or articles. All inquiries
should be addressed to Skyhorse Publishing, 307 West 36th Street, 11th
Floor, New York, NY 10018.

Skyhorse Publishing books may be purchased in bulk at special discounts
for sales promotion, corporate gifts, fund-raising, or educational
purposes. Special editions can also be created to specifications. For
details, contact the Special Sales Department, Skyhorse Publishing, 307
West 36th Street, 11th Floor, New York, NY 10018 or
info@skyhorsepublishing.com.

Skyhorse® and Skyhorse Publishing® are registered trademarks of
Skyhorse Publishing, Inc.®, a Delaware corporation.

Visit our website at www.skyhorsepublishing.com.

10 9 8 7 6 5 4 3 2 1

Library of Congress Cataloging-in-Publication Data is available on file.
ISBN: 978-1-62087-360-1

Printed in the United States of America

Ah, where are the soldiers that fought here of yore?
The sod is upon them, they'll struggle no more,
The hatchet is fallen, the red man is low;
And near him reposes the arm of his foe.

.   .   .   .

Sleep, soldiers of merit; sleep, gallants of yore.
The hatchet is fallen, the struggle is o'er.
While the fir tree is green and the wind rolls a wave,
The tear drop shall brighten the turf of the brave.

—From an Old Poem.

FOREWORD

The Boys' Book of Indian Warriors told of the deeds by the red Americans in defense of their lives and to keep their homes. This second book tells of the deeds by the white Americans, in defense of their lives and also to clear the way for their homes. It commences with the pioneers and hunters in the East, and continues on to the frontiersmen and soldiers in the West.

These are stories of bravery and of pluck amidst great odds. In many of the stories victory was won by the aid of powder, ball and steel, used manfully. In others it was won by sheer nerve and wit alone—for a good fighter fights with his heart and head as fully as with his hands.

Americans have always been great fighters, when called upon to fight in self-defense. They never quit until they are killed or triumphant; and although many may be killed, those they leave press forward again. In France the Americans "never gave up an inch." We Americans of to-day, looking back, may be proud not only of the part played by our blood in the World War, but likewise of the part it played in the days when, rifle in hand, we were hewing the peace trail in our own country.

Clothes do not make the soldier. Whether in buckskin, wool, cotton gown or army uniform, those men and women—yes, and boys and girls—of frontier times in the forest and upon the plains and prairies were soldiers all, enlisted to face danger.

It is largely the quick, dauntless spirit inherited from the American pioneers, hunters and Indian fighters of the old days that shone so brightly in the recent days when, in record time, we raised a gallant army of fighters, at home and abroad, against a desperate enemy.

CONTENTS

CONTENTS

LIST OF ILLUSTRATIONS

CUSTER'S LAST STAND

BOYS' BOOK OF FRONTIER FIGHTERS

CHAPTER I

THE CAPTURE OF OLD CHIEF ANNAWAN (1676)

BOLD CAPTAIN CHURCH IN THE LION'S DEN

CAPTAIN BENJAMIN CHURCH, born in Plymouth Colony of old Massachusetts, was a rousing Indian fighter. He earned his title when in 1675 the Pokanoket League of nine Indian tribes, under King Phillip the Wampanoag, took up the hatchet against the whites. Then he was called from his farm in Rhode Island Colony, to lead a company into the field. So he bade his family good-by, and set forth.

He was at this time aged thirty-six, and built like a bear—short in the legs, broad in the body, and very active. He knew all the Indian ways, and had ridden back and forth through the Pokanoket country, between his Aquidneck home on Rhode Island, and Plymouth and Boston on the Massachusetts coast. In his Indian fighting he never turned his face from a trail. The famous Kit Carson of the West was no bolder.

King Phillip's War lasted a year and two months, from June of 1675, into August of 1676.[1] Captain Church soon became the Indians' most hardy foeman.

He was constantly trailing the King Phillip warriors

[1] See "Boys' Book of Indian Warriors."

15

to their "kenneling places," routing them out and killing them, or taking prisoners, whom he spared for scouts.

At the terrible battle of Sunke-Squaw, when in dead of winter the colonist soldiery stormed the Indian fort in southern Rhode Island, he was struck by three balls af once. One entered his thigh and split upon the thigh-bone; one gashed his waist; and one pierced his pocket and ruined a pair of mittens—which was looked upon as a real disaster, in such cold weather.

It was while his wounds were still bandaged, and he was yet unable to mount a horse, that the bold Captain Church had a fierce hand-to-hand tussle with a stout Netop, which gave him great renown.

Now the Netops were of the allies in the Pokanoket League, and this warrior had been captured by a Mohegan ally of the Captain Church men. Captain Church wished to save him, in order to get information from him; but owing to a wound in the leg the Netop could not travel fast, therefore the Mohegan was granted leave to kill him, that night.

Accordingly the Netop was seated by the large fire, with a Mohegan at either side of him, to hold him fast until the tomahawk had been sunk into his head. Although Captain Church had seen much blood-shedding and had made short work of many other Indians, to-night he walked away, with his heart a little sick.

The Netop had appeared to be waiting for the tomahawk, as if he intended to die like a brave. But when the Mohegan struck, he suddenly jerked his head aside so cleverly that the tomahawk not only missed him

16

entirely, but flew from the Mohegan's hand and almost killed one of the others.

That was a surprise. With a quick writhe the Netop broke loose, and bolted headlong, fairly into Captain Church himself, among the baggage and the horses. This was a surprise for the captain, too. He grabbed him but could not keep him, because he was a naked Indian and as slippery as an eel.

Away they two went, both lame. The captain had not wished the Netop to be killed, but he was bound that he should not escape. In the darkness the Netop stumbled, and again the captain grabbed him. No use. This Netop was an eel and a panther as well— slippery and strong. A second time he wrenched free. Once more away they went, with the captain now grasping for his hair. On through the surrounding swamp they pelted, crunching the ice so loudly that the captain thought everybody within a mile should hear. And he knew that the swamp was full of other Pokanokets. However, that did not stay the angry Captain Church.

The Netop was getting off, when he was barred by a fallen tree, breast high. He began to shout for help from his own people, hiding in the swamp. Captain Church charged into him—and found *himself* seized by the hair! The Netop tried to twist his head and break his neck. Captain Church gained a hair hold; and he, too, tried neck-breaking. Thus they wrestled in the swamp, in the darkness, with their hands in one another's hair, and the captain bunting the Netop in the face whenever he might.

17

On a sudden there was a new sound. Somebody else came running. They could hear the ice crunching under rapid footsteps. Each hoped that it was one of his own party; but the captain hung on, like a bull-dog, and called in English.

Horrors! The on-comer did not reply, which was a bad sign for the captain. Very soon the man arrived. They could not see him and he could not see them; and the next thing the captain knew, a pair of hands were feeling him over, as if to pick out a good spot on him. They crept up to where his own hands were fastened in the Netop's hair. While the captain was still hanging on grittily, and expecting to feel a blow, down thudded the hatchet, right between his hands, into the Netop's crown.

It was the Mohegan!

Now that the fight was done, the Mohegan hugged his captain and thanked him for holding the prisoner. He cut off the Netop's head, and together they bore it back to the camp fire.

Of such bull-dog stuff Captain Church was made. His fight with the Netop, in the darkness of the dangerous swamp, raised him high among his scouts.

He finally cornered King Phillip in another swamp, August 12, 1676. There King Phillip fell, with two bullets in his breast from the gun of a deserter. Captain Church's Indians hacked King Phillip into quarters, to be hung upon a tree.

Only a remnant of King Phillip's people were left at large, under two principal chiefs, Tispaquin and old Annawan. Of these chiefs Annawan was the more

18

important; he had ranked as Phillip's head captain. In the swamp battle where Phillip was killed, his great voice had boomed through the mist of morning, calling "Iootash! Iootash!"—"Fight stoutly! Fight stoutly!" But in the mix-up he had escaped, and when the dew had dried the Captain Church scouts could not trail him.

Having shattered the league of the Pokanokets and killed King Phillip, Captain Church withdrew to Plymouth headquarters, to report. For the campaign his men were granted only about $1.10 each, and he himself was well tired out.

But right soon a message reached him, from Rehoboth, of southern Massachusetts north of Rhode Island, that Head Captain Annawan was "kenneling" in Squannaconk Swamp, and plundering the farms outside. Being a true citizen, and knowing that the settlers looked to him for aid, Captain Church, instead of resting up, sought his faithful lieutenant, Jabez Howland, and others of his former company.

"Old Annawan is out," he said. "He is among the last of King Phillip's men. I have reliable word that he is kenneling in Squannaconk and doing much damage. You have been poorly paid, but I want hands to go with me to hunt him."

"We will go with you wherever you please to take us, as long as there is an Indian left in the woods," they answered. Which made him very glad.

So again he set forth, from Plymouth, with Lieutenant Jabez Howland and a few soldiers, and with Scout Captain Lightfoot, the friendly Sogkonate Indian who had charge of the scouts. He led westward across southern Massachusetts to the eastern border of Rhode Island Colony. He arrived there at the end of the week. He had hoped to spend Sunday, at least, with his family on Aquidneck Island, just opposite, in the bay; but in the morning there came a courier to tell him that Indians had been sighted, landing from canoes upon Poppasquash Neck.

Poppasquash Neck was a narrow point, northwest of him, in the upper portion of Narragansett Bay. It is a fork of the same point upon which King Phillip had his "royal seat" of Mount Hope, and upon which the present city of Bristol is located.

Captain Church marched for Poppasquash at once; he was that kind of a man. He had to cross the arm of the bay here in canoes. By the time that he had made a round trip and a half, such a wind was blowing that he was stranded on the point side with only two white soldiers and fifteen or sixteen scouts.

Yet no whit daunted was bold Captain Church.

"My brave boys, if you are willing, we shall march on across to Poppasquash and see whether we may not catch some of those enemy Indians," he said.

March they did, through the thickets and swamps of the base of the main point, to enter the upper part of the Poppasquash Neck. Here the captain sent forward Lightfoot the Sogkonate, with three other Indians, to scout. Lightfoot took with him, as one, a Wampanoag of King Phillip's defeated army, named Nathaniel. He explained that Nathaniel knew the signals of the Annawan band, and would be a good decoy.

20

"If you come upon any of the rogues, do not kill them but take them prisoner, so that we may learn where Annawan is," Captain Church directed, to Lightfoot; and Lightfoot promised.

Lightfoot was gone ahead a long time. Captain Church and his little band proceeded, until they reached the narrowest part of upper Poppasquash Neck; and here he posted his men, and waited for Lightfoot to drive the enemy to him, or else appear and report.

He waited until dark, but Lightfoot did not come, nor did any of the enemy. So night fell without news or stir. This night he dared make no fire, and they had nothing at all to eat, for the supplies were behind with Lieutenant Howland. The scouts began to fear that Nathaniel had deserted—perhaps had given Lightfoot the slip or tolled him into ambush, for there had been several gunshots in the distance.

In that case, old Annawan himself was likely to turn up and make serious trouble. Therefore the night passed gloomily and hungrily, on this lonely, swampy Poppasquash Neck, with water at two sides.

As soon as day dawned, Captain Church took his party to a better position, on a brushy little hill just outside the neck. Scarcely had he done so, when they saw an Indian come running. It was Lightfoot.

"What news?" Captain Church hailed anxiously.

"Good news, great captain," Lightfoot panted. "We are all safe and sound and we have 'catched' ten of the Annawan people!"

Nathaniel had done this. First there had been
21

sighted two strange Indians skinning a horse in an old Indian burying-ground. Nathaniel had decoyed them on by howling the Wampanoag wolf signal. After they had been taken they had told of eight others near by. Nathaniel had howled those in, also. The ten had been carried to the rude fort built last year on the main point, of Mount Hope. Lieutenant Howland was waiting there, with them.

This August 28 was to be Captain Church's busy day. He and his men had had nothing to eat for twenty-four hours; but without pausing to eat of the horse-flesh brought by Lightfoot they hastened across eastward, to talk with the prisoners, and see what they knew about Chief Annawan.

They found the prisoners happy. Nathaniel had assured his friends that it was better serving Captain Church than hiding in swamps, and they now agreed with him. Indeed, they wished the captain to send out for their families, who were not far away. First the captain ordered that enough horse beef be roasted to last a whole day. Then he easily bagged the prisoners' families, until his captives numbered thirty.

These Wampanoags had been with Annawan only yesterday, but one and all declared that they did not know where Annawan might be to-day, for he never stayed long in one place. Then a Wampanoag young man asked leave to go out and get his old father, four miles distant in a swamp. Captain Church decided to go with him and explore. So taking a soldier, Caleb Cook, whom he especially liked, and five scouts, he

22

went—for he was a man who did things. He never missed a chance.

This time he rode horseback, being tired. At the swamp the Indian who was looking for his father scurried ahead, to howl the wolf signal. While waiting for him, the captain saw an old Indian man coming down through the swamp, with a gun on his shoulder, and with a young squaw close behind, carrying a basket. They were quickly ambushed and seized. The captain questioned them separately, after telling them that if they lied to him they should be killed. He questioned the young squaw first.

"What company have you come from last?"

"We come from Captain Annawan's."

"How many are there with him?"

"Fifty or sixty."

"How many miles is it to the spot where you left him?"

"I do not know how to count in miles," she said. "He is up in the great Squannaconk swamp."

The old man proved to be one of Annawan's councillors. He gave the same answers as the young squaw, his daughter.

"Can we get to Annawan by night?" Captain Church queried.

"If you start at once and travel stoutly, you might get to him by sunset," replied the old man.

"Where were you going when I seized you?"

"Annawan had sent me down to look for some of his Indians who were to kill provisions on this Mount Hope Neck."

"Those Indians have all been taken by me," Captain Church informed him. "They are with my men and will not be harmed. Now I mean to take Captain Annawan."

He asked his little squad if they were willing to pay Annawan a visit. That rather startled them. They made their reply.

"We are your soldiers and ready to obey your commands," said the scouts. "But we know Captain Annawan to be a great soldier, too. He was a captain under Massasoit, Phillip's father, and under Phillip also. He is a man of courage and strong mind, and we have heard him say that he will never be taken alive by the white people. We know the men with him. They are warriors and very determined; and we are but a handful. It will be a pity if after all your great deeds you should throw your life away at last."

"I do not doubt that this Captain Annawan is a valiant man," Captain Church admitted. "But I have hunted him a long time, and not until this moment have I got exact news of his quarters. So I am loth to let him escape again. If you will cheerfully go with me, by the protection of Providence we shall take him, I think."

The scouts agreed to go.

"What is your mind, in the matter?" the captain next asked, of Caleb Cook.

Caleb Cook was brave: a Plymouth man who had been in the fight when King Phillip was killed. Yes, he had tried a shot at King Phillip, there, but his gun had failed him.

"Sir, I am never afraid of going anywhere when you are with me," asserted Caleb Cook.

Captain Church made ready. No time was to be lost, for Squannaconk swamp contained three thousand acres, and if he did not start at once he might lose Annawan in the darkness. He sent his horse back. The old Indian said that the swamp was too thick with brush, for a horse. He sent the Indian young man and two other prisoners back, with the horse. They were to tell Lieutenant Howland to move on to the town of Taunton, but to expect him in the morning on the Rehoboth road—where he would surely come out, if he were alive, with Chief Annawan.

He kept the old man and the girl.

"Now if you will guide me to Captain Annawan, your lives shall be spared," he said to them.

The old man bowed low to him.

"Since you have given us our lives, we are obliged to serve you," he answered. He was a courtly old man. "Captain Annawan and his people are camped under a great rock in the midst of the swamp, north from here. Come and I will show you."

Thereupon Captain Church pressed forward to the vast swamp, with his one white man and five Indians, to capture Chief Annawan and his fifty or sixty.

The old councillor was nimble. He scuttled fast, but whenever he got out of sight from them, he would wait. They traveled all the rest of the day, until sunset. Then when amidst the twilight deep in the swamp they came upon the old man again, he was sitting down. They all sat down.

"What news now?" Captain Church demanded.

"We must wait here," the old man replied. "Captain Annawan is not far. At this time he sends out his scouts, to see that there are no enemies near about. They return at dark, and then we may move without fear."

When the swamp was dark, the old man arose.

"Let us go on," he said.

"Will you take a gun and fight for me," Captain Church invited.

The old councillor bowed lower than before.

"I beg you not to ask me to fight against my old friend, Captain Annawan," he pleaded. "But I will go in with you, and help you, and will lay hands upon anybody that shall offer to harm you."

They moved forward, keeping close together, for the swamp was growing dark indeed. Suddenly Captain Church heard a strange sound. He grasped the old man by the arm to hold him back. They all listened.

"It is somebody pounding corn in a mortar," they agreed; and by that they knew they were approaching the Chief Annawan camp.

Presently a great outcrop of rock loomed before them, and there was the glow of fires. The corn pounding sounded plainer. Now Captain Church took two of his scouts, and crawled up a long slope of brush and gravel to the crest of the rock pile, that he might peer over. He saw the Annawan camp. There were three companies of Wampanoags, down in front of the rock pile, gathered about their fires. And right below, at the foot of the cliff, he saw big Annawan himself.

Chief Annawan and several of his head men had made their own camp here. They had leaned brush against a felled tree trunk to keep the wind from the cliff face. The rocks overhung, forming a sort of cave that narrowed upward in a split; and at the mouth of the cave Annawan and his young son were lying watching the squaws cook meat in pans and kettles upon the fires.

The guns of the party had been stacked along a stick set in two crotches, and covered with a mat to keep the dampness off. Annawan's feet, and his son's head, opposite, almost touched the gun butts.

It was a snug, well-protected kenneling place, surrounded by the swamp.

The face of the rock pile was so steep that there was no way of getting down except by holding to the shrubs and small trees. That did not look very promising. So Captain Church crept back to ask the old man guide if there was not some other trail. The old man shook his head.

"No, great captain. All who belong to Annawan must come in by that way, down the cliff. Whoever tries to come by another way will likely be shot."

"Very well," said the captain. He made up his mind to beard the lion in the den. "You and your daughter shall go down before us, so that Annawan shall suspect nothing. We will follow close behind, in your shadows."

This they set about to do. The old man and his daughter climbed the slope of the rock pile, and passed over, and down by the narrow trail, for the fires at the bottom. Captain Church, his hatchet in his hand, followed close, stooping low and keeping in the shadow of his guides, cast by the firelight. His six men trod after.

The corn pounding helped them. Whenever the squaw paused to shake the corn together, they paused also, and crouched. When she began to pound again, they hastened. The trail ended just at one side of Captain Annawan. The old man and daughter passed on —and suddenly darting forward Captain Church stepped right over the son's head, at Annawan's feet, and stood by the stacked guns.

He was here. They knew him well. The surprise was perfect. Young Annawan, seeing, instantly "whipped his blanket over his head and shrunk in a heap." Old Annawan straightened half up, astonished.

"Howoh (I am taken)!" he gasped.

Then he fell back, without speaking farther, while Captain Church, with his men on guard, gathered the guns. No one dared to resist. None, there, dreamed that he had only the six men.

"Go to those other companies," ordered Captain Church of his scouts, "and tell them that I have taken their captain, Annawan, and it will be best for them to surrender peaceably; for if they try to resist or to escape, they will find themselves entrapped by a great army brought by Captain Church and will be cut to pieces. But if they stay quiet till morning, they will have good quarter and be carried to Taunton, to see their friends already there. As for you," he spoke to

Annawan, "you will be well treated, also; and at Plymouth I will ask my masters to spare your life."

The scouts made the talk, and brought in all the guns and hatchets, so that now Captain Church was in possession of the whole camp. His nerve had won out for him.

So far, Chief Annawan had not uttered another word. He seemed dumb with his astonishment.

Captain Church maintained a bold front, as though he truly had a great army at his back.

"What have you for supper?" he asked. "You see I have come to sup with you."

Chief Annawan aroused. He was a strong, burly man, and spoke in a deep voice.

"Taubut (beef)." He called to the squaws, bidding them bring food for the Captain Church men. "Will you have cow beef or horse beef?" he queried.

"Cow beef would pleasure me the most," answered the captain, in Indian. So he supped heartily upon cow beef and the dried corn that the squaw had been pounding into meal in the mortar.

He had not slept any for two days and a night and had traveled hard upon only one meal. Now he stretched himself out by the fire, to sleep for two hours while his party watched. But he was so nervous that he closed his eyes in vain. When he opened them, he saw that everybody was asleep except himself and Chief Annawan!

This was a curious situation—and not very comfortable, either. The moon had risen, flooding the swamp with pale light. He and Annawan lay for a few minutes, eyeing one another—the white captain and the red captain. Captain Church would have given a great deal to know what Captain Annawan was thinking. Presently Annawan cast off his blanket and stood up. Without a word, he walked away through the moonlight, until he disappeared among the trees.

Captain Church did not call out. That would have been sign of fear. But he was much alarmed. He drew the guns closer to him and shifted over to lie against young Annawan, so that if the chief found a gun outside he would not be able to shoot in without risk of hitting his son.

Pretty soon, here came Annawan back again, through the moonlight, with a bundle in his arms. He knelt beside Captain Church and spoke in good English:

"Great captain, you have killed Phillip, and conquered his country, for I believe that I and my company are the last that war against the English. Therefore, these things belong to you."

He unwrapped the bundle. It contained the royal treasures of the Wampanoags. There was a large wampum belt of black and white beads woven into figures of persons and animals and flowers. Hung upon Captain Church, it reached from his shoulders to his ankles, before and behind. There was another wampum belt, with flags worked into it, and a small belt with a star. And these all were edged with red hair got in the country of the Mohawks. There were two fine horns full of glazed powder, and a red blanket.

They had been the tokens of kingship, when King Phillip had sat in state. They had passed to Annawan, as the next chief. Now they had passed to Captain Church, the conqueror of both.

After having given them, Chief Annawan seemed to feel relieved. While the camp slept, he and Captain Church spent the rest of the night talking like brother warriors. Annawan told of the mighty deeds that he had done, as a young man under Phillip's father Massasoit, in battles against other Indians. Captain Church gladly listened. He appreciated bravery.

There was great joy, the next morning, when with all his prisoners Captain Church was met by Lieutenant Howland on the Rehoboth road—for nobody had expected to see the captain alive again. He sent the most of the prisoners to Plymouth, by way of Taunton, but he took Annawan and the scouts to his home in Rhode Island, and there kept them for two or three days. Then he went with these also, to Plymouth.

If Captain Church had stayed at Plymouth, very likely he would have saved the life of old Annawan, whom he much admired. However, he was ordered out upon another hunt, which resulted in the surrender, this time, of Chief Tispaquin. That over with, he went to Boston; and when he returned to Plymouth from Boston he found the heads of Annawan and Tispaquin cut off and stuck up for all to see.

This is what had occurred: Tispaquin had claimed to be a wizard whom bullets could not harm. "In that case," said the Plymouth people, "we will shoot at you, and if your wicked claim is true, you shall live"; so the government soldiers stood him up and shot at him, and of course he died. And as old Annawan could not deny that he had put some of his prisoners to death, he was shot, also.

Captain Church served New England in other Indian wars through almost thirty more years. He was made commander-in-chief of all the Plymouth Colony forces, and as major and colonel campaigned by horse, foot and boat clear up to Canada. He prospered in business, and likewise grew very large in body, until, in January, 1718, he was killed, aged seventy-eight, by a fall from his horse.

CHAPTER II

UPON the old Indian frontier of Virginia and Kentucky the year 1777 was known as "the three bloody sevens." The American settlers had crossed the Cumberland Mountains dividing Virginia and Kentucky, to make new homes in a fair land reported upon by the great Daniel Boone.

John Findlay of North Carolina had been the first to explore Kentucky, in 1767. His story of his trip and of the wonderfully fertile realm that he had discovered stirred the hearts of the Boone brothers. In 1769 Daniel Boone, his brother-in-law John Stuart, Joseph Holden, James Mooney and William Cooley, guided by the old but stout-limbed Findlay (a peddler by trade and a hunter by nature) crossed the Cumberland Gap Mountain of eastern Kentucky, and with horses and packs traveled still westward into that country where white foot had only once before trodden.

But they had confidence in John Findlay. Daniel Boone had scouted with him a dozen years back, when General Braddock, his British regulars and his Virginia riflemen, had been shattered by the French and Indians south of Pittsburgh.

They found Kain-tuck-ee to be all that fancy painted.

33

So four years later, in September, 1773, the two Boone brothers, Daniel and Squire, with their families and five other families and a total of forty men, started out to open the way in earnest. But before they had crossed the Gap, on October 10 their rear was attacked by the Shawnees and Cherokees. It was a sad day for Daniel Boone—his oldest son, James Boone, aged seventeen, was killed, and five others.

They had been on the road only fourteen days. So, to save the women and children they turned homeward.

But Kentucky was not forgotten. Nothing stops Americans when their faces are set westward, and the long trail beckons.

The next year Daniel Boone and party went into Kentucky again. They found James Harrod of Virginia building Harrodsburg, south of the Kentucky River in central Kentucky. He had come in from the north; Daniel Boone and companion Michael Stoner from the east.

This James Harrod was a man of valor. At sixteen years of age he was a young soldier in the French and Indian War. He loved the scout trail, and grew up to be one of the best sign-readers among all the "Long Hunters of Kentucky." He was tall, silent, swarthy—as dark as the Indians whom he tracked. They called him the "Lone Long Knife." When he was fifty years of age, or in 1792, he left his wife and daughter, on his last journey through the forests. After that February day he never appeared again, nor did word of him come back.

But in 1774 he had founded Harrodsburg—or Harrod's Fort, as it was known. Daniel Boone visited with him and his thirty. A company was formed of North Carolina and Virginia settlers, who by treaty with the Cherokees purchased all southern Kentucky. In March of the next year, 1775, Daniel Boone led thirty men who with their hatchets blazed a bridle-trail of two hundred miles, from southwestern Virginia across Cumberland Gap and on into the northwest clear to the Kentucky River. "Boone's Trace" and the "Wilderness Road" was the name of the path.

April 1 they commenced Boone's Fort of Boonesborough, on the south bank of the Kentucky eighteen miles southeast of present Lexington. Then there came the women, in September: for Boonesborough, Daniel Boone's wife Rebecca and their daughters; for Harrod's, Mrs. Hugh McGary, Mrs. Hogan and Mrs. Denton. These were the first white women in Kentucky.

There came, also, the same year, from the Holston River in southwestern Virginia, the noble Benjamin Logan, of Irish birth but as dark in hair and complexion as James Harrod. Since the age of fourteen he had been caring for his mother, his brothers and sisters.

While Boonesborough was being built and Harrod's Fort was not yet completed, he founded his own settlement of Logan's Station, or Fort Asaph, at Stanford of to-day, about thirty-five miles southwest of Boonesborough, and twenty miles southeast of Harrod's. Now, by the close of 1775, here was a triangle of three

35

white men's settlements, in central Kentucky. The "Long Hunters" had arrived, to stay. The first homes of any human being had been planted.

No Indians had placed villages in Kentucky. The Indians only hunted and warred here. It was to them the Dark and Bloody Ground. The Cherokees had sold, but the Shawnees and their allies of the Northern Confederacy—the Miamis, Wyandots, and all—with headquarters in Ohio, also claimed Kentucky for their hunting reserve. The Shawnees had not been consulted in the treaty with the Cherokees. Following the fierce and bloody battle of Point Pleasant in October, 1774, peace had been declared between the Northern Confederacy and the Long-Knife Virginians; nevertheless, here just before the war with England, British agents were stirring the Indians up against the colonists. Kentucky, said the Shawnees, must be cleared.

They swooped down upon the young settlements. On the day before Christmas, 1775, they attacked half-finished Boonesborough. After that, through some years, it was rare for a young man to die except from wounds.

By reason of the outbreak of the Revolution, in 1776, the Kentucky settlements seemed to be cut off entirely. The next winter the people of Logan's Station and the post of McClelland's Station fled to Boonesborough and Harrodsburg. In all that region there were only one hundred and fifty white men, to protect the women and children; but they were men such as Daniel Boone and his brother Squire Boone; the tough-skinned Simon Kenton whose touch-

and-go escapes are related in Chapter V; tall
James Harrod and Benjamin Logan; George Rogers
Clark, soon to found Louisville and to conquer the
"Illinois country" bordering upon the Mississippi
River; William Whitley, captain of Rangers; and many
another, every one an expert with the flint-lock rifle.

The year of the "three bloody sevens" dawned
peacefully. The Logan's Station families returned
home from sheltering Harrodsburg, to till their farms.
In March the Kentucky men were organized into a
militia: their posts supposed to be Boonesborough,
Harrodsburg and Logan's Station; their officers,
George Rogers Clark as major, Daniel Boone, James
Harrod, Benjamin Logan and John Todd as captains.
This same month some two hundred Shawnees entered
Kentucky, to wipe out the little forts.

On March 7 they first attacked Harrodsburg. Harrodsburg resisted so bravely that they drew off, to try
Boonesborough. A great storm of sleet and snow
halted them, and not until April 24 did one hundred of
them appear before Boone's Fort. Daniel Boone and
Squire Boone, their less than twenty men and their
heroic women fought the good fight and won; but it
was a close shave. Daniel Boone almost was tomahawked, and owed his life to young Simon Kenton.

The Shawnees under Chief Black Fish marched for
Logan's Station.

They should have tried Logan's Station first. It
mustered a garrison of only thirteen rifle-bearers, and
was the weakest of the three stockades. Now it had
heard from the two other forts, and had done its best

to get ready. But it was short of provisions and of ammunition.

The Indians cunningly took their time. At last the Logan people grew hopeful that there would be no attack, for nearly a month had passed since the attack upon Boonesborough. Early in the morning of Friday, May 30, Mrs. Ann Logan, Mrs. William Whitley and a negress servant went out to milk the cows; William Hudson, Burr Harrison, John Kennedy and James Craig were their body-guard. Suddenly, from a brake of cane, there burst a volley. The Indians!

The persons in the fort rushed to the pickets. They saw the three women and James Craig running wildly in. They saw John Kennedy staggering after. He had four bullets to carry. They saw William Hudson, dead, and being scalped, and Burr Harrison limp upon the ground.

In through the gateway rushed the three women and James Craig; protected by the rifles, John Kennedy lurched through, also. The heavy gate was quickly barred, while bullets pattered against the close-set palings. Then there arose the cry:

"Harrison! Look at Burr! He's trying to make in!"

He had fallen in the full open, half way between the fort and the cane brake. Now he was working hard to crawl for the gate. He could drag himself only a few feet at a time. The Indians let him alone; the men and women peered anxiously through the cracks in the palisades—his frenzied wife and children cried piteously, urging him on.

38

But he collapsed in a patch of thin brush, and lay lax, plain to see.

Captain Logan sprang to the gate.

"Who will go with me to rescue Burr Harrison?" he thundered.

The voices of the women were stilled; the men hesitated, looking one upon another. The Indians evidently were waiting for just such a try. How many lurked in the thicket? Who might tell? A report from those days says fifty-seven; chronicles say one hundred, two hundred. It is difficult to count Indians skulking amidst bushes and trees. At any rate there were plenty. One hundred had attacked Harrodsburg; a like number had attacked Boonesborough; probably one hundred guns commanded the gateway of Logan's Station.

It looked to be certain death for any two men venturing outside.

"Who will go with me to rescue Burr Harrison?" Captain Logan repeated, seeking right and left with his dark face and flashing black eyes. His brave wife uttered never a word to hold him back.

"I'd be your man, Cap, but I'm weakly yet," spoke one.

"I'm sorry for Burr, but in a case like this the skin is tighter than the shirt," muttered another.

"Will you let Captain Logan go alone?" reproached the women.

"No. I'm with you, Cap," exclaimed John Martin. "A man can die but once, and I'm as ready now as I'll ever be."

"Open the gate. Keep the savages off us. That's all we ask," Captain Logan ordered.

He and John Martin stood, braced for their dash. The gate was swung ajar, and instantly they dived through. But as if he had gained strength, Burr Harrison rose to his knees. Seeing, John Martin whirled and leaped back under cover again. He afterward explained that he thought Burr was coming in of himself, and rifles would be needed more in the fort than outside.

Captain Logan only paused; then, crouched, he darted on, for Harrison had toppled. During the space of just a moment or two the Indians were silent. Now, before he had reached his goal, a musket whanged, from the thicket—a second followed—the firing swelled to a volley, while the stockade answered.

Was he down? No, not yet. He had seized Burr, and hoisting him in his two arms was coming at a plunging run through the spatter of bullets and the drift of powder-smoke.

The gate swung wider. He was here—he panted in, out-sped by the balls but still on his feet. Eager hands received him and his burden; the gate slammed to and the bar fell into place.

"Hurt, Logan?"

"No. Never mind me; watch the walls."

There were bullet-holes in his shirt and hat. The gate and the pickets enclosing it were riddled, but by a miracle the lead had not touched his flesh.

The women tended to Burr. He was grievously wounded—he lived six weeks and died in his bed, which was better than dying by torture or the tomahawk. So Captain Logan's hero deed had not been in vain.

The rescue made the Indians very angry. They laid themselves to the siege, and so briskly they maintained it that there was no rest for the little garrison of only ten able-bodied men, nor was there any chance for succor from Harrodsburg or Boonesborough.

Within less than a week the ammunition was almost spent, and the food alarmingly low. Help must be summoned from the Holston settlement on the Holston River in southwestern Virginia, two hundred miles by Boone's Trace.

How many might be spared from the feeble garrison? Not more than two—not more than one; and after a short debate, Captain Logan himself set out, in the night of June 6.

It was a forlorn hope, but he slipped out amidst the darkness, by way of a loosened picket in the rear of the stockade, and vanished. The garrison strained their ears, listening. They heard nothing, and breathed a sigh of relief. For an hour more they listened, fearing sudden burst of whoops and shots. Silence reigned. Good! Captain Logan was through the lines by this time.

But could he make it, when all the surrounding country was being watched by the Shawnee scouts? He had planned to avoid the Boone Trace. That surely would be guarded close; it was the white man's road. He was to follow no trail at all, and the wilderness had swallowed him.

Two weeks passed. There was no token of any

nature from Captain Logan. Likely enough he had perished; the bullet, the tomahawk, perhaps the torture stake, had stopped him. His wife was in despair, and the garrison were beginning to despair, for the powder had dwindled, and the Indians had relaxed their relentless circle for never an instant. It seemed impossible that a man could get through them, going or coming.

In the night of June 23 the guards heard a scratching on the loose picket. A trick? Be careful.

"Hist! It's I—Logan."

What! They stood aside, with hatchets lifted; but he it was, for he poked a pack ahead of him, and slipped in after.

He told his story. Five hundred miles, at least, he had trudged, always at top speed, day and night; making his own trail, through tangled vines, across streams, up and down lonely gorges; and now he brought powder, and the promise of reinforcements.

In all his journey eastward and westward he had not been sighted by an Indian. It was a trip long remembered in the border country.

With such a leader, no garrison would yield. Logan's Station was filled with courage and hope renewed. It fought on, day after day, night after night, constantly expecting the reinforcements. Finally it seemed that Captain Logan's venture had been for naught; a month had elapsed since his return, and the reinforcements had not arrived. Once more the powder was low, and by this time the scanty provisions had been reduced to miserably small rations.

This was August 23. The end appeared near. On August 25 gun shots sounded, in the timber behind the Shawnee lines. Indians were running. Relief had come—the reinforcements were breaking through! Hurrah!

No! The gun-fire ceased. Hope died again. The Indians were too thick. Logan's Station settled for another night of waiting.

But the next morning, where were the Shawnees? From the stockade weary eyes searched to locate the shadowy forms. All was quiet. What had happened? If the Indians actually were gone, that could mean only one thing: relief. Could it be true, at last?

Within a short time, amidst the cheers of the men and the sobs of the women Colonel John Bowman led his column of Virginians straight into the widely open gate of the fort.

He had brought from the Holston one hundred riflemen. He had already been at Boonesborough—therefore his delay. From Boonesborough he had advanced for Logan's Station, sweeping the timber. The Shawnees had ambushed six of his advance scouts, and killed two. But here he was, just in nick of time, with his hardy Long Knives, whose rifles were as much feared as the rifles of the Long Hunters.

Logan's Station, Harrodsburg and Boonesborough were saved, for the present. The Shawnees, Mingos and warring Delawares continued to watch them close.

Benjamin Logan lived on, as scout, soldier and Kentucky statesman, and died peacefully in 1802, aged fifty years.

CHAPTER III

IN THE STOCKADE AT WHEELING (1777)
AND THE GREAT LEAP OF MAJOR MC COLLOCH

WHILE from Virginia, North Carolina and soon from Tennessee the American settlers were pushing on through Kentucky for the closed trail of the broad Ohio River, farther north another out-post had been placed at the river itself.

This was the Zane settlement away up in the panhandle of North-Western Virginia; to-day the city of Wheeling, West Virginia.

The Zanes, first there, were three brothers: Colonel Ebenezer, Silas and Jonathan. They all were of the roving "wild-turkey" breed, and bolder spirits never wore buckskin or sighted a rifle. A fourth brother, Isaac, had been taken by the Indians when nine years old, and had chosen to stay with them. He married a sister of a Wyandot chief; rose to be a chief, himself. but never lifted the hatchet against the whites. On the contrary, he helped them when he might.

It was in the summer of 1769 that the three Zanes led a party from present Moorfield, on the South Branch of the Potomac River in eastern West Virginia, to explore northwest into a country where Ebenezer already had spent a season. They reached the Ohio and looked down upon the shining river, and the lovely vales surrounding, where Wheeling up-sprang.

Ebenezer Zane, then twenty-three years old, built a cabin on a knoll near the river above the mouth of Wheeling Creek. The Zane family home was here long after Wheeling became a town. Jonathan lived with Eb; Silas put up a cabin beside the creek. The next year they went back for their wives and children; other settlers returned with them. Among these were John Wetzel, whose five sons, Lewis, Jacob, Martin, John and George grew to be such frontier fighters that Lewis was called the Boone of West Virginia; there were the McCollochs—John, William and Samuel— whose sister Elizabeth had married Eb Zane; and another of the Zanes, Andrew.

Those were days of large families.

Up and down the east bank of the Ohio, north and south of Wheeling Creek, the number of cabins gradually increased, until in the year of the "three bloody sevens" they numbered some twenty-five or thirty.

They were scattered here and there under the protection of a fort that had been built three years before by the Government. At first it was named Fort Fincastle, after Fincastle County of Virginia; the name had been changed to Fort Henry, in honor of the great Patrick Henry, orator and governor of the State of Virginia; but it was known also as Wheeling Fort.

And considerable of a fort it was, too—ranking second to only the famed Fort Pitt at Pittsburgh. It stood near the river edge of a flat bluff about a quarter of a mile up the Ohio from the mouth of Wheeling Creek. Its stockade of sharpened white-oak pickets seventeen feet high enclosed more than half an acre, with small block-houses or bastions in the corners, and with a commandant's log house of two stories, in the middle.

Inland, or east from it, there arose a high hill—Wheeling Hill. Between the fort and the base of the hill were the Ebenezer Zane cabin and the other cabins, on the bottom-lands, forming Wheeling.

To this time young Wheeling had been little bothered by the Indians. But the Ohio River was the border country; it flowed through a No-Man's Land. On the east and south the white people were pressing toward it, on the west and north the red people were seeking to keep its banks clear. The struggle waged back and forth. All the territory of present Ohio was red, and in Ohio and adjacent Indiana the Shawnees, Miamis, Wyandot Hurons, the Mingos, the war Delawares, and such, had their principal towns. The Wheeling settlements in the pan-handle were within short striking distance of the Indian strongholds.

The War of the Revolution had been in full stride for a year. The majority of the Indians of the northwest sided with the British, in the hopes of keeping their country from the Americans. It is said that Isaac Zane, the white Wyandot, sent the word of danger to the commanding officer at Fort Pitt. At any rate, on the first day of August, 1777, Chief White-eyes the friendly Delaware appeared there with warning that the Indians of the Northern Confederacy, helped by the British, were making ready "to take Wheeling home with them."

General Edward Hand of Fort Pitt dispatched a

THE GREAT LEAP OF MAJOR McCOLLOCH

(From an Old Print)

runner to Colonel David Shepherd, of Fort Shepherd, six miles up Wheeling Creek.

"The Indians are planning to attack Wheeling. You will therefore remove your forces from Fort Shepherd and rally all the militia of your district between the Ohio and the Monongahela at Fort Henry."

No regular troops might be spared by General Washington; they were needed at the front—and these were dark days for the Buff and Blue. The home guards, or militia, needs must protect the settlements on the far border. But Fort Henry itself had no garrison of any kind. The settlers around-about were supposed to defend it when defending themselves.

Colonel David Shepherd was lieutenant in charge of the pan-handle—which at that time included a slice of Pennsylvania on the east. He had under him a number of small block-houses. From these and the settlements he summoned eleven companies of militia. He also worked hard to put Fort Henry in good repair.

Had the Indians struck at once, they might have scored heavily, in spite of the fighting Zanes, Wetzels, McCollochs, and all. But they delayed, and by the last week of August Colonel Shepherd reported to General Hand:

"We are well prepared. Fort Henry is Indian proof."

He relaxed, and dismissed nine of the militia companies, so that only two remained: the companies of Captain Joseph Ogle and Captain Samuel Mason, composed mainly of Wheeling men. There were about sixty, in all.

The night of the last day of August Captain Ogle returned to the fort from a scout with twelve of his men. He had been watching the trails.

"Never a sign of Injun anywhere around," he and Martin Wetzel and the others declared.

The warning by White-eyes seemed to have been a false alarm, or else the Indians had learned of the preparations and had backed out.

That very night, however, the Indians cunningly crossed the Ohio below the fort, instead of above; there were almost four hundred of them—Shawnees, Wyandots, Mingos, accompanied by a white man interpreter. They saw the lights in the fort, and planned their favorite morning surprise instead of a direct attack.

So they formed two lines from the river to a bend in the creek, facing the fort and surrounding the settlers' cabins. A corn field hid them. The main road from the fort down through the corn field led right between the two lines. Then they posted six warriors, who should show themselves and decoy the garrison out.

Some of the militia-men were in the fort; others were with their families in the cabins, for after the first alarm the cabins had been used again. Wheeling slept well this night of August 31, with no inkling that three hundred and eighty or more red enemies were occupying its own corn fields.

A heavy fog dimmed the sunrise. Andrew Zane, Samuel Tomlinson, John Boyd (a mere lad) and a negro slave started out to hunt the horses of James

McMechen, who had decided to leave. All unsuspecting, they passed right through the first line of Indians. They met the six decoys.

For a few minutes there was lively work. A single shot brought poor young Boyd to the ground; in making for the fort Andrew Zane leaped a terrific distance (the stories say, seventy feet) down a cliff bank; but the six Indians did not pursue far, none of the other Indians took part, and Andrew Zane, Samuel Tomlinson and the negro reached safety.

"How many out there, Andy?"

"Six is all we counted. We saw no sign of more," panted Andrew Zane.

"By thunder, we can't let Boyd lie unavenged, without a try. That's beyond human nature. With Colonel Shepherd's permission I'll take some men and shake the rascals up," Captain Mason exclaimed.

Out he marched, with fourteen of his compapny. The six Indians decoyed them on. Those scores of fierce eyes that had been peering from trees and corn-stalks, waiting for the morning to break and for this very sally to occur, focussed on the sight.

Suddenly the war-whoop rang. Behind, and on either flank of the Captain Mason party the painted scalps and faces of the Indians rose above the tassels and brush—their muskets belched smoke and lead through the fog.

Wellnigh by the one volley two-thirds of the men fell; the others turned in retreat. Soon it become every man for himself. William Shepherd, son of Colonel Shepherd, almost gained the stockade. Shelter beckoned, faintly seen. But his foot caught in a grape-vine, down he pitched, head-long, and a war-club finished him. Captain Mason and his sergeant burst through the Indian line, and raced up the slope, for the protection of the loop-holes. The captain had been twice wounded, and had lost his rifle.

Midway, the sergeant dropped. Captain Mason paused for a moment, to help him.

"No use, Cap. I've got to stay. Take my gun and save yourself. Better one, here, than two."

It had to be. Captain Mason took the gun. Without a weapon, the brave and crippled sergeant died like a hero.

An Indian, tomahawk in hand, pursued the captain close. Captain Mason sensed the lifted hatchet poised to split his head. He was too weak to run farther—he whirled, to grapple. He had not noticed that the sergeant's rifle was loaded. By a vigorous shove he pushed the Indian backward, down hill, and the tomahawk blade was buried in the ground. The gun! It was loaded and capped! He leveled and fired just in time, and the Indian, at the very muzzle, fell dead.

The captain made onward. He concealed himself under a large felled tree; remained there for the rest of the day and into the night.

The people of the cabins and the fort had heard the fracas out in the fog. They could see little. Still not knowing how many Indians there were, Captain Ogle and twelve men sallied to the reinforcement. They, too, were ambushed, and wiped out. Captain Ogle himself hid in a fence-corner, until darkness.

Only Sergeant Jacob Ogle, his son, Martin Wetzel and perhaps one other man, escaped to the fort.

From the Captain Mason party only Hugh McConnell and Thomas Glenn came. Of the twenty-six men under the two captains these five, alone, ran gasping in from the deadly fog; and two had been badly wounded.

By this time the women and children, carrying the babies, and many of them still in their night-clothes, had scurried from their cabin homes into the fort. The mists were lifting; and barely had the gates of the fort been closed again when the Indian lines advanced upon the village. They appeared, marching to beat of drum, with the British flag flying; crossed the corn-field bottom-land and took possession of the village. The cabins and out-buildings swarmed with them.

From a window of a cabin near to the fort the white savage shouted a message. He promised mercy to all the people who would join the cause of their sovereign, King George; he had come to escort them safely to Detroit. And he read a proclamation from Lieutenant-Governor Henry Hamilton, the general commanding the British Northwest, offering pardon to the "rebels" who would renounce the cause of the Colonies. The people here would be allowed fifteen minutes to decide.

There were no faint hearts in Fort Henry. Colonel Ebenezer Zane replied at once.

"We have consulted our wives and children, and we all are resolved to perish, sooner than trust to your

51

savages, or desert the cause of liberty. You may do your worst.''

"Think well of that," retorted the Indian's spokesman. "I have a thousand warriors. They are rich with powder and guns furnished by their father at Detroit. Once you enrage them, I will not be able to hold them back. Then it will not be possible for you to escape. Better for you to save your wives and children by accepting the offer of the governor and yielding to your rightful king."

But a rifle bullet made him duck. The attack opened at once.

There were thirty-three men and grown boys in the fort; and as many women and children. Led by the white savage, the Indians charged the gate with battering-ram logs; the log-carriers fell, but a hundred warriors stormed the palisade and tore with their knives and tomahawks and fingers at the pickets.

From the loop-holes the long rifles cracked in a steady drum-fire. Every man and boy who could raise a muzzle aimed and fired and aimed and fired again. Every woman was busy—running bullets, filling powder flasks, loading rifles and leaning them ready for the eager, groping hands, and serving out water and food.

Two of the strongest women, Mothers Glum and Betsy Wheat, took station at loop-holes and shot the same as the men. Border women, they, who well knew the uses of a rifle.

A dummy cannon, of painted wood, had been mounted upon the flat roof of the commandant's quarters. But the Indian soon saw that it did not awaken. They laughed and jeered, and grew bolder.

Within the fort all was a reek of powder-smoke; the stout pickets quivered to the pelting balls—every loop-hole was a target. Never did a garrison work harder; there was not an idle hand, for the wounded crawled about, helping.

The Indians withdrew as quickly as they had come, and from the cover of the cabins shot furiously. In the afternoon they tried once more. They divided, and launched a heavy attack upon the south end of the fort. The garrison rushed to repel. A cry arose:

"Here! In the front! Quick!"

The attack had been a feint—battering-rams were crashing against the gates again. Back to defend the gates ran the men, and the enemy did not get in.

Toward evening the attacks lessened. The little garrison had a breathing space, sorely needed. Their faces were grimy, their eyes wearied, their rifles fouled in spite of the frequent cleanings by the women. Fortunately the fort had its own well—but how long would the ammunition and provisions last?

That proved to be a hideous night. About nine o'clock the Indians rallied, in a third attack. They fired the cabins and out-buildings before the fort; the blaze gave them light. All was pandemonium. Colonel Zane saw his home go up in flame and smoke, while the feathered, shrieking foe danced and capered and deluged the fort with lead. The whole village blazed, and the frightened cows and horses and dogs scampered in slaughter.

The fort showed no lights; the Indians' figures were outlined blackly, and the rifles of the Zanes, the Wetzels, and the others—every man a dead shot—picked them off.

So the night attacks failed. Morning brought a pleasant surprise. Colonel Andrew Swearingen, Captain Bilderdock and Private Boshears entered at the rear of the fort, having climbed up from the river. They brought the news that they had left twelve men, near by, from Fort Holliday, twenty-four miles above. But they had feared, by reason of the burning houses, that Fort Henry had been taken.

"Not yet, sir," reproved Colonel Zane. "Not while we have a bullet for a rifle."

Back went the three, to the boat, and the twelve men were brought in.

The Indians had been strangely quiet since before daylight. Had they actually quit, defeated! Who might say? It was decided to send out two scouts, to see. The scouts stole as far as the corn-field and sighted nothing but the plundered, smoking homes, the carcasses of the cattle, and the bloody trail of bodies that had been dragged off. Not a shot was fired at them.

Scarcely had they returned, hopeful, and Colonel Ebenezer Zane was about to lead out a larger force, when they all heard a cheer. They looked. Hurrah! Another company of men, ahorse, were galloping across the bottom, for the top of the bluff, and the fort gates.

"It's Major McColloch! It's Sam McColloch, from Short Creek! Huzza! Huzza!"

Short Creek was a dozen miles north. The McCollochs lived there. Here they came—the Short Creek settlers, business bent.

And on a sudden, as the battered double gates of the fort swung, the Indians sprang from the very ground, and charged to cut off the galloping company. 'Twas a race for life or death. Shooting right and left, the Short Creek riders tore on. They were winning, they were winning. Major Sam McColloch veered aside, to let his men pass. He was resolved that not one should fail. It was a generous act—the act of a real captain. But he lingered too long. The Indians were upon him—they out-stripped him, as he turned late, and before his horse had caught its stride they were between him and the gates.

He wheeled around, and bending low to avoid the bullets he sped at a tangent in the opposite direction, for the timber of Wheeling Hill. The Indians afoot could not catch him, no bullet caught him; he would make it— he would make it; there he goes, up the hill. He was safe—but was he?

He had planned to reach another fort: Van Metre's Fort, a block-house beyond the hill. And he himself thought that he was safe, until, galloping more easily along the brow of the hill, he ran squarely into another band of Indians, trooping to the siege of Fort Henry.

The Indians recognized him. They all knew Sam McColloch and his white horse; they asked no better prize.

"Sam! Now we got you, Sam!" They spread, to take him alive.

Again he wheeled. There were foes in front of him, foes closing in hot behind him, and a dusky line extending on his right. On his left the hill ended in a precipice. He chose the precipice, and with his moccasined heels hammered his horse straight for it.

Yelling gleefully, the Indians ran after. Now they had Sam.

Just as the foremost arrived at the spot where Major Sam should be at bay, they heard a crashing of brush and branches, a grinding of rock and gravel. They peered over. It was three hundred feet to the creek below—and plunging, scrambling, now on its haunches, now on its nose, the white horse was bounding, leaping, sprawling, already half way down, with the major firmly astride, reins in one hand, rifle in the other.

For one hundred feet there was a sheer drop that might have daunted even a deer. But the horse had taken it—he had struck on his feet, where the rougher slope commenced; from there he had slid, braced, and scratching fire from the rock; he was still sliding and pitching. Other Indians panted in, to peer. Presently the defiant shout of Major McColloch echoed up to them. He flourished his rifle, and splashing through the creek went clattering into the timbered flat on the other side.

Major McColloch's Leap was a famous spot through many years.

The reinforcements to the fort discouraged the Indians. It was saved. Major McColloch also had been saved, but the red enemy did get him, at last, five years later.

That was the fall of 1782. He and his brother John were looking for Indian sign, out of the same Fort Van Metre which was located east of the Short Creek settlement, over near the Monongahela River. They made a circuit west, almost down to Wheeling, and on July 30 were circuiting back by way of Short Creek, for Van Metre's again, without having discovered a single track, when from the bushes half a dozen guns opened on them.

Major Sam wilted in his seat and fell to the ground dead. John's horse crumpled under him, dead also, but he himself was wounded only by a scratch across his hip.

He saw that Sam was dead; the Indians were yelling—and as quick as thought he had sprung to his brother's horse, and was away, to give the alarm at Van Metre's. He looked back. The Indians were flocking into the trail, and one was about to scalp Sam. John drew rein, threw his rifle to his shoulder, the ball sped true. That Indian took no scalp.

John reached Van Metre's. The next day Major Sam McColloch's body was rescued. The Indians had eaten his heart, to make them as bold, they said in after years, as he had been.

CHAPTER IV

BIG TURTLE BREAKS THE NET (1778)
AND MEETS HIS FATHER AT BOONESBOROUGH

AT the beginning of the year 1778 the settlers of Boonesborough found themselves again out of salt. Salt is a habit. White people, red people and all animals get along very well with no salt, until they have learned the taste of it; and then they will travel almost any distance to get it. Salt licks are famous places for deer.

The Licking River of northeastern Kentucky was named by reason of the salty springs along its course. It lay about forty miles northeast from Boonesborough. Boonesborough itself had been planted only some sixty yards from a small salt lick, but this proved not enough. So on January 8 Daniel Boone led thirty men and several horses packed with large "boiling pans," to the Lower Blue Licks of the Licking River.

The process of making salt here was slow. Eight hundred and forty gallons of the water needs must be boiled down, to obtain one bushel of salt. But there was no great hurry. It was the winter season, when the Indians usually stayed home.

Two or three of the men hunted for meat, while the others made salt. They all lived well; game was plenty in the neighborhood of licks. A month had passed.

58

On Saturday, February 7, Daniel Boone was hunting by himself, with horse and rifle, in a snow-storm. He had killed a buffalo, tied the best of the meat upon his horse, and was trudging for camp, when four Indians surprised him.

For a few moments he worked fast, to defend himself, untie the meat, mount his horse and escape. But the thongs were stiff with the cold. He, too, was stiff, and his fingers grew numb. He sprang behind a tree, his rifle ready, but saw himself surrounded.

The four Indians were shielded, likewise. They laughed at his efforts, and waxed bolder. They had Daniel Boone!

"Come out, Boone," they called. "Come out. No fight, no get hurt. Many Injuns near."

So he wisely surrendered before he lost his scalp.

It was well that he had done this. The four Indians took him to their main party. There were one hundred and two Shawnees, altogether, and two white allies, marching down under Chiefs Munseka and Black Fish to attack Boonesborough and avenge the murder, last fall, of the Chief Corn-stalk party when prisoners in the American fort at Point Pleasant on the West Virginia side of the Ohio River.[1]

The capture of Captain Daniel Boone was hailed with great joy. The Shawnees scarcely had expected to achieve this feat. Once before he had been taken, but had escaped while his guards were drunk. He was a hard man to hold; now they were determined to keep him.

[1] See "Boys' Book of Indian Warriors."

They seemed to know that he and his men had gone out from Boonesborough, salt-making. That was why they had chosen this time for the attack. Now they demanded that he tell his men at the licks to surrender likewise.

"We will surprise them, too, and kill them. Or let them surrender and they shall not be harmed," said Black Fish.

Daniel Boone had been thinking rapidly. He understood Indian nature. The Shawnees were treating him kindly—they respected him as a great chief who had always met them fairly. He had killed a number of their warriors, but only when fighting man to man against odds. He trusted the word of Black Fish.

Burdened with prisoners got at a bargain, so to speak, the Shawnees might prefer to go home rather than attack Boonesborough. But if his men fought and killed, they likely enough would be cut to pieces; the Shawnees, blood maddened, would attack Boonesborough—and woe to the women and children!

"I will tell them to surrender," he promised. "I have your word."

"That is good," Black Fish answered. "They shall not be harmed."

In the morning they all marched the few miles to the Blue Licks camp. Covered by the Indians' tomahawks and guns, he stood forth, at the edge of the snowy timber, and hallooed. He stated just what had happened, and what was likely to happen now if they resisted.

At the Siege of Boonesborough

(From an Old Print)

The fact that he himself had surrendered scored heavily. He was not a man to give up without good cause.

"Boone is prisoner!"

The sight rather took the tuck out of the salt-makers. They knew him for a man of sound common-sense; his word, in Indian matters, was law; and they surrendered, also. But it was a bitter pill.

However, Chief Black Fish proved true. Two of the camp hunters, Thomas Brooks and Flanders Callaway, were still out; and two of the salt-makers had returned to Boonesborough, with salt and the news that all was prosperous at the Licks. This left twenty-seven to march with the Shawnees.

As Daniel Boone had hoped, instead of continuing on to Boonesborough the Shawnees hastened northward, to display their triumph in their town of Little Chillicothe on the Little Miami River in southwestern Ohio. Twenty-seven prisoners, without the loss of a scalp! And American prisoners were worth money, these days. The British father at Detroit was paying $100 for each one brought in to him.

Knowing this, the Boone men were encouraged to believe that none of them would be tortured; for their bodies were more valuable than their scalps.

It was a ten days' journey, in very cold weather, to Little Chillicothe. Daniel Boone says that on the way his party "received as good treatment as prisoners could expect from savages." The good treatment was not broken. He recalled that last year James Harrod, of Harrod's Fort, had wounded a Shawnee, then had nursed him in a cave and let him go. Possibly this was one reason for the kindness of the Shawnees.

At any rate, he was given the name Big Turtle, because he was so strongly built, and was adopted as a son by Chief Black Fish. Sixteen of the men likewise were then adopted, by chiefs and old women and warriors.

Big Turtle tried to bear his new honors modestly. He and the others worried considerably about their families, down at Boonesborough. What would be the feelings there, when nobody returned from the Blue Licks! Still, they could not help themselves. Big Turtle counseled patience, and set the example. He was a silent kind of a man, who bided his time until the right opportunity should come.

On March 10, about three weeks after their arrival at Chillicothe, he, and the ten men who had not been adopted were taken north to Detroit. There the ten men were sold, for $100 apiece, in goods. Big Turtle was proudly placed on exhibition, but he was not for sale.

The fame of Daniel Boone of Kentucky had spread widely. Now here he was—a tall, strongly-framed, slightly stooped man, with a long and noiseless stride and a low and quiet voice. He wore buckskin. His face was high-cheeked and thin, his nose a little hooked, his chin firm.

The lieutenant-governor at Detroit, General Hamilton, offered Black Fish $500 for him. Black Fish refused.

"I will not sell. He is a great captain. He is my

son. He will stay with me. You see that I have him."

The English in Detroit made much of Daniel Boone. They liked his manners. They entertained him, and questioned him about his adventures, and offered him money.

"I thank you," he answered, "but I cannot accept, for I should not be able to repay."

Governor Hamilton also treated him well; insisted that he be ransomed in some way, so that he might return home on parole; otherwise he might yet be killed, should the Indians get angry. But Big Turtle shook his head. He had rather go back to Chillicothe and take his chances.

Having exhibited him for two weeks, Chief Black Fish and warriors escorted him back to Chillicothe. They left Detroit on April 10, and were fifteen days on the trail: another disagreeable march. Big Turtle made no complaint, he acted as much Indian as they, and they thought more highly of him than ever. They marveled that a white man should equal them.

Pretty soon, as he had not tried to escape, and did not sulk or shirk, they grew to look upon him as one of them forever. Did he not mingle with them, and eat as they ate, and sleep as they slept, and appear perfectly satisfied? Other white men had become Indians; so why not he? The Indian life was the best life, the Shawnees the greatest of nations, and he would be a chief!

A cunning man, was Daniel Boone. They could not see behind his face. At the shooting matches he allowed them to beat him. This pleased them immensely; they did not suspect that he planted his balls precisely where he had purposely aimed; and that he was wise enough to know that if he beat an Indian, the Indian would be his enemy. Instead, he gained a friend with every shot. They sent him out hunting, under guard. He brought in deer, and gave the meat away.

Finally, to test him, they sent him out alone—but they watched him. He did not attempt to run off; he came back, with more meat. He was well aware that they had watched him, but he said nothing about it. Then Chief Black Fish decided to trust him completely. He only counted the bullets, each time, by doling out two or three.

"Here are your bullets. We know you never miss. For each bullet, a deer."

"That is good," replied Big Turtle.

He was smarter than they. In the woods he cut a bullet in two, and used half charges of powder. Two deer, to each ball and each full charge of powder! In this way he gradually laid aside ammunition for future use.

He frequently wondered about Boonesborough. How was the place getting along? How were his family? No words came up from there. But if it had been attacked, he would have heard.

On the first of June the Black Fish family took him eastward to some salt licks on the Scioto River, and put him at work making salt. This caused him to think of home more than ever, if that were possible. After he had been there ten days he was taken back to Chillicothe, and he beheld an alarming sight.

One hundred and fifty chiefs and warriors were already "painted and armed in a frightful manner," about to start against Boonesborough! They had made complete preparations while he was absent. Now he heard the talk, which he pretended not to understand, but he saw that he must escape at once and carry warning.

He had to wait a week before his chance opened. All that time he was on pins and needles, lest the Indians leave before him. Yet he dared not so much as flicker an eye. He had to laugh and loaf and eat and sleep, the same as usual.

He dared not hurry, either. If he tried to hunt, before-time, likely enough he would be frowned upon and maybe tied up. So he waited. He felt certain that once started, he could out-travel the warriors, did they not have too much of a lead.

Toward the close of the first week they were still in the town, waiting for other bands and for orders from Detroit. On the night of June 15 Big Turtle said to his father Black Fish:

"The meat is low. To-morrow morning I will hunt for more."

"You are right, my son. It is time. Go, as you say."

The bullets were doled out: two or three. The powder was measured. Early in the morning of June 16 Big Turtle strode forth, into the forest. He did not hurry; but when far from sight of spies he went to his

65

câche of ammunition, scooped up the powder and lead hidden there, and ran.

Before night there would be four hundred and fifty Shawnee warriors eager for Captain Boone; if he was caught, he surely would be tortured and killed; even Black Fish could not save him. And Boonesborough would fall.

Luckily, the Indians would not be looking for him until later in the day. He was supposed to be hunting. Now, with this head-start, could he but reach the Ohio River! Once across the Ohio, and he would feel safe, for he knew the Kentucky country.

Never had he traveled so fast; never before had he taken such pains to leave a blind trail. He did not stop to eat nor to sleep; and when, on the second day, he emerged upon the banks of the broad Ohio River, the current was swirling full and muddy, swollen by the June freshets.

Daniel Boone was no swimmer to brag of; not with rifle and powder, in such a river. For a moment he was daunted, but he swiftly scouted along the shore, seeking a partial ford, or islands that would aid him. By a miracle he came to a canoe—an old canoe, half concealed in the bushes at the water's edge, with an end stove in.

Laboring rapidly, he stuffed and patched the hole. By paddling with his hands and a branch he crossed, and still he heard no whoop of pursuit.

He was in his loved Kentucky. The Ohio River and the Shawnee country lay behind him.

Near sunset of June 20 he sighted the clearing of

Boonesborough. He saw the log walls of the fort, the rudely shingled sloping roofs of the rows of cabins lining it, the supper smoke gently wafting from the clay chimneys. Everything looked to be as when he had left, except that the season was smiling summer instead of white winter. Yes, his home was safe, and so was he. Afoot he had covered one hundred and sixty miles, breaking his own trail through the forest and across the streams, in four days, and had eaten only once. That was a record, white or red.

He hastened down in. His eye rapidly grasped details. The gates of the fort were widely open; women were outside, milking cows; men were chopping wood in the timber; children were fetching water, and playing about, even straying almost beyond call. No guards were posted, on the look-out. The logs of the defences had sagged by weather—some appeared to have rotted. One of the double gates, swung inward, hung crookedly. It was a Boonesborough gone to seed in a fancied peace.

He arrived unchallenged. Indians might have done the same. The first persons whom he met stared at him blankly, then amazed.

"What! Boone? We thought you dead long since, man! Hooray!"

At the cry, the people flocked to greet him. He had been absent five months and twelve days; four of these months he had been among the Indians. Shawnee paint was still on his face; his hair was unusually long, and he himself uncommonly thin and gaunt—weary but keen.

"Where's Rebecca? How are my wife and children?"

There was silence. Then Simon Kenton spoke up frankly.

"Well, you see, Dan, they'd give you up. We all thought you dead—you and likely the rest of the boys. You'd escaped once from those same Injuns; 't ain't their nater to let a man escape twice. So Rebecca got heart-sick. After waitin' a bit, and hearin' naught, she packed what she could and took the children, and set out hossback for her father's home in North Caroliny."

Daniel Boone grew pale.

"Alone?"

"Yes."

"Did she get there?"

"Yes; all right. Never harmed."

"Thank God. I do not blame her."

"But Jemimy's here. Here's Jemimy! She didn't go."

That was the pleasant surprise. Jemima, aged seventeen, rushed into his arms.

"Father! Father!"

"Gal, gal! Bless you, gal! But why didn't you go with ma?"

"I wanted to be here if you came back, father. I knew you'd come."

Daniel Boone wiped the tears of joy from his tired eyes. He thrust Jemima aside, for sterner duty.

"Gather everybody into the fort. We must repair it and be ready for a siege. When I left Chillicothe four days ago the Injuns had armed and painted for the war-path and they'll be on us any moment.''

That changed the scene. There was calling and running. Boone ate a few mouthfuls, while directing. As they all worked he told his story; he answered a hundred questions about the other prisoners; wives and brothers and sisters were eager to know how they were getting along.

Within twenty-four hours Fort Boonesborough had been repaired. It was a roomy fort; the walls of palisades a foot thick and twelve feet high fenced almost an acre. They were helped by the rows of cabins, blank to the outside, the hewn-shingle or ''shakes'' roofs sloping sharply. In the corners there were block-houses, projecting out like bastions, so as to sweep the walls with their port-holes. Boonesborough had been well planned, and ranked as the strongest settlers' fort in Kentucky.

But the clearing around was small. The brush and forest were within gun-shot, and the river, flowing between high banks, was only sixty yards in front. The old salt lick extended from the very walls. Inside the fort a well had been excavated, at sign of a spring.

The Indians did not appear. Soon second-stories had been added to the block-houses, making double bastions. Then, on July 17, William Hancock came in. He also had escaped from Chillicothe; but he had been twelve days on the way, and was almost famished.

''There was rare racin' and chasin' up yonder when they found you'd cleared out, Daniel,'' he reported. "It over-set their plans, I can tell you! So they put off their march for three weeks." ·

Daniel Boone at once sent a messenger eastward to Colonel Arthur Campbell, lieutenant commanding the militia at the Holston settlements in southwestern Virginia; said he expected an attack soon; could hold out three or four weeks—and then "relief would be of infinite service."

Still the Shawnees did not show up. A few spies were seen, near the fort. Evidently they had found the fort rebuilt and ready and had gone back with discouraging news. About six weeks had passed since William Hancock had reported; the cattle collected in the fort were turned out to graze, and with nineteen men Captain Boone the Big Turtle started upon a scout northward to learn what had happened to the Shawnees.

Young Simon Kenton (who was known as Simon Butler) was his lieutenant. Their goal was the Shawnee village of Paint Creek in southern Ohio east from the town of Little Chillicothe on the Little Miami.

They were not far from Paint Creek, when Simon Kenton, scouting before, stole upon two Indians riding a pony through the brush and laughing heartily. He shot them both with a single ball; off they tumbled, pierced through the breast, one dead, the other wounded; away ran the pony; on ran Simon, to finish the business with his tomahawk and take the scalps— and just in the final act he ducked his head aside barely in time to dodge the bullets of two more Indians.

That was a close call. Now the brush seemed full of Indians. He made for a tree. The firing and the galloping pony had carried the alarm to the main party; Daniel Boone and all came in a hurry, and cleared the neighborhood. The Indians had numbered thirty. The wounded warrior was borne off, but Simon took the scalp of the dead brave, after all.

He and his true friend, Alexander Montgomery, were sent ahead, to spy upon Paint Creek town. Paint Creek town was empty.

"Back to Boonesborough!" Captain Boone exclaimed. "The varmints are rallying. We've no time to lose."

At best speed they traveled for Boonesborough. All signs pointed to the fact that the march of the Shawnees was under way. They scouted for the trail of the red army, and found it. It was broad and fresh. On the sixth day southward they were right at the heels of the Shawnees, and circuited their camp at the Blue Licks itself, only forty miles from the fort. Indeed there had been no time to lose.

But the next afternoon they trooped, breathless, into Boonesborough, with word that the Shawnees—in full force—were close at hand.

At ten o'clock the following morning, September 7, the enemy appeared. They had crossed the Kentucky at a ford a mile and a half above the fort, had marched around by the rear, and now filed down for it from a timbered ridge on the south.

They made an imposing sight. They had flags, both French and British. They had horses with baggage.

They mustered some four hundred warriors, a dozen Canadian white men, and a negro named Pompey who was an adopted Shawnee. Their red chiefs were Black Fish himself, Moluntha, Black Wolf and Black Beard; their captain was a French-Canadian named Isidore Chêne, of the British Indian department at Detroit.

Under a white flag, Captain Chêne demanded the surrender of Fort Boonesborough. Counting the old men and boys, and several slaves, Daniel Boone had sixty persons who could handle a rifle; only forty of them were really shooters. He asked for two days in which to consider surrendering, but his mind was already made up.

The Shawnees had not donned their war paint for nothing; old Black Fish had come, looking for his "son"—and the rest had come, looking for whatever they might get.

Captain Chêne, a pleasant enough man, consented. He posted his hideous array in the forest, to cut off any escape; Captain Boone spent the two days in gathering loose cattle into the stockade and putting last touches upon the defences. He looked in vain for the militia from Virginia.

Of course, while he knew what he himself would rather do, he had no right yet to speak for the rest. He held a council with them. If they surrendered, he said, likely enough their lives would be spared, but they would be prisoners in far-away Detroit, they would lose all their property, their fort and homes would be burned. If they fought, they might hold out, but the Indians were led by white soldiers and it would be a desperate siege, much worse than the other sieges. If they were overcome, they could expect no mercy, for the few whites would be unable to keep the tomahawks and scalping-knives from them.

Every voice declared:

"Let us fight."

Therefore on the morning of the third day Captain Boone made reply to Captain Chêne.

"Sir, we have consulted together and are resolved to defend our fort whilst a single one of us is living. But we thank you for giving us notice, and time in which to provide for our wants. As for your preparations, we laugh at them. We do not fear painted faces. You shall never enter our gates."

"We know that you are brave men," Captain Chêne the soldier courteously answered, and the daubed countenances of the Shawnees, peering from the thickets behind him, tried to leer. "Governor Hamilton appreciates your situation. The force against you is over-whelming, but he has charged me not to destroy you. He does not wish even to treat you with harshness. If you will send out nine of your men for a talk, we will come to some agreement by which you will evade further trouble, and I will then withdraw my forces and return whence we came."

Governor Hamilton certainly had acted kindly toward Daniel Boone, in Detroit. The "hair-buying general," he was dubbed by the American colonists because he gave out rewards for scalps and prisoners taken by the Indians. But he had a good side, and Captain Boone felt moved to experiment again. His men agreed with him. There was a slim chance of favorable terms.

He took his brother Squire Boone, Stephen and William Hancock, Colonel Richard Callaway, Settler Flanders, and three others. They carried no arms, for Captain Chêne was unarmed.

"We will halt within fair rifle-shot," said Captain Boone, to the remaining men. "Do you cover us well and watch every movement."

The nine sallied out and met Captain Chêne about forty yards in front of the gates. Captain Chêne proposed the terms. He was all politeness and smiles. So were the Shawnee chiefs—although Black Fish eyed the Big Turtle rather darkly. He thought him a very ungrateful son.

The terms were these, said Captain Chêne: only these. If the Boonesborough men would but sign a paper, promising not to fight against His Britannic Majesty King George, and submitting to the rule of Governor Hamilton, the whole garrison might march away unharmed, with all their goods.

The nine looked upon each other questioningly. "That's ag'in all reason," thought Daniel Boone; and so thought his comrades. Those four hundred Indians would never permit it. They had been fooled by him twice; they had come a long distance for plunder; they had been led to expect rich prizes as their reward. Merely to see the garrison move out, leaving a bare fort, would not satisfy them. Indians go to war for scalps, horses, guns, powder, iron, captives."

"We will sign," remarked Daniel Boone. It was

the quickest way to learn what would happen next. Something was due to happen, whether they signed or not.

Now Chief Black Fish had his turn. He stood forward and made a speech. An oily old rascal, he. This was a treaty between two great white nations, and with a red nation, too, he said. It must be sealed in Indian fashion. Each Long Knife chief should shake hands·with two Indians. Such was the Shawnee custom. Then they would be as brothers.

That struck the Daniel Boone men as something new. However, they had got in too deep to stick at trifles, but they smelled a mouse.

"It is good," said Daniel Boone. His muscles tense, his eyes bright. he stretched out his hand; he was strong and active, the Hancocks, Colonel Callaway, Squire Boone, Flanders, and all—they were as stout as buffalo and as quick as panthers; rifle muzzles that rarely missed were resting upon the port-holes only forty yards to rear, and the gates were open, waiting.

He stretched out his hand; two Indians at once grasped it—clutched his arm—

"Go!" shouted Chief Black Fish, exultant.

Instantly Captain Big Turtle was being dragged forward; other Indians had sprung at him—his eight comrades were wrestling and reeling—with a twist and a jerk he had flung his captors sprawling—his comrades had done likewise with theirs and while muskets bellowed and rifles spat they ran headlong for the gates; got safely in, too, with only Squire Boone wounded; the gates creaked shut, the bar fell into place, the peace treaty had been broken almost as soon as made, and Fort Boonesborough was in for a fight.

A deluge of hot lead swept against the walls. The bullets drummed upon the logs and the palisade, whined through the port-holes, tore slivers from the roofs. Urged on by the white men, the Indians charged under cover of the muskets. They were bent backward, and broke and fled, leaving bodies. With flaming arrows· they set fire to a roof; their sharpshooters, in trees, would keep water from it. A stripling young man scrambled on top, stood there, seized the buckets passed up to him, doused the blaze and amidst cheers leaped down again.

Some of the brave women, Jemima Boone and other girls, donned men's clothes and showed themselves here and there, to deceive the enemy. Jemima was wounded; two of the men were killed. Somebody, in the timber, was doing good shooting, with a rifle.

It was the black Indian, Pompey. He was known to be a crack marksman. They watched for him. Daniel Boone glimpsed him, high up in a tree; waited for a chance, took quick aim—and down from the tree crashed Pompey, dead before he struck the turf. After the siege they found him, shot through the head by Daniel Boone's long-barreled "Betsy," at a distance of one hundred and seventy-five yards.

Directed by Captain Chêne, the Black Fish Shawnees started a tunnel, from the river bank, to under-mine the walls. The clay that they threw out behind them made the river current muddy, and the keen eyes in the fort saw and read.

The defense started a counter tunnel, which should meet the other and cut a trench across its course. The Indians' tunnel became rain-soaked and caved in; they knew that the fort was digging also, and after having bored for forty yards, they quit. Fighting was more to their taste than burrowing like moles.

More than a week passed, without a let-up day or night. The powder smoke hung, veiling the clearing and the edge of the forest, and the surface of the river. Inside the fort there was not an idle hand, among the living. The losses had been very small indeed, in spite of the hubbub; no one had any notion of surrender, yet.

Then, on the morning of September 20, the sun rose in silence. After a parting volley the enemy had gone. The siege was lifted.

Daniel Boone sent out scouts. They reported the coast clear. The gates were opened. The corpses of thirty-six Indians and the negro Pompey were awaiting. How many other bodies and how many wounded had been carried away was never learned.

One hundred and twenty-five pounds of lead were gathered, inside the fort and outside; nearly as much more had entered the logs. That proved the fierceness of the ten days' attack, but did not pay for the cattle killed or stolen, astray in the timber.

However, this was the last siege of Boonesborough. The Shawnees gave up hopes of ever getting their Big Turtle, but they admired him none the less.

CHAPTER V

SCOUT KENTON HAS A HARD TIME (1778-1779)

HOW HE PAID FOR HIS HORSE-STEALING

WHEN Boonesborough was besieged this last time, Daniel Boone's most trusted man (excepting his own brother) did not take part in the defence. Young Simon Kenton—or at present Simon Butler—was absent, with his friend Montgomery also.

After the gleeful Simon had shot the two Indians at once, near Paint Creek town, and had spied upon the town itself, he and scout Montgomery had stayed while the others hastened back to Boonesborough. They were not at all satisfied to have come so far and to have taken only one scalp.

Now this Simon Butler or Simon Kenton was a daredevil pure and simple: a youth of roguish but extremely obstinate spirit. He had started upon the adventure trail at sixteen, and here at twenty-three he already had many hair-breadth escapes in his memory and many notches in his rifle-stock.

First, when he was sixteen he had fallen in love, at his home in Virginia, and had fought a rough-and-tumble with his man rival, by name William Veach or else Leitchman. He seemed to be holding Leitchman pretty even, too—until his rival's friends jumped in and pummeled Simon well.

78

Lad Simon limped away, bruised and bleeding, scarcely able to walk—for such fights were wild-cat fights with claws and teeth. He bided his time; he grew rapidly, and by April, 1771, being six feet tall at last (the true border height) and strongly muscled, he challenged Leitchman again.

They stepped into the timber, and fought. It was nip and tuck. No friends were at hand. But Simon was still too young; down he went, under the rain of blows, and Leitchman, taunting him with the loss of his sweetheart, proceeded to "give him the boots."

Simon lay and took it, saying no word. His mind was active. He noted his enemy's long hair, reaching to the waist—a fashion among the border beaux. An idea occurred to him. He grasped one of the piston-like legs and sank his teeth into it. Yelling, Leitchman dragged him and sought to get free. Down he tumbled, also, tripped in his efforts. Simon grabbed at his hair, wound it around the trunk of a small sapling, and had him!

He saw red, did Simon; a moment more, and the man was gasping as if dying. This was more than bargained for. Horrified, Simon plunged into the wilderness, just as he was. He was a poor boy, a hard worker on the Kenton farm, and had not learned even to read or write; now he thought himself a murderer; he changed his name to Butler and the forests swallowed him.

In those days there was always hunting and exploring and Indian-fighting to occupy the wanderer. Anybody accustomed to a rifle could be of use in opening new country. He speedily fell in with another wanderer, driving a pack-horse. They lived like Indians in the Alleghany Mountains region of southwestern Pennsylvania.

Two years passed. In March, 1773, Simon Butler, aged eighteen, was camped with two other hunters, named Strader and Yager, beside the Great Kanawha River of northwestern West Virginia. They were trappers as well as hunters: white Indians who traded their furs in at Fort Pitt.

This day Indians attacked the camp; Yager toppled over, dead; and when Simon and his older comrade, Strader, managed to gain the highway of the Ohio River, westward, they were nearly dead, too, from starvation.

Simon soon became a scout. He achieved fame as a spy against the Indians. From Fort Pitt he and another Simon—Simon Girty—employed by the military government of Virginia traversed the forests far and near, watching the movements of the Indians. Simon Girty deserted to the Shawnees, during the Revolution, and was a cruel enemy to all his former fellow-Americans; but Simon Butler remained true blue.

When in the fall of 1774 he entered Kentucky the lovely, he had reached full stature. Six feet one inch he measured, in his stockinged feet—a real Long Hunter; weighed one hundred and ninety pounds, and could spare not an ounce; was the light-haired, blue-eyed, gentle-mannered, laughing type of fighter, with a great good-nature and a single-track, simple mind; but

Simon Kenton in Trouble

(From an Old Print)

when he was desperate or angered his blue eyes blazed and his strength was prodigious.

So, at nineteen, Simon Butler had turned out a personage to be reckoned with.

He was at the Lower Blue Licks country, where Daniel Boone was captured later, before the founding of Boonesborough. He built a cabin at Washington, south of the Ohio River in northeastern Kentucky, and from there prowled about with two comrades. In September of 1775 another white wanderer told them that American men and women were living on the Kentucky River in the interior to the south.

Rejoicing, they abandoned Washington, and traveled down to new Boonesborough. It seemed good to see white women again.

Simon still thought that he had killed his rival Leitchman. He kept his name of Butler. Daniel Boone was glad to have such reinforcement. Soon he liked the young man. In the course of the sieges of 1777 Simon rescued him, before the gates; shot his nearest foe and grabbing him carried him, leg broken, into the fort.

Daniel Boone was a man of few words. But he spoke roundly—for him.

"Well, Simon, you have behaved yourself like a man, today—indeed, you are a fine fellow."

It was a great tribute from Daniel Boone.

However, even the excitement of the daily life at Boonesborough palled on young Simon Kenton-Butler or Butler-Kenton. He was the restless kind. When danger did not come to him, he went out to seek it.

He delighted in the daring foray and in spy work. A narrow squeak was a joke to him. The greater the risk, the more heartily he laughed about it.

The two Indians whom he had tumbled from their frisky pony at one shot, near Paint Creek, and the whish of the bullet grazing his head, and his dive for a tree, only whetted his appetite for more fun; consequently when the Daniel Boone party turned about, he and his comrade Montgomery lingered, to experiment with Paint Creek town itself.

All the rest of that day they hid in the corn-field on the edge of the town, waiting for Indians to appear and gather roasting-ears. That was sheer nerve; they were in the heart of the Indian country and more than one hundred miles from any protection except their own wits and their rifles. But they saw no Indians other than a few little children. The town certainly was deserted for the war trail.

Therefore at dusk they slipped into the town, stole four horses, led them out, mounted two, drove the others, rode all night, to the Ohio River, swam it, and avoiding the trail of the Indian army to Boonesborough galloped gaily into Logan's Station beyond the Kentucky.

One scalp and four horses! Simon laughed easily. The trip had been worth while.

He "loafed" only until the danger to Boonesborough was past. For that space all the Kentucky forts sat tight. But Colonel John Bowman of the militia was here, at Logan's. Boonesborough had come safely through the red tempest; the Indians had retired; he planned a counter blow, and wished to learn just what were the conditions at the Chief Black Fish town of Little Chillicothe on the Little Miami River: whether it was on guard, whether the warriors had left to strike at another point, and so forth. That called for skillful work.

Who more willing to act the spy than the happy-go-lucky young giant, fair-haired Simon Kenton alias Butler? With him he took his comrade Montgomery again, and Ranger George Clark. Alas, it was to be Montgomery's last outward trip. The Simon Kenton trail was always the danger trail, and he made it doubly dangerous by his recklessness.

They had no difficulty in reaching Little Chillicothe. It was a large town, of the Shawnee round bark houses, and surrounded by a rude palisade fence. When all the families seemed to be asleep, and silence reigned, they went inside—gliding here and there and wakening not even the dogs.

Simon sought out his two comrades, and touched them, as a signal. They followed him. At the edge of the town he had found the Shawnees' horse-pound, or yard. It contained more than a dozen horses. The opportunity was too good to be passed by. Nothing would do but that they must have each a horse, upon which to ride back.

Even with that all might have been well, had they not waxed greedy. Now they did a very foolish thing —the first of several foolish things. Simon was determined to steal all; the two others agreed to it. They rapidly fitted the hide halters that they discovered, mounted, and began to lead and drive the loose horses through the opened gateway.

But the horses were wild; did not like the smell of white men. They snorted alarmingly, and cavorted and reared. Dogs commenced to bark, voices arose, inquiring and scolding; the three men worked desperately with the stubborn animals. And suddenly the voices swelled.

"The horses! The Long Knives are here, stealing our horses!"

The town was in an up-roar.

"To the tall timber and keep goin'," Simon panted. "Lead all you've got. I'll follow."

So instead of riding free, out they hustled, Clark and Montgomery each with a fistful of halter thongs, Simon lashing and whooping and laughing behind.

They dashed at top speed through the forest, never minding the branches. They had seven horses. Such a mad-cap prank it was! The village rang with the hue and cry, and the forest aisles echoed. Presently the tumult died away. The blind course had plunged into a swamp, and the three mischief-makers were forced to halt uncertainly. They listened keenly. They heard no sound of pursuit. The town evidently was reconnoitering.

So they side-stepped the swamp and resumed their own noisy route. They did not stop again that night; they rested at day-break, long enough to eat a few mouthfuls; all that day they rode, and all the night again; with the morning they had arrived upon the bank of the Ohio.

They had left a trail plain enough for a five-year-old child to follow. But here they were, and—

"Across the Ohio and we're safe, boys," quoth Simon. "Hooray! Didn't we come it over 'em proper?"

The wind was blowing a gale, up-stream, and the Ohio was whipped into white-caps. It looked like a stormy passage.

"You fellows tote our fixin's over on a raft; I'll swim with the hosses," bade the nimble Simon.

They worked; made a raft of logs and branches; loaded the guns and blankets and ammunition upon it; herded the horses into the stream, and while his two comrades threw stones and sticks at them from the shore Simon himself forged into the stream, to swim just below them.

He was a strong man, but the high waves choked him, the current carried him down, down in spite of his efforts; pretty soon he and the snorting horses were separated. They had had enough, and turned back to the shore. Montgomery and Clark could not head them; out they all scrambled.

Pshaw! Around turned Simon, and staggered out, too, for another try. The same thing occurred. He could not keep up with the horses, and they refused to cross without a guide. In fact, they wanted to go home.

He sank exhausted upon the bank.

"Plague take 'em! I've got to rest a spell."

"What next?" queried Montgomery. "Shall we leave 'em and ferry ourselves over on the raft?'

"The Injuns are hot after, you can be sure of that," said Clark. "But I for one hate to lose a bunch of hosses as fine as these are."

"Lose 'em we sha'n't," Simon asserted. "I intend to risk my scalp by stayin' with 'em. We've twenty-four hours the start."

"We can't cross 'em; that's sartin, in the state o' the water; hoss or man either can't swim it," Montgomery declared. "I vote to stay with 'em, myself. But we might keep goin' up or down stream, and mebbe throw the beggars off the scent. It'd give us distance, anyway."

"We've twenty-four hours the start," Simon repeated, "and we're dog tired. This wind'll fall at sunset; we'll still have time to spar'. Then by crossin' and travelin' all night we'll be beyond reach, for good and all."

They agreed. They had their rifles and plenty of powder and ball, and each was unwilling to let the others out-brave him. So they lolled about all that day; dozed, laughed and joked. At sunset the wind increased. The water had become so rough that even the raft would be swamped; and to try with the horses was beyond reason.

"Well," proffered Simon, lazily, "we can wait till mornin'. The pesky wind will have blown itself out by then."

And so it did. The river was smooth and peaceful in the sunrise. They hustled to gather their little herd and drive them in—but remembering their fright of yesterday, not an animal would take to the water.

They all balked, and scampered. Soon they were scattered on the back trail.

"By cracky, it's no go, boys!" Clark gasped. "Our time's up. I feel Injuns. Let's mount and make off—for I tell you, scalpin' knives are near."

"No, sir! Not a step without those hosses," vowed Simon. "I'll leave not a one. We've 'armed 'em and we'll keep 'em."

"All right. Hosses and all, then. Hooray!"

Horseback, they started in to round up the loose animals, on the back trail. They rode in a line, Simon at the middle—and he had gone scarcely one hundred yards when he heard a halloo behind him, asking him to wait.

Somebody was coming from their camping place; the hail had been in good English, but he was suspicious. Nevertheless—

"Whoever you are, I'm your humble sarvant," Simon laughed, to himself. "And for your politeness I'll give you as little trouble as possible."

Thereupon what did he do but dismount, and with his rifle in the hollow of his arm leisurely stroll back in the direction of the voice! He had full faith that he could take care of himself, afoot as well as ahorse. In a moment he found himself facing three Shawnees and a white man, riding straight for him.

He threw his rifle to his shoulder, for a scalp, and a signal shot to his comrades. He drew fine bead upon the heart of the leading warrior, pulled trigger—the dampened powder only flashed in the pan.

At the click and the sputter the four horsemen

shouted and charged him. Drat such a gun! All that he might do was to whirl and run like a deer for the nearest thicket. He crashed into it, head-first; they could not follow. He tore through, and was commencing to chuckle at his success—when just out of the farther edge of the fallen trees and tangled underbrush he bolted almost into an Indian, horseback, galloping as if to overhaul him.

"The goose is cooked," thought Simon. He had had no time in which to freshen his priming. He stopped short. He heard the sound of pursuit in the jungle behind him. No use.

The Indian on horseback acted very good-natured; smiled widely, held out his hand, as he approached, and greeted with: "Brudder. How-do, brudder?"

"Consarn your yaller hide, I'd 'brudder' you if my gun would fire," thought Simon. But he did not say so. He leveled his piece, and called:

"Hey, you! Wait a minute. If I surrender, you treat me well? No hurt?"

"No harm, brudder. Treat good. No shoot, no get hurt. Fine man."

"I'll bet you're lyin'," thought Simon.

The Indian arrived, to shake hands. Simon watchfully consented. His hand was grasped, the grip instantly fastened upon it, would not loosen—"Tarnation! Let go, I tell you!" growled Simon, and with his other arm swung his gun wrathfully.

At the moment the Indian who had followed him through the thicket landed like a panther upon his back and pinioned him tightly. It all was up with Simon.

He struggled in vain. The horseback Indian "seized him by the hair of his head and shook him until his teeth rattled." Other Indians rushed joyously in. They scolded him with shrill tongues and belabored him with their ramrods.

"Hoss tief, hey? Big rascal, hey? Steal Injun's hoss, hey? One rascal white man, hey?" At every "hey" their ramrods fell; they cuffed him until his ears rang, and he rather believed that they were going to beat him to death then and there. Plainly enough they were the owners of the horses.

On a sudden they ceased, and stared. Brave Montgomery had appeared, summoned by the noise. He was standing yonder, among the thinned trees, trying to freshen the priming of his rifle. Two Indians darted for him at once. They pursued him amidst the trees—all vanished—two rifle shots spoke; the Indians came back waving a scalp, which they thrust into Simon's face as promise that his own should soon join it.

Thus Montgomery perished, in a long chance of rescuing his partner. But he could have done nothing. He only proved himself to be the kind that never leaves a friend. George Clark did not know what had happened; he heard the rumpus and made off. Maybe he acted wisely. It was a hard problem. If he had killed an Indian in the party, the party would have killed Simon. Anyway, he arrived at Logan's, by himself.

The angry Shawnees, with their white Indian looking on, had a very good time beating Simon, until they all, including Simon, were tired out. Then they staked him flat on his back, stretched by arms and legs and neck—his ankles drawn taut to two stakes, his elbows and wrists held by a stout pole laid across his chest, and his neck enclosed in a halter. He could not move an inch!

They cuffed him a little more, for full measure— "Tief! You big hoss tief! Hey? Hey? How you like tief? Hey?"

Simon spent an uncomfortable night. The matter had passed the joking period; he saw only torture ahead of him, at Little Chillicothe.

The Indians were not yet done with him, here. In the morning they seemed to be more enraged than ever. The longer they thought about this "tief," the wrathier they grew. Simon's hunting shirt had been stripped from him, so that he was naked from the waist up. Now they brought in the wildest of the horses—an unbroken young colt. They mounted Simon upon him bareback, his hands tied behind him and his feet tied together under the colt's belly. They turned the frenzied colt loose; away he fled, prancing and rearing through the brush, bearing Simon—they after, whipping and shrieking.

It was a rough ride while it lasted; but the colt simmered down, and much to the Indians' disappointment fell in line with the other horses, to jog soberly by the best trail.

"Thank you," thought Simon. "If ever I own you I'll see to it that your ribs never show."

In this fashion he rode all that day, and part of the next. He had not the slightest opportunity to escape.

Chillicothe was in sight. An Indian galloped before, to carry the word, so that the town might get ready. The "big hoss tief"—Simon the "big hoss tief"—was being brought in!

Chief Black Fish himself came to meet the procession. He, also, was in bad humor. He had not got over the loss of his son, Big Turtle, and of scalps at Boonesborough. Simon could not have chosen a worse time for seeking trouble.

Black Fish was armed with a heavy hickory switch. He eyed Simon scowlingly, Simon eyed the switch.

"You been stealing hosses?" Black Fish demanded in English.

"Yes."

"Captain Boone, he tell you to come steal our hosses?"

"No. I did it of my own accord."

That was the limit of impudence. This white man actually defied him! Huh! Chief Black Fish vigorously applied the switch, and Simon took another threshing. His naked back and shoulders speedily were ribboned by bloody welts. Whew! Compared with this, his first beatings had been as nothing.

They proceeded on for the town. By the manner with which the whole population boiled out, like crazy persons, to hoot and yell and shake fists and clubs, he had a hard row to hoe, yet. Beyond doubt, he would be burned alive. His reputation was bad.

They could not wait to get into town with him. They planted a stake at once—they tore off the remainder of his rags—they stretched his arms to the utmost above

his head and tied his hands together to the top of the
stake. There he was. He heartily wished that he had
let horses alone, but resolved to die manfully.

But they did not burn him. The men, women and
children danced around him, and yelled and hooted and
screamed and made faces, switched him and slapped
him, until midnight. They wanted to make the most of
him, so they untied him and hustled him on into the
town, for another day's sport.

The first thing in the morning he saw the scalp of
his friend Montgomery, bound upon a hoop and drying
in the sun, before a house. That was a reminder. The
next thing, he was led out, to run the gauntlet.

The people were waiting, lined up in two rows facing
inward. The rows bristled with clubs, switches, hoe-
handles and tomahawks. The two persons at this end
were warriors, holding butcher-knives! They would
initiate him! Gosh! The lines were closed by a man
beating a drum. Back of the man was the council-
house.

Simon knew that he was to run between the lines,
from the butcher-knives through the clubs and hoe-
handles and tomahawks past the drum, to the council-
house—if he could.

"Not for me," thought Simon. "I'll fool those
yaller varmints."

He stood braced, two warriors grasping him. The
drum suddenly boomed with a new note, the warriors
shoved him—"Go!" The air trembled with the ex-
pectant clamor. But Simon, a bloody white-skinned
giant, veered aside. He avoided the butcher-knives;

92

he struck for the clear, the lines broke in furious pursuit, headed him off, he doubled like a rabbit, doubled again, sighted an open place, felled two Indians with his fists, headed for the opening, was tackled, stumbled under the blows, recovered, lunged on, and gasping clutched the post at the council-house doorway. It was sanctuary.

He was seized none too kindly, wrenched from the post, and with his arms bound was seated under a guard, outside the council-house, while the council of chiefs, surrounded by squatting warriors, voted upon whether to burn him now or later.

The white man came out to bring him the news.

"You are to be taken to Wakatomica."

That was another Shawnee town, about seventy miles north.

"What will they do with me there?" Simon asked.

"Burn you, by thunder," the white man snarled; and swore at him, and strode away as angrily as any of the red men.

All the Black Fish people, whatever their color, evidently were bent upon the destruction of Simon. A great pother, this, over the theft of a few horses, taken as the spoil of war! But it was not the horses alone that counted. There was the escape of Big Turtle, and the defeat at Boonesborough, and the shooting by Simon of the two Indians on the pony, and to cap the climax, there was his nerve in taking horses from the town pound, under the very noses of the Shawnee warriors.

Simon cogitated. The council broke up and to his

alarm he was treated more kindly. He was unbound, his clothes were given back to him, and he was left unguarded. That looked bad; it meant that he was being saved for the stake. The white Indian had spoken truly.

A firm resolve surged in his breast. If he could but plunge into another thicket, on the way to Wakatomica, he might yet escape. And if they recaptured him, why, the fire could be no hotter for that. He had a fighting chance.

The Shawnees did not delay. Within a half hour a large band of the chiefs and warriors started out, he in their midst. Several times, on the way, he almost darted aside—and each time his heart failed him. He dreaded more beatings—he was very sore and worn.

But after they had marched a distance unknown to him, although it seemed long, they commenced to beat their drum, and raise the scalp halloo. The next village was near; they were calling for the gauntlet, and the stake. This made his flesh cringe, and pricked him to action. Now, or never! With a great spring and a wild whoop he bolted into the brush.

He tore through; his sudden strength was that of a buffalo, his speed that of a stag. He was running for his life; and he was getting free, too, for they did not catch him. He left them behind, their pursuit whoops grew muffled and uncertain, he had the wide forest before him, and hope swelled; he had distanced bullet and horse and foot. Then, full tilt he fairly rammed into the very midst of a party of other Shawnees, who had come out from the village.

It was a sickening disappointment. He quit, breathless, and they seized him, put a rope around his neck, this time, and led him to the town.

The village was Pickaway or Piqua, just south of present Springfield in west central Ohio, on the road to Wakatomica. They tied him to a post in front of the council-house here, and held another debate. After that the village and its visitors danced around him and threatened him and scolded him, until late at night. Simon really did not care. He had done his best, they might do their worst.

In the morning he was taken on up to Wakatomica. It was a larger town. On this trip he had been closely watched; and here he was punished by the gauntlet in earnest. It about finished him. Then they painted him black, the death color. Half clothed, battered and spent, he was sitting upon the dirt floor of the bark council-house, while the Shawnees squatted in a circle and discussed the next event (which probably was to be the burning at the stake), when a new party entered the doorway.

They were three white men in Indian garb, a white woman and seven children as prisoners, and one Indian bearing a bunch of seven fresh scalps!

The woman's name proved to be Mrs. Mark Kennedy. A pitiable object she was, too. Simon recognized the three white men: Simon Girty himself (his scout-partner at Fort Pitt), James Girty, a brother, and John Ward—all squaw-men who were aiding the Shawnees against the Americans.

None of them appeared to know him; and before

they spoke to him he was put outside, while the council heard their report and decided what to do with the women and children.

Surely, Simon Butler-Kenton realized that he was in a very nest of trouble. The council-talk continued for a long, long time. It was late in the afternoon before he was hauled inside again, to hear his fate pronounced. He had given up hope. He could expect mercy from the Girtys least of all. They had deserted the American service in a huff, and were noted as the bitterest enemies of everything and everybody connected with it. Their hearts were hot and red.

He was greeted with a general, savage scowl. Simon Girty pointed to a dirty blanket spread upon the floor.

"Sit down."

Simon the victim tottered a moment; the insulting tone angered him. Girty grabbed him by the shoulder and forced him down.

"How many soldiers are there in Kentucky?"

"I don't know. I'm only a private and it's not my business to know. I can tell you the number of officers and you can judge for yourself."

"Do you know Captain Stuart?"

Captain Stuart was a leader of the Virginia militia, had tried to save the life of Chief Corn-stalk at the Point Pleasant fort, and had defended settlements against the Shawnees.

"I know him well. He is an old friend."

"What is your name?"

"Simon Butler."

Girty stared as if paralyzed. Simon Butler! This wretched man Simon Butler, the young comrade whom he had loved when they were scouts together, back "home"?

With a strange choked cry he rushed from his seat and hugged him.

"Butler! You? I've got to save you."

He turned upon the astonished warriors, who did not understand. He made an earnest speech, in the Shawnee tongue, with many gestures. Simon caught only the drift of it, but Girty the renegade was arguing for the life of a friend. He explained that here was a man as dear to him as a brother. They had traveled the same trail, slept under the same blanket, lived in the same house. He had never asked a favor before. He had been with them three years and helped them. Now he wished only the life of this man, his former brother.

Several of the older chiefs grunted approval. Simon's heart rose. But others spoke opposing. They said that the council already had decided; the Shawnees should not change their minds like squaws. Here was a very bad man. He had taken scalps, had stolen their horses, had flashed a gun at them when they tried to get their horses back again. He was too bad to be a Shawnee. He was from Kentucky, and henceforth all Kentuckians were to be killed. Even Captain Boone had deceived them. Besides, people had come to Wakatomica, to see the fun, and ought not to be disappointed!

Simon's heart fell.

Girty leaped up and spoke again, at length. He was answered. The debate lasted for an hour and a half. The council proceeded to a vote. The war-club was passed from hand to hand. Those who struck the floor with it, voted for death. Those who merely passed it on, voted for life. An old man, sitting in the center, kept tally by cutting notches in the two edges of a stick—one series of notches for the yeas, one series for the nays.

Simon watched intently. He dared not show any sign of joy, but his heart thrilled to bursting when he saw that the nays were winning. The old man announced the result. Simon Girty turned to Simon Butler.

"Well, my friend, you are safe. Come with me."

It was the shortest speech yet, and the best.

He led Simon outside. No Indian opposed. He took him to the trader's store and fitted him with moccasins, leggins, shirt, a handkerchief for his neck and another for his head. Took him home; had his own squaw dress the wounds from club and knife and switch. Made him one of the family.

For twenty-one days Simon lived in clover. The Indians all treated him kindly. He wandered where he pleased, in the neighborhood. It seemed too good to be true.

At the end of the blissful three weeks, he and Simon his friend were at Solomon's Town, a short distance from Wakatomica. They heard a shrill whoop; an Indian came running from Wakatomica. The heart of Simon Butler sank again. He did not like whoops in that tone of voice, and the Indian was signaling *them.*

"It's the distress halloo. We are summoned to the council-house," said Simon Girty. "We must go at once."

They and their friend Red Pole, a Shawnee, went to meet the runner. He shook hands with Red Pole and Simon Girty, but he refused Simon Butler's hand and scowled upon him.

Matters looked bad once more. Fortune was playing tricks, still. Matters looked worse in the council-house. The place was thronged with chiefs and warriors. There were a number of strange chiefs. Hands were shaken, but not the hand of Simon. He received only scowls.

A war party of the Shawnees had been defeated on the border; the spirits of their slain required revenge. The stranger chiefs gazed upon Simon indignantly. Why had he not been killed before? The Shawnee nation were getting childish. Let him be executed. The councils had so voted. Who now wanted him to live?

Simon Girty made another speech. He was hotly countered, by the stranger chiefs. They carried the day. He again turned to Simon Butler.

"My friend, I think you must die. But I have persuaded them to burn you at Upper Sandusky, where there will be many more Indians than here, receiving their presents from the British. I will ride ahead and see what I can do for you."

He left. Simon was immediately hustled out by

the collar and arms, and led by a rope around his neck was marched afoot, guarded by horsemen, for the north.

What a sudden change! First he had been beaten; then he had been painted black, for death. Then he had been released. Now he was to be killed. He had faint hope. It flickered when Girty passed him, and saying "I have friends in the next village," continued. It died completely when he arrived at the next village, and no Girty was there. His friend Simon had failed, and had gone back by another trail.

By this time he himself was already in torture. On the way the march had been interrupted by an old Indian who was sitting on a log, smoking a pipe and watching his squaw chop wood. The sight of the roped prisoner enraged him. He had lost a son, by a white man's rifle. In a twinkling he had sprung up, grabbed the ax from the squaw, and at one blow had cut Simon's arm wellnigh off at the shoulder.

The ax whirled high for a more deadly blow, but another Indian caught at it just in time.

"Shame on you!" he scolded. "You act like a fool. This man is for the stake. Would you cheat us out of him, when the people ahead are expecting great pleasure?"

Half dead from loss of blood, poor Simon arrived at the village. It was the town where the sullen Logan, once the firm friend of the whites, lived. Here he was eating his heart, with grief over the wrongs done to him.[1]

[1] See "Boys' Book of Indian Warriors."

Chief Logan the Mingo walked over to Simon and surveyed him. Simon did not know who he was, he may have heard of Simon.

"Well, young man," he said, in good English, "these other young men seem very mad at you."

"They certainly do," Simon admitted ruefully.

The dark Logan slightly smiled.

"Don't be discouraged. I am a great chief. You are to go to Sandusky. They talk of burning you there. But I will send two runners to speak good of you."

Simon's heart bounded. When he learned that this handsome, determined-looking Indian was Chief Logan the celebrated Mingo, he thought himself rescued, sure.

True to promise, the two runners took the Sandusky trail early in the morning. The Shawnee guard waited, and left Simon to the care of Logan. Things had brightened wonderfully. Chief Logan would not say, but he acted as if in hopes of success. He and Simon spent most of the day together. In the evening the two runners returned. They sought out Chief Logan, and talked apart with him, and Simon scarcely slept, so anxious was he to know their report.

The next morning he saw his guards coming, with Logan. Alas, the chief's face was sober. He brought a piece of bread.

"You are to be carried to Sandusky at once," he uttered shortly. That was all. He walked away without another sound. Plainly enough his good words had been of no use.

Simon sighed. Was ever a man so buffeted about, before, from high to low, and low to high, and high to low again! It was a case of the mouse and the cat, with fortune playing as the cat, and he serving as the mouse.

The five guards from Wakatomica took him in tow, for Upper Sandusky, and he gave over hoping any more.

Upper Sandusky, northern Ohio, was a Wyandot Huron town. It was a center for the Indians of many tribes. The Shawnees and Mingos gathered here to receive payment of gifts, from their British father. Simon was roundly welcomed, but was not made to run another gauntlet. Only, for a fourth time a council, and this time a grand council, sat to discuss him. He was wearied of councils; they usually condemned him.

The council had just opened, when a white man in the gay red uniform of a British captain entered. He was Pierre Drouillard, a French-Canadian in the British Indian department. Simon did not know, yet, but Chief Logan's runners had been sent to this same Drouillard, to tell about the prisoner. Chief Logan was smart.

The British captain looked at Simon sharply, and stood forward to make a speech.

"It is true," he said, with Simon listening hard, trying to understand the words, "that the Americans are a dangerous people. They are the cause of this bloody war. There can be no peace until they are either killed or driven out of the country."

"Good, good!" the council grunted.

"But we must meet them with cunning as well as bravery. To learn their plans, so to defeat them, is worth twenty prisoners. I think that if we take this man to Detroit, we might learn a great deal. The governor would find out from him the secrets of the Americans. I should like to take him. You would be rewarded, for your British father is good to his red children. When I bring him back, you may do with him as you choose. Have I spoken well?"

There were grunts and nods. It was a wise idea.

"As for you," said the captain, to the five Shawnees, "I can see that you have been put to a great deal of trouble, to carry the prisoner here. It is not right that you should have no pay. I will smooth your path by giving you rum and tobacco, or anything else, to the amount of one hundred dollars so that you may be happy while I am in Detroit."

That was indeed a pleasing as well as a crafty speech. The affair had been settled. The man in the British uniform grasped Simon by the arm.

"You are reprieved. Now you will come with me."

Again reprieved? Thoroughly bewildered, Simon followed him out. They mounted horses, and rode north, with one chief.

"I am Captain Drouillard," explained the officer. "This is what I said to the council." And he repeated. "You appreciate that I took a great risk by interfering. You were to have been burned at the stake in the morning. The Indians do not like to be robbed of their spoil, and I have engaged to return you. You will certainly be burned, if I do. But that rests with you. You have information of value. Reply to my questions, and talk straight, and all will be well. You shall stay in Detroit. Now, what is the American force in Kentucky? And how many men are there in Fort McIntosh?''

Fort McIntosh was an American post erected only last spring at the mouth of the Big Beaver River, beside the Ohio twenty-six miles below Fort Pitt.

"Lor' bless you," laughed Simon. "I'm nothin' but a private soldier, else a scout, and 'tain't my business to deal in such large matters. So I can't answer your questions, in any way, shape or manner. Fact is, as you can plainly see, I've enough to do to look out for myself.''

Captain Drouillard eyed him, and laughed also.

"I believe you," he said. "You've made a bad bargain of it, at that. Perhaps so have I.''

But they went on, to Detroit.

Simon was saved. The British did not send him back to the Indians. They sent presents, instead, and kept him as a prisoner of war. His arm healed, he grew strong, and stayed there from this October until the next June, 1779. He was by no means the only such prisoner in old Detroit. A great many others, taken in battle or on the trail, were here; among them, the majority of the ten Daniel Boone men sold by Chief Black Fish a year ago, to the British.

He and two of the Daniel Boone men planned to escape together. Mrs. Harvey, the wife of an Indian trader, agreed to aid them. She was particularly fond of Simon, who never complained and who had suffered so much.

It was more than two hundred miles to the nearest post on the Ohio River. Every mile led through the country of war Indians. They would be only too glad to catch Simon again. So he must have guns for himself and his companions. Mrs. Harvey said that she would get the guns.

On the night of June 3, Simon, in his quarters, heard a rap on his door and a low voice. He opened. Mrs. Harvey was there. She beckoned him into the darkness, and spoke rapidly. She was out of breath from running.

"Sh! I have the guns—three. They are Indians' guns. I picked the best three while the Indians are on a big drunk. They stacked their arms near the house. I've hidden what I took, in the pea patch in my garden. Come at midnight. You will find a ladder waiting for you, by which to climb the garden wall. The guns will be in the pea patch. There are food, ammunition and blankets in the hollow tree you know of, at the edge of town. Don't fail. Goodby." She scurried away.

"God bless you for an angel," murmured Simon, peering after her. And he hastened back to tell his comrades.

He knew that the Indians would have no thought of their guns before the morrow. At midnight the three climbed the wall, by the ladder. The guns were in the garden; so was Mrs. Harvey, waiting anxiously. In after years he said that her dim figure, sitting there, was the most beautiful thing that he ever saw. He never forgot Mrs. Harvey.

Outside, in the town, the yells of the drunken Indians were making the night hideous. There was little time for thanking the good woman. By daylight the three ought to be far from sight—and the hours seemed all too few.

Trailing the guns, and stooping, using their best scout methods they scuttled through the by-ways. They safely won the open; then ransacked the hollow tree, and plunged on, to head south, through the forest, for distant Louisville at the Falls of the Ohio. Upon a great circuit, to throw off the pursuit, they traveled, traveled, traveled by a series of night marches, until after thirty days they arrived at the Colonel George Rogers Clark settlement, to-day the city of Louisville, Kentucky.

Simon had been absent from Kentucky nine months. In one space of four weeks he had been beaten eight times by the gauntlet or otherwise; had three times been condemned to burning at the stake, had been painted black and was being condemned a fourth time, to certain death, when rescued by the accident of meeting Chief Logan. But he lived to be over eighty and died peacefully in his bed at last—which proves that the most desperate peril is never hopeless. Dangers do not surely mean death.

He went right out upon another scout against the Indians. He continued to be a scout, and a soldier, and was with General "Mad Anthony" Wayne at the decisive battle of the Fallen Timbers, in 1794, when the backs of the Shawnees, Miamis, Wyandots, Delawares, Senecas, and all, joined together by Chief Little Turtle, Chief Blue-jacket and Simon Girty, were broken to fragments.

He fought the Shawnees again in the War of 1812. He had been living at Urbana, Illinois, and was appointed brigadier general of the Illinois militia; but he enlisted as a private.

When he died, in April, 1836, it was in his cabin on the site of that very Wakatomica, the Black Fish town where he had suffered tortures. Long before this he had become Simon Kenton; he had learned that he was no murderer, after all; he had met his one-time rival, Leitchman, and they had "made up."

CHAPTER VI

THE SCRAPE OF LEWIS AND JACOB WETZEL (1778)

AND THE NERVE OF TWO BOY SCOUTS

SEVERAL kinds of frontier fighters seem to have been needed in order that from the white strip along the Atlantic coast the American cabins should move on to the Ohio River and into the red Northwest.

The patient, untiring Daniel Boone was one kind. He was a settler. He explored only to plant a family home; he killed Indians only to preserve the home, his people and himself. He commanded respect.

Simon Kenton was another kind. He was an adventurer. He planted no home of any value to the country; he took the trail as a scout, and killed Indians who got in his way. He won hatred as well as respect.

The Wetzel boys were a third kind. They were settlers, they were scouts, but they were professional Indian-hunters. The trail had one object to them: scalps and revenge. They spread fear and hatred both.

There were five Wetzel brothers: Martin, Lewis, Jacob, John and George. Not so much is heard about George, but the four others became famous bordermen.

The Wetzel family removed with the Zane families and neighbors from the South Branch of the Potomac River, West Virginia, in 1770, to help form the Wheel-

108

ing settlement at the Ohio in the pan-handle. Father John Wetzel was a daring man; a great hunter, a venturesome explorer; and finally he took chances once too often and lost his life.

When he arrived in the Wheeling district he located his cabin fourteen miles up Wheeling Creek, where he had little company except his wife and children. Besides the five sons, two daughters were born: Susan and Christina. So the cabin did not lack excitement, even had there been no Indian scares.

Of the sons, Martin was the eldest. He and his father aided in the defense of Fort Henry, in 1775. Lewis was the next; he was born about 1764. Jacob probably was the next to Lewis.

It was in 1778, when Lewis was about fourteen and Jacob was about twelve that they two had their celebrated affair with the Indians, which proved them to be made of the right stuff for bordermen.

They were playing near the corn-crib some little distance from the cabin when Lewis, standing up, saw a rifle-muzzle pointing straight at his breast, from a corner of the crib. As quick as thought he sprang backward—but the ball was on its way. It tore across his breast, and took a piece of his breast bone. However, he had done well; the rifle had been aimed to kill, and only the smartness of his frontier training had saved his life. The children of the border days were brought up to act fast in self-defence.

He fell. Indians rushed him at once, seized him and little Jacob, and clapping a hand across their mouths carried them away.

These were a small party of Indians, prowling about in hopes of doing something just like this. When they had seen Lewis, they had decided to shoot him. He was a stout, chunky lad, and looked to be older than his real age; they feared that he would run from them and give the alarm.

Now they had him and Jacob too. In the timber, pretty soon they set the two down, and dragged them forward by the arms. There was no use fighting, there was no use crying; to cry would have been a sign of weakness, in a border boy, and to fight would have brought only a beating.

Lewis grew sick with his pain, for his breast had been laid open clear to the mangled bone. But he uttered never a whimper, and being the older he of course had to encourage Jacob to keep a stiff upper lip. He was resolved, though, that the Indians should pay for this, some day. And he did make them pay, not only for this but for other matters.

"Aren't you bad hurt, Lewis?" panted Jacob.

"Kinder. But if I complain they'll tomahawk me rather'n be pestered."

This night they all slept upon the ground in the woods north of Wheeling. The Indians tied the boys tightly. There was no chance of escape and it was a very uncomfortable night, what with Lewis's wound and Jacob's fear, and the cold and the hunger and the thought of the cabin on Wheeling Creek.

"Don't you beller, Jakie," Lewis bade. "We won't stay with 'em any longer'n we have to. We're Wetzels."

In the morning they were taken over the Ohio River in a canoe. That day they were made to travel twenty miles farther. Like other frontier boys (and like the girls too) they were raised bare-foot; by this time on their hustling journey their feet were cut and bleeding, so to-night the Indians did not tie the two prisoners.

They were foolish Indians; they had little idea of the nerve of white boys, especially these settler boys.

When all was quiet and the Indians were breathing deeply, Lewis sat up. It was bright moonlight, and he could see plainly. He could see Jacob, and the forms of the Indians stretched around. He moved more. Nobody else stirred, not a breath was interrupted. Then, to find out if the Indians were playing 'possum, he stood on his feet.

Not an Indian even so much as turned over. He began to walk about, treading carelessly, to test them out. He was a wise boy; he spent an hour, experimenting, while his heart beat more and more hopefully. He might have stolen off, but of course he had to take Jacob.

Jacob was asleep. Lewis crept to him and touched him and woke him.

"Come on," he whispered. "We're going."

Jacob shook his head, afraid.

"No."

"Yes."

Jacob's eyes widened.

"We'll be caught."

"No, we won't. They're asleep. Listen? I know they're asleep. Hurry up."

Jacob was only twelve. Lewis was his bigger brother, whom he admired. So he got up, staring—took long breath, and he holding to Lewis's hand, into the moonlit timber they scooted with never a backward look.

"We can follow our own trail back to the river," said Lewis. "It'll be easy."

"Ouch!" And Jacob began to limp.

Lewis stopped.

"You wait here. I'll get some moccasins."

"No, Lewis! They'll catch you."

"No, they won't. We've got to have moccasins."

Lewis scudded for the camp. In a minute he had found moccasins and had brought them. That was better. Now they might travel faster. But Lewis halted again.

"Wait. I'm going to get father a gun!"

"No, Lewis! Let's hurry. We don't want a gun."

"Yes, we do. Maybe we'll have to defend ourselves or kill meat. You wait right here."

Back Lewis scudded, a second time. He was a boy without fear. He brought a gun and ammunition. Then they hastened on. This time they had not gone far before they heard muffled voices behind them. The Indians had wakened and were on their trail.

"Hurry!" Jacob gasped. "Run!"

"No. They'd catch us sure. Our legs are too short. You do as I say, Jakie. When they get near, we'll hide and let 'em pass us. That's the way."

They hurried, but they kept listening. At what he thought ought to be the right time—when the voices and the twig-crackings were louder—Lewis grasped Jacob's arm.

"Now! Into the brush on this side, quick! No noise!"

They hid in a good place. Not a minute later two or three of the Indians filed past, like hounds upon the trail. Lewis, clutching Jacob to keep him quiet, waited. No more Indians came. Lewis chuckled.

"We'll follow on behind, but we'll have to be watching sharp for 'em to turn back," he whispered.

So they followed their pursuers, instead of their pursuers following them. The regular Indian trick had worked finely. But even a rabbit knows enough to do that: to hide beside its trail while its hunters race on. Lewis and Jacob felt smart indeed.

They kept their eyes and ears alert. Soon they heard the Indians coming back, on the trail, as if puzzled.

"Hide," Lewis whispered.

It was done at once, by a silent dart to the left and a squatting behind bushes. Again they held their breaths. Lewis's wound throbbed and stung, but he uttered not a murmur. The Indians passed; their keen eyes noted nothing suspicious; their sounds died away—

"All right, Jakie."

They set out once more, hastening on down the forest trail flecked by the moonlight; Lewis led, lugging the heavy gun, Jacob trotted close at his heels. Rabbits hopped and flattened, a fox or two glided, there was nothing dangerous, until—

"Listen!"

They two stopped short, and poised, heads turned. Lewis painfully stooped and put his ear to the ground.

"They're following us horseback. We'll have to hide again."

They came to a good spot, and hid. This time it was two Indians on horses, sure enough, moving rapidly to catch them. Morning was near. The forest paled with the first tinge of dawn. They straightened up cautiously.

"I think we'd better leave this trail, Jakie," Lewis said. "We'll strike right east, for the river. We can't get lost now."

The sun rose, and they were still trudging fast, and no Indians had followed them. The Indians had been fooled nicely. About eleven o'clock they sighted the Ohio—they came out almost opposite the mouth of Wheeling Creek! Their father and Martin could not have beaten this, for a scout feat.

"There's Zane's Island!" Lewis panted. "Hooray, Jakie! There's the smoke of Wheeling settlement. We're nearly home."

He was just about worn out. For a boy of fourteen, with a big gash across his chest, and a gun to carry, and a little boy to look after, it had been a tough stunt —that fifteen-mile tramp by night and day, on an empty stomach.

"Let's yell, Lewis, so somebody'll come for us."

"No. Injuns might hear us. We'll have to make a raft. We'll find logs and tie 'em together."

They did. They found two logs, lashed them to-

LEWIS WETZEL LOADS ON THE RUN

(From an Old Print)

gether with grape-vine, and half swimming, half paddling, launched out. Shortly after noon they landed below Wheeling, and were safe.

The people of Wheeling were much astonished to see them toil in. Long before they had reached home they were heroes. They received many compliments upon their work. And it goes without saying that there was a great ado over them in the Wetzel cabin, which had given them up for lost.

Nine years later Father Wetzel was killed by the Indians. He and a companion had been down river in a canoe, hunting and fishing. Neighbors had warned him that this was risky business, but he only laughed. Now he and his partner were paddling upstream, along shore, about eight miles below Wheeling. From the brush a party of Indians hailed them and ordered them to land.

"What! Surrender to you, you yaller varmints?" old man Wetzel rapped. "Not whilst we live."

They turned the canoe and paddled fast, but the guns spoke and he received a ball through his body. He felt that he was wounded to death.

"Lie down in the bottom," he gasped. "That'll save you. I'm gone anyway, but I can get us out o' range."

He acted as target, while paddling his best. They made the opposite shore, at the mouth of Captina Creek, and he died at Baker's Bottom settlement, a short distance above. He was buried here. For some years a stone marked his grave. It said, only: "J. W., 1787."

At the Wetzel home the Wetzel boys vowed relentless war against all Indians. Their hatchets should never be dropped until not a redskin roamed the woods.

Lewis was now twenty-three: a borderman through and through and skilled almost beyond all others. He was not of the "long" type; instead, he was five feet eight inches; darker in complexion than his swarthy brothers, pitted with small-pox scars, broad-shouldered, thick in body, arms and legs, fiery black-eyed, and proud of his deeply black hair that when combed out fell in rippling waves to his calves.

All the brothers had long hair, black and oiled and curled. His was the longest; when not loose it formed a bunch under his fur cap.

He grew to be the most famous of the West Virginia Indian-fighters. In daring, and in trail-reading, he won first place. He practiced reloading his thirty-six-inch barreled, flint-lock patch-and-ball rifle on the run (no easy job), and by this trick out-witted many Indians who thought that they had him when his gun had been emptied. The West Virginians looked upon him as their Daniel Boone, and their "right arm of defence."

He was credited with twenty-seven scalps, on the West Virginia border, and as many more elsewhere on the frontier. His brothers swelled the number to over one hundred.

Jacob reached six feet in height, and a weight of two hundred pounds—a powerful man like Simon Kenton. He and John also were celebrated Indian-hunters. But although Lewis himself once was out-lawed by the military government for shooting an Indian needlessly, Martin was the really vindictive killer. No Indian of any kind, and whether surrendered or not, was safe from him, his rifle and his tomahawk.

Indian-hunting and Indian-killing was a business with the Wetzels, and the name "Wetzel" carried terror through the forests.

Strange to say they, like Simon Kenton and other bordermen who scorned danger, lived on to a round manhood in spite of the chances that they took. Lewis died in his bed, of a sickness, near Natchez on the southern Mississippi River, in the summer of 1808, aged forty-four. John had died, a few years before, at Wheeling, in similar manner. Martin and Jacob also passed away peacefully.

Such men as the Wetzel brothers were "shock" troops. They did not occupy a country, but they broke the enemy's line.

CHAPTER VII

CAPTAIN SAMUEL BRADY SWEARS VENGEANCE
(1780-1781)

AND BROAD-JUMPS LIKE A WILD TURKEY

SAMUEL BRADY the Ranger: the Captain of
Spies, the Hero of Western Pennsylvania—he indeed was a famous frontier fighter in the years following the Revolution, when the Indians were determined
that "no white cabin shall smoke beyond the Ohio."
The struggle to keep the settlers out of present Ohio
and Indiana (the Northwest Territory) proved long
and bloody.

In western Pennsylvania and northern Ohio the
name Captain Samuel Brady ranks with that of
Daniel Boone in Kentucky and Kit Carson in the Far
West. Up the Allegheny River above Pittsburgh there
are Brady's Bend and East Brady, to remind people
of his deeds; near Beaver, Pennsylvania, at the Ohio
River below Pittsburgh, there are Brady's Run,
Brady's Path and Brady's Hill; in Portage County,
northeastern Ohio, over toward the Pennsylvania line,
there are Brady's Leap and Brady's Lake. So Captain Samuel Brady left his mark upon the map.

He came of fighting Irish stock. He was born in
Shippensburgh, Pennsylvania, in 1756, during the
French and Indian War. His father, John Brady, was
out upon the battle trail at the time.

CAPTAIN BRADY SWEARS VENGEANCE

When he was nineteen, or in 1775, he joined the volunteers from Pennsylvania, to march for Boston. The War of the Revolution was just bursting into flame, and he intended to be in the thick of it. The next year, 1776, his father and his younger brother, James, enlisted with the Pennsylvania troops, also to fight for liberty.

The men of the Brady family did well. Father Brady was appointed a captain; James Brady was wounded at the battle of Brandywine, soon after he had enlisted, and had to quit for a time; Sam was appointed a first lieutenant when he was twenty, and became captain.

Then, in 1778 his brother James was killed by a band of Senecas under Chiefs Bald Eagle and Corn Planter. He fought bravely, single-handed, against them all. They tomahawked him five times in the head, and scalped him, but he crawled to safety and even used a rifle. That was the Brady way. He told the story, and died.

In the next year, 1779, old Captain John Brady, the father, was ambushed and murdered, by other Indians. Captain Samuel Brady had vowed vengeance for his brother James; now he vowed vengeance also for his father; he swore never to suffer torture, but to kill right and left, and henceforth, as the chronicles say, he "made Indian killing his business."

When he had the opportunity to be captain of spies against the Indians, he accepted gladly. This was in 1780, and by orders of General Washington.

The Indians of the upper country, above Pittsburgh,

or Fort Pitt, were threatening trouble. General Washington decided to reconnoiter them. He directed Colonel Daniel Brodhead, commanding at Fort Pitt, to send out scouts, locate the Indians and count them. Colonel Brodhead well knew that for this kind of a job there was no better man than Captain Samuel Brady; and Captain Brady went.

He took with him John Williamson, Martin Wetzel, and several Chickasaws. The three whites dressed as Indians, in paint and feathers. Captain Samuel spoke the Wyandot tongue. They set their trail for the great Wyandot Huron town of Upper Sandusky, in north central Ohio.

This was the heart of the Indian country. The sound of a white man's voice, the print of a white man's foot, in all that region, would call the rifle, the tomahawk and the stake. It was forbidden ground.

When near the town, the Chickasaws deserted, taking part of the ammunition with them. Likely enough they had gone on, to the Wyandots, with their news. But the three white Indians did not turn back; they continued, until at dusk one evening they reached the Sandusky River, close to the Wyandot town.

Captain Brady made his arrangements. He left Scout Wetzel, and taking John Williamson waded the river to an island separated from the town by only a narrow channel. Here he and John hid themselves in the brush, and waited for morning.

The morning dawned in such a fog that they could not see a rod. Captain Samuel fidgeted. He hated to waste time.

THE RENOWNED CAPTAIN BRADY OF PENNSYLVANIA

(From an Old Print)

"If it does not clear, I shall go into the village and see what I can see at close quarters," he said.

However, about eleven o'clock the fog lifted. All the great town, of hundreds of lodges, lay spread before them, with thousands of Indians hastening to and fro, preparing to race horses.

It was a gala day for the savage Wyandots. A war party of them had returned from the south, bringing a fine bag of Virginia and Kentucky blooded animals. The starting post of the races was squarely in front of the two spies' hiding place; they could have thrown a stone to it. For several hours they watched. There was one gray horse that won every race, until two Indians together mounted him, as a handicap; and then he barely lost. Captain Brady's fingers itched to grasp that gray champion's bridle thong—and he was the kind of a man to do so, with half a chance. But it was not to be, this time.

At dusk that night he boldly entered the town. He did not find the horse; nevertheless he slipped about, as much an Indian as any Wyandot—and his heart was in his throat at every step. The air fairly bristled with danger. One false move on his part, and another Brady would have fallen to the hatchet.

He strolled carelessly—he gained the edge of the town again and away he went, to John Williamson on the island.

"Did you make it, Sam?"

"Yes; but be quick. We must cut loose. They suspicioned me—they smelt a mouse."

They lost no time in joining Scout Wetzel. All this

night they traveled hard, to the southward. At daylight they sighted the sign of Indians, on their trail. They set out again. Now it was Indian against Indian, for they three were up to all Indian tricks. They took to the streams, they stepped from dry log to dry log, and from rock to rock. On the afternoon of the third day they thought that they had out-witted their pursuers, and halted to rest.

John Williamson stood guard. Captain Brady had only one fault, on the trail: he was a prodigious snorer. He began to snore so loudly that the very trees quivered.

"You're enough to alarm all the Indians betwixt here and Sandusky," John Williamson complained; and got up and turned him over, hoping to quiet him.

John sat down again by the fire. Then he heard a twig crack, and looked, and amidst the forest aisles he saw an Indian cautiously stealing forward.

He did not move; he pretended to have heard and seen nothing. The Indian stole on, rifle and tomahawk ready. John seemed to be nodding—until, just at the right time, he whirled, leveled his own rifle, it cracked sharply, and with a single bound the Indian crumpled, dead.

Up sprang Captain Brady and Scout Wetzel, their own guns in hand.

"What's that?"

"A dead Injun. Get out o' here. There may be more—drat your confounded snoring!"

They dived for shelter; but evidently the warrior had been alone, for no others were seen until they had arrived at the Big Beaver, not far north of Fort McIntosh which is to-day Beaver City.

By this time they were out of food. Captain Brady shot an old otter, but the flesh was so musty that they could not eat it. Now the charge in his reloaded gun was the only ammunition they had. He found a fresh deer track in a narrow trail, and left them eating strawberries while he followed the track.

"I'll bring back meat, or my name's not Brady," he promised.

He trailed the deer, and came upon it standing broadside while it browsed. Good! He took aim, but the rifle flashed in the pan. Off ran the deer.

"Tarnation!" muttered Captain Brady, and sat down to prick the touch-hole. Then he determinedly set out after the deer.

He had gone only a little way, when at a bend in the trail he saw, before him, a large Indian, horseback, with a white baby held in front and a white woman on the horse's rump, behind. There they were, coming, the three on one horse, the baby tied fast to the warrior.

Captain Brady sank down, out of sight. His quick eye had taken it all in. The woman's face was bruised; her arm broken; her hair was flowing loosely—she was a captive, and he *knew* her! The baby's head was rolling from side to side. It was asleep! Close following the Indian, there rode in single file a full company of other Indians. They were a returning war party, laden with spoils.

Captain Brady raised his rifle. He had only the one load, but he did not hesitate to use it. He waited; he must take care not to harm the baby or the mother. Presently he had fair show. The rifle spoke; off from the horse plunged the big Indian, bringing the baby and mother with him.

"Why did you risk your one shot?" Captain Brady was afterward asked.

"Well," he grinned, "I figgered on getting plenty more powder off the Injun."

At the rifle's crack the file of warriors bolted hither-thither, scattering like quail for covert. Captain Brady rushed forward, shouting loudly.

"Surround 'em, boys! Kill the rascals! At 'em, at 'em! Give 'em Brandywine."

The Indians would think that he had an army. He ran to the fallen brave and the struggling woman and baby. First he grabbed at the powder-horn—but he could not tear it free.

The woman glared at him wildly. He looked like an Indian, himself.

"Why did you shoot your brother?" she cried. She did not understand.

"Jenny Stupe (or did he really say: "Jenny, stoop!"?), I'm Sam Brady. Quick, now! Come with me and I'll save you both."

The Indians dared not charge, but they pelted him with bullets as he dashed through the brush, carrying the baby and dragging Jenny by the hand. Never a ball touched them.

They gained the strawberry patch. It was vacant—for his whoops had alarmed Rangers Williamson and Wetzel as well as the Indians; and being without ammunition they had legged it. Sam Brady had stirred up a hornets' nest. There was no use in their staying.

The next day he and Jenny Stupe and the baby, tired and hungry, entered Fort McIntosh on the Ohio River at the mouth of the Big Beaver. His gun was still empty, but that had not mattered.

As an expert at leaving a blind trail or no trail at all, Captain Sam Brady had no equal. Nothing pleased him more than to lose himself to his own men; while to deceive the Indians, and lure them on, was his constant joy. Consequently when, along in 1781, they captured him, quite by accident, in his lone camp up the Beaver, they gladly hustled him northward for a jubilee.

All the Wyandot town of Sandusky welcomed him with clubs and shrieks. He was painted black—the paint of death—and tied loosely to the stake by the ankles and the waist, so that he might squirm. He had been pretty well beaten, and seemed so exhausted that they had no fears of his escaping.

The next year the Wyandots ceased to burn prisoners. But now they heaped the fagots around Captain Brady, and applied the torch for a slow fire.

"We got you, Sam Brady," they jeered. "You no lose Injun; Injun no lose Sam."

They danced about him, awaiting his agonies. He said no word, but he had his wits keenly sharpened. He was not a "gone coon" yet. The squaws were worse than the men. There was one squaw, a chief's squaw, with a baby in her arms, especially aggravating. She darted in, to strike him. Instantly his two hands flew out, tore the baby from her and dropped it into the blaze.

She screamed; she and the warriors dived to rescue it—and on the second Captain Brady had snapped his bonds and was plunging at top speed for freedom. He knocked down two warriors, and cleared a way, then he was into the open, and out and on like a deer, with the town in pursuit.

Bullets and hatchets missed him. He bounded into the nearest brush; won the river, first; wading and swimming crossed it, and a wide country lay before.

He knew better than to turn south for Fort McIntosh. That was expected of him, but only in the unexpected might he find safety. So he headed eastward for the Pennsylvania border. He ran steadily, using every trick in his pack. Up hill and down he ran, day and night, scarcely pausing to rest; a party of the Indians continued to press him closely, and at the end of one hundred miles he was being forced to the Cuyahoga River in present Portage County, northeastern Ohio.

He knew of a ford there—the Standing Stone, it was called. But when he had almost arrived, naked and torn and bleeding, he found himself out-guessed. The Indian whoops sounded; the enemy were there before him—they held the ford and they hemmed him in on either flank.

Straight onward, in front, the river had cut a gorge, thirty feet deep and some twenty-five feet in width: a sheer up-and-down. That was the trap laid for him; and just a moment he despaired. Had he come so far, merely to be taken at last?

126

No! Not yet. He increased his speed, and set all his muscles. The Indians were yelling triumphantly. They had Sam Brady again. But their yells suddenly died. What was that? They had witnessed a marvelous sight. From the brink of the gorge the figure of Sam Brady had launched itself into the air; arms and legs extended it had been out-lined for an instant, in space, then had landed—Crash!—amidst the thin bushes clinging to the opposite edge, had scrambled, recovered, hauled itself a few feet, and was disappearing.

Their rifles cracked hastily. But with a bullet in his leg Captain Brady ran on.

The Indians clustered for just a moment, to stare with amazement.

"White man jump; Injun no jump," they jabbered, excited. So they crossed by the ford, and striking his blood spatters easily followed his trail.

Captain Brady was about all in. His wounded leg bothered him, his great leap had shaken him. But he knew of a lake, ahead, and made for it. It was his last resort. He got there, in time, and like a mad thing surged neck deep among the pond lilies. By quick work (he heard the yells coming nearer) he snapped a lily stem; and sinking to the bottom he held himself down, with the hollow stem in his mouth and the other end at the surface. He might stay there, and breathe!

The broad leaves of the pond lilies covered his hiding place; the stem gave him air. The Indians reached the pond, and saw his tracks leading in. He faintly heard them splashing about. All that day they searched and waited; they were there until late into the night; soaked and cold and cramped, he felt as though he could not stand it much longer; but he gritted his teeth and determined that he would die, of himself, rather than yield them his scalp.

At last, having heard no muffled sounds through the water or through the hollow stem for some time, he risked rising to the surface. All was quiet. The darkness concealed him. He might straighten his limbs and breathe freely. By thunder, he was safe!

Several days afterward, Captain Sam Brady limped into Fort Pitt. For a long time the Indians believed that he had drowned himself. They never quite understood how he had managed to leap that gorge. Even the exact spot of the famous Brady's Leap is disputed. One gorge, claimed to be the place, measures twenty-five feet across. Another measured twenty-seven feet and a half.

Here the Indians, traveling to view it, carved a turkey foot in a rock.

"Sam Brady no man; he turkey. No jump; flew," they declared.

None of them ever managed to capture Sam Brady and keep him. He defied them and lived on. In 1786 he married the lovely Drusilla Swearingen—daughter of another noted soldier and Indian fighter, Captain Van Swearingen who was called "Indian Van."

Captain Swearingen did not favor the match.

"It will only make Dru a widow," he said. "I do not wish her to mate with a man who is always on the trail."

They were married, just the same; and to state the truth, the young wife did suffer "untold miseries" while waiting for her daring Sam to return from his long forays. He was lame, from the wound in his leg; and partially deaf from his plunge beneath the pond; but he hated to leave the Injun trail.

Finally he was worn out, and consented to spend a few years at home, in West Liberty, West Virginia. Here he died, aged about forty-four, or in 1800, an old man before his time, but with his years crammed to over-flowing with brave memories.

CHAPTER VIII

THE FLIGHT OF THREE SOLDIERS (1782)

ON THE TRAIL WITH THE CRAWFORD MEN

FOLLOWING the last attack, in 1778, upon Boonesborough, Colonel John Bowman of Harrod's Station had led a revenge expedition into the Ohio country. At Little Chillicothe, where Daniel Boone had been son to Chief Black Fish, he had fought the Shawnees and their allies the Wyandots and others; and although he had been driven back his men had killed old Black Fish. That was a blow to the enemy.

More important than this, beginning in 1778 the great Long Knife chief, General George Rogers Clark, had "captured" the Illinois country clear to the Mississippi River at Kaskaskia below St. Louis; had marched northward one hundred and fifty miles, laid siege to the British garrison of St. Vincents (Vincennes, Indiana), and taken prisoner no less a personage than the noted Lieutenant-Governor Henry Hamilton of Detroit; and in 1780 had destroyed the Shawnee towns of Pickaway and Little Chillicothe also.

These events and others stirred the Northern Confederacy to action afresh. They saw the Ohio Valley being cut in two. They had given up Boonesborough; but there were many other forts and stations and settlements and they sent their parties against the Ameri-

130

cans of western Pennsylvania, West Virginia, and the outskirts of Kentucky along the Ohio.

The principal Wyandot town of Upper Sandusky (where Simon Kenton had been rescued by Pierre Drouillard the British Indian agent), in central north Ohio, seemed to be the rallying place for the bloody forays. General Washington could spare no regular troops yet, to campaign on the Indian trail; so in order to "shake up" the red rascals volunteer militiamen and Rangers for miles back in southwestern Pennsylvania and northwestern West Virginia and adjacent Kentucky were summoned to gather, secretly, May 20, 1782, at Mingo Bottom (present Mingo Junction, Ohio) on the west side of the Ohio River about forty miles up from Fort Pitt.

Three hundred had been called for; four hundred and eighty arrived—mainly Pennsylvanians, and the bulk of them crack-shot bordermen in moccasins, leggins, fringed buckskin hunting shirts, armed with the long patch-and-ball rifle, tomahawk and scalping-knife, and mounted upon the best of their horses. It was to be an earnest expedition—a stroke at the heart of the Indian country. Before leaving home, many of the men had made their wills.

The popular William Crawford was elected commander. He had been an ensign with Washington in the General Braddock campaign of the fatal 1755; had been colonel under General Washington in the Buff-and-Blue Continental Army, and was General Washington's intimate friend: but Lord Cornwallis, the British general, had surrendered at Yorktown last fall,

131

the War of the Revolution appeared to be almost over, and he had returned home as a veteran.

The guides were Jonathan Zane of Wheeling (one of the fighting Zanes) and John Slover, another Virginian.

Much dependence was placed upon John Slover. When eight years old, or about in 1760, he had been captured by the Miami Indians and taken to Upper Sandusky town. He had lived there among the Miamis and Wyandots, had mingled with the Shawnees, Delawares and Mingo Iroquois, for twelve years, and they had treated him well. He rather liked being an Indian. Then during a peace council at Fort Pitt in 1773 he had met his real kindred again. They had persuaded him to be a white man; therefore he had bade his Indian brothers goodby, and had walked away with his new-found relatives.

He, also, had served in the Revolution, as a sharp-shooter. Now he felt badly at having been asked to guide the Long Knife column against his old-time Indian friends, and the town that had sheltered him; it seemed to him not an honorable thing to do. Still, he was an American soldier and citizen; there was war between the white and the red, and dreadful deeds had been done by hatchet and knife, upon his very neighbors. His duty was plain. He could not stay behind or refuse to aid. Therefore he consented to guide and fight, in the cause of his fellow settlers and the protection of the women and children.

The surgeon of the column was Dr. John Knight—a small but gritty little man. Among the Rangers was

132

James Paull, of West Virginia, a young Buckskin of twenty-two who had left his widowed mother in order to march to Sandusky.

The column met with such a defeat as had been known but once since the day of Braddock's Field. For the Indians were ready. Their spies had reported upon the secret gathering at the old Mingo town of Mingo Bottom. To all the villages of the north and even to Detroit the word traveled that the Long Knives were coming.

Captain Pipe, the old war-chief of the Delawares, and his aide, Chief Wingenund, arrayed two hundred warriors and marched from the eastward to join the four hundred Wyandots of Chief Half King and Chief Shaus-sho-to, and defend the Sandusky. In the south the Shawnees of Black Hoof and Black Beard and all, prepared. The Miamis rallied from the west. The white captains, Alexander McKee and the Girty brothers, urged the warriors on. A messenger to the British father at Detroit brought back promise of reinforcements from there. The British father was sending his Butler's Mounted Rangers and three cannon, and the great white captain Matthew Elliott to command the whole army.

All the long, long way up from the Ohio River the Colonel William Crawford column had seen only two Indians. On June 4 they sighted their goal, the old Wyandot town of Upper Sandusky. It showed not a sign of life. They marched upon it. The buildings had been leveled and grass was growing in the crooked streets. Some months before, Chief Half King had

moved his people eight miles northward, down the Sandusky.

Guide John Slover had led in vain. He, also, was
mystified. The volunteers were disappointed; they
wished to turn back. The council of officers decided
upon one more day's march; then if nothing happened,
back they would go and glad to get out of the land
alive.

It was a wide, grassy, forest-dotted country strange
to the Long Knives. Few of them, not even the Zanes
and the Wetzels and their like, had ever been here
except as prisoners. They did not know, John Slover
did not know, that only eleven miles to the east was
the eager village of Chief Pipe and his Delawares; that
only eighteen miles north was the principal village of
Chief Half King and his painted Hurons: and that six
hundred warriors of the two nations had come together,
with guns loaded and hatchets sharpened, to await the
Shawnees, the Miamis and the British Rangers guided
by Matthew Elliott, and wipe the Americans from the
trail.

The Long Knives moved fearfully on. To them, the
air was full of threat. The Delawares and Hurons met
them, and held them in check. June 5 the Shawnees,
Miamis and the Rangers tore in. Matthew Elliott, in
his brilliant uniform, had taken command; his comrade
renegade, Simon Girty, as his lieutenant raged hither-
thither on a white horse. Beset amidst the timber islands and the cranberry swamps the Long Knives broke
in retreat. Their horses mired. The best efforts of
Jonathan Zane, Lewis Wetzel, brave Colonel Craw-

134

ford the Continental, other men and officers, availed little.

Four hundred and eighty, the flower of the border, were over-matched by one thousand, the full strength of the Northern Confederacy.

The battle ended on the night of June 6. Three hundred of the Long Knives remained together, and reached the Ohio. By ones and twos and threes others straggled in. But many did not come. Among them were Colonel Crawford, his son John Crawford, Major John McClelland of a famous border family, Dr. Knight, John Slover, young James Paull—and he, and he, and he, a score of them whose fate might be guessed at only with a shudder.

Of these, few ever did return. The noble Colonel Crawford had been captured. He was the "Big Captain"—he must die, and Chief Pipe, another "Big Captain," ordered him to terrible torture. Boyish John Crawford and Major McClelland also were killed in the Indian way. But little Doctor Knight the surgeon, Guide John Slover and young James Paull finally turned up, at home, with remarkable stories now to be told.

Doctor Knight had been taken, along with his colonel and several comrades. They were eleven in number, prisoners to the Delawares. Captain Pipe had marched them to his own town. Their hopes had been flickering, they thought that Simon Girty might help them, but on the way Chief Pipe and Chief Wingenund had painted them black. Then nine of them were killed by a mob. And at Pipe's Town Doctor Knight had sickened in watching his colonel burned before his eyes. That was an afternoon and night of horror.

"You," said Chief Pipe to him, "will be taken to the Shawnee towns to see your friends."

To see his *friends!* Doctor Knight did not know whether this meant his "friends" the Shawnees, or his other friends who had been tortured like Colonel Crawford. It all amounted to the same thing. He resolved to escape or die while trying. Already he had been given a broken jaw.

In the morning he was painted black again, and sent away afoot in charge of a large Shawnee, who drove him with a hickory whip. They were bound for the Shawnee towns, forty miles southwest—probably to Wakatomica. The doctor, who was not much over five feet tall and weighed scarcely more than one hundred and twenty, trotted valiantly, glad that he had not been tied by a rope. But because he was so small, and was not a warrior, the Shawnee seemed to think him harmless.

A warrior armed with gun and hatchet and knife should have no fear of a midget white man who had been well beaten.

"There lie the bones of your Big Captain," the Shawnee jeered, when they passed the charred Crawford stake.

The doctor only smiled as well as he could, with such a jaw. He showed no fear. He pretended to feel safe, for he was going "to see his friends." He began to make up to his guard, whose name was Tutelu.

For all his surly looks Tutelu proved to be good-

The Fight of the Privates

natured. He and the doctor proceeded to fool each other.

"When we reach the Shawnee towns, you and I will live together in the same cabin, as brothers," the doctor proposed.

Tutelu grinned. He grinned to think that this white man was so simple, and he grinned to think that this white man wished to live with him.

"Yes," he said. "You make good cabin! Know how?"

"I will build us such a great cabin that the council-house will look small," assured the doctor.

"Heap cabin maker, huh?" answered Tutelu, much impressed "See, to-morrow." And they journeyed on like friends, except for the whip.

But the wool was not yet pulled over Tutelu's eyes. In camp to-night he tied his prisoner; and whenever the doctor stirred, to loosen the knots, Tutelu's gaze glowed upon him, through the darkness. There was no chance to do a thing.

"Reach Shawnee town to-morrow when sun is high," Tutelu had announced, before lying down. And all night the doctor thought and thought, and worked vainly at his knots.

When at daybreak his keeper untied him, he determined that he would attempt escape, somehow, at once. The Shawnees should not torture him as all the rest had been tortured.

They did not start immediately. Tutelu squatted, to renew the fire, in order to get breakfast. The mosquitoes and gnats were very bad; they hovered in clouds, lit upon his naked back and bit him severely. With one hand he poked the fire, with the other he slapped and scratched, while grunting angrily about the pests.

"Brother, I will make a smoke behind you," spoke the doctor, who had a desperate idea. "Then we can sit between two smokes and be at peace."

"All right," Tutelu grunted.

There was a little stick near at hand. It was a dog-wood stick, only eighteen inches long and not thicker than two fingers—not much of a weapon. But the doctor was desperate. He picked it up, rolled a coal upon it, held the coal in place with a smaller stick, and walked around behind Tutelu, as if to start another fire. He laid down the coal, and drew long breath. It was now or perhaps never. Suddenly he turned, and half rising struck with all his strength. The dog-wood fork fairly bounced upon the Indian's head.

"Wagh!" gasped Tutelu. He had been knocked forward, so that he fell with his two hands and almost with his face into his fire. Instantly he was up, before the doctor might strike again. He ran howling, with his head bloody. He had no stomach for another blow. His prisoner had changed to a demon.

The doctor sprang for the rifle. He must kill, or else the alarm would be spread. But he was so excited that in cocking the rifle he broke the lock. Tutelu feared a bullet. As he still ran, howling, he dodged and doubled like a rabbit, until he had disappeared in the timber and his howls soon died away.

Now the doctor worked fast. He grabbed up Tutelu's powder-horn and bullet-pouch, blanket and moccasins, and ran, too.

In about an hour he came to the open prairie. He did not dare to cross it in the daytime, so he hid in the edge of it. That night he traveled by the north star, gained the other side by morning, and kept on until late in the afternoon.

He was no woodsman. He could not fix the gun, and finally threw it away. He could not chew, but he knew the herbs and weeds that were good to eat, and he sucked on these. He found plenty of green gooseberries; they upset his stomach, and he relieved himself with wild ginger. He ate three fledgling black-birds, from a nest; and he ate the soft parts of a land tortoise, torn apart with his fingers and sticks, because he had no knife.

After wandering twenty-one days he reached Fort McIntosh on the Ohio below Pittsburgh.

What of the cowardly Tutelu? Tutelu, still in great terror, arrived at Wakatomica. He panted in with a big story. He showed his head. It was laid open, four inches long, to the bone! He showed his feet. They were filled with thorns. He said that his prisoner had been a giant, with the strength of a buffalo. While they had been talking together, the giant had pulled up a young tree and battered him first on one side of the head and then on the other. They had tussled. He had stabbed the giant twice, in the belly and in the back, and had left him for dead. At least, the fellow would die soon, for he had not been able to pursue.

But a white man was here in Wakatomica. He was

John Slover; he spoke three Indian languages—Miami, Shawnee and Huron; and when he heard Tutelu's wonderful tale, he laughed. He told the other Indians the truth: that the prisoner was a little doctor and not a warrior—only five feet and a half tall and weighing no more than a boy! The Indians laughed long and loud. They bombarded Tutelu with broad jokes, and the best he could do was to go off to get his head dressed.

John Slover had been captured. He and James Paull and four others were threading homeward from the battle trail when several Indians had ambushed them; with one volley killed two, then had summoned the rest to surrender.

He and young James were the only men with guns. John Slover leveled his from behind a tree, to fight; but the leader of the Indians had called: "No shoot, no hurt. Treat good." Therefore he and two others had yielded. James Paull dived aside into the brush and ran. It seemed as though he got away.

One of the Indians was an old Miami who had helped to make prisoner of John Slover when a boy twenty-two years before. He knew him at once—called him by his Indian name Man-nuch-cothe, and scolded him for "bearing arms against his brothers." That was hard luck. Scout Slover saw himself trapped, and could not reply. He figured that unless he could explain matters he was in for a bad time.

The Indians took the three of them to Wakatomica; painted the oldest man black and made them all run the gauntlet; killed the man who had been painted for death, but let John and the other man reach the posts

140

of the council-house. Then the other man was led away, to another town; he never appeared again, and John Slover was left alone in Wakatomica.

He was rather blue when Tutelu had come in. He had found some friends, but he had more enemies. The worst was James Girty, a brother to Simon Girty.

James Girty told the Indians that he had asked Man-nuch-cothe how he would like to live with old friends again; and Man-nuch-cothe had laughed and said: "I will live here long enough to take a scalp. Then I will steal a horse and go back to the whites."

This enraged the town. A grand council was held, to decide about John Slover. It lasted fifteen days. John spoke in his own defence, in the Shawnee tongue. He knew many of the chiefs by name. They knew him. He spoke well.

"I am here. I am not ashamed. I lived with you twelve years. You treated me kindly. On my part I never tried to escape. You gave me many chances, but I was red. Your cabins were my home. You were my fathers and brothers. When I left, I did not run away. I had found my own blood. It called to me. I said good-by, and shook your hands. You were willing. It was done in the open, there at Fort Pitt. That was a peace council. You had no thought of war again. I had no thought of war again between the red people and the white people. We all were to be brothers. When I lived with you, I would have helped you fight your enemies. That was my duty. A warrior's duty is to serve his country. Your country was then my country. When I went to live with the whites, I became a warrior there. Their country was my country. If you think I deserve death for acting like a warrior, you may kill me. I am in your power. I am alone. As for the words of James Girty, they are lies. I have not spoken with him. You know me. Do you take me for a child? I am not a child; I am a man. If I had thought such a thing that he says, would I have been foolish enough to say it to him? No. He is an enemy to all whites. Everybody knows that. Then why should I have told my thoughts to him, as he says? He lies, in order to kill me. I am done."

The council listened keenly. Some of the chiefs believed, and softened. The speech rang true; it came from the heart. The sentence was postponed and John Slover was released and kindly treated. He took up quarters with an old squaw, who called him her son. He went to the dances. He was an Indian again. All this might mean little, but he took hope.

The town was eager for news of the war between their British father across the water, and the Long Knives.

"The war is over," John explained. "A great British general and all his army have surrendered to the Long Knives of Washington. His name is Cornwallis. He surrendered many moons ago. There is peace talk. Are your ears stopped up, that you have not heard?"

"We have not heard," they answered, astonished. "No one has told us. We will ask if it is true."

They asked James Girty and Alexander McKee. James Girty was frequently drunk, and altogether worthless; but Captain McKee, the British trader, lived in a large house of hewn white-oak logs, wore a fine uniform, kept by himself, and was highly thought of.

He and James Girty laughed at the story of John Slover.

"That is a lie," they said. "He tries to frighten you. The British soldiers have been eating up the Americans. They soon will capture that man Washington. We say so, and we know."

Another white Indian reported that Slover had agreed with him to escape. This angered the town, again. A general council was called. The council-house was filled with Shawnees, Mingos, Chippewas, Delawares and Hurons. Two Indians came to the old squaw's cabin to get her "son." She covered him with a large bear-skin, in a corner, and drove the two Indians out with a club and her tongue.

John waited. He knew what would happen. Presently, in strode George Girty, another of the brothers, in Delaware paint. He brought forty warriors with him. They threw the old squaw to one side, and dragged John Slover through the door; tore off all his clothes, painted him black, tied his hands, and triumphantly marched him away, by a rope around his neck.

Evidently the council had decided. The old squaw wailed vainly. She had only hastened his doom.

"We have waited long enough," gibed George Girty, swearing horridly. "Now you'll get what you deserve. You'll eat fire."

They took him to a smaller town of Wakatomica, five

miles distant. There they and the other people beat
him for an hour. It was the beginning. They hustled him on to a third town, named Mequa-chake—Red
Earth. John Slover lost all hope. He was Indian
enough to know. Mequa-chake was to be his finish.
He had no friends here.

The stake was ready, for hoots and howls and shaken
fists greeted him. The people—warriors, squaws, boys
and girls—old and young they could scarcely wait.
He was towed and shoved and jostled to the council-
house. It was only half roofed. The stake, a stout
post sixteen feet high, had been planted in the center
of the unroofed part. Four feet from its base there
were three piles of wood—dry hickory, that makes the
hottest kind of a fire. But he was to be scorched, not
consumed at once.

In a moment more he had been bound to the post: one
thong around his neck, one around his waist, one
around his shins. They strapped him as tightly as a
mummy. It was fast work. He saw no sign of mercy;
he saw no chance of rescue, like Simon Kenton had.

The evening was beautiful, save for a hard wind.
The wind would fan the flames. A warrior thrust a
torch into the piles of hickory. A chief commenced to
speak, bidding all watch the prisoner die but not to
let him die too quickly. The wood was crackling, the
heat of the flames wafted across John Slover's black-
painted skin; he stiffened and held himself taut. He
would bear himself like a man, and utter never a groan.

The heat increased; the orator was still haranguing;
whew! Hah! What was that? The wind had ceased,

the sky had darkened, there was a roll of thunder and the rain pattered! The drops pelted thicker, the cloud burst and a regular deluge descended, hissing into the fire, smudging it, drenching John Slover, driving the crowd away, under the roof—and putting out the fire completely.

A gasp of astonishment, almost awe, arose. The Great Spirit had interfered! The storm passed in twenty minutes, and left the sky clear for the setting sun. The Indians gained courage. Some were for rekindling the fire; but the wood was wet. There was no sport in burning a man with wet wood. So they untied him and seated him upon the ground. Then they danced the scalp dance around him for three hours, the while they kicked him, and beat him with sticks. At last they grew tired. He had again lost hope.

"You will burn in the morning," they jeered.

"Are you not sleepy, brother?" asked a tall young chief, Half Moon.

"Yes, I am," John answered, although that was a queer question to ask of a man battered like he was.

"Very well; we will all sleep, so that you may be fresh to eat fire to-morrow."

"A pleasant night for me," thought John.

Now it was eleven o'clock, by the stars. He was taken to a log cabin, under three guards. They tied his wrists and elbows together behind his back, with buffalo-hide thongs that bit into his flesh. They put a noose close around his neck and fastened the end of the rope to a beam above, giving him just enough slack so that he might lie down.

145

The three guards smoked their pipes and made themselves disagreeable by telling him about to-morrow. It seemed as though they never would go to bed and let him alone. After a time two of them did stretch out; they began to snore. The other sat up; smoked and smoked and talked and talked; described to him all the ceremonies of "eating fire," wondered with him how long he would hold out, encouraged him to stand the torture bravely and not forget that he once had been an Indian.

This was decidedly an aggravating old man, but John Slover answered not a word. Nevertheless, he was suffering tortures already. He traced the first paling of the air—token of dawn; and still the old man did not sleep. There was no chance of escape. Did the fellow intend to talk all night?

Ah! He had dropped his pipe; his voice drawled off; he turned upon his side, and snored!

The air was gray; in an hour it would be daylight. John wrestled fiercely with his tied wrists until the sweat beaded his forehead. He writhed, as he lay; he dared make no noise, but how he did strain!

Hurrah! He had slipped one arm—his left—past the other. The blood tingled in the numbed, swollen veins; his heart beat furiously. Then he sank back, his heart pounding worse than ever. The old man had sat up. Confound him! Was he going to talk again—and daylight so near? No. He only stirred the fire, cast a sharp glance at the prisoner, and stretched out, to snore once more.

John instantly busied himself. He clawed at the

noose around his neck; he tugged at the rope, he took a little slack, and half sitting up, gnawed at it. But it was green buffalo-hide, as thick as his thumb, and he might as well have gnawed wire cable. His teeth did not even break the surface. He tugged until his fingers bled.

He sank back again, exhausted. Must he die at the stake? How light the air was getting! "One more try," he said, to himself. He inserted his raw fingers between the stubborn noose and his throbbing neck, and hauled.

A miracle! It was a slip noose, with a knot in it to hold it. The slip knot passed the other knot—his very blood and sweat had helped; the noose widened, he ducked out of it, and was free. Now he might die fighting, at least.

He wasted no time. The village would be astir early, eager for the sport. Old squaws likely were about already; dogs prowling. Day was at hand. He carefully stepped over the three figures, he glided through the doorway, and was into the fresh open air. How good it felt!

Silence reigned in the village, but in the sky the stars had almost vanished. He had not a half hour of leeway. He ran for the nearest corn-field—well-nigh stumbled upon a squaw sleeping out of doors in the midst of five children, but managed to leap them. It was a narrow escape.

He gained the corn-field, and had glimpsed some loose horses. In the corn-field he paused and untied his right arm, which had swollen black. He must have a horse, or he never would get away with such a short start. So he ran back for a horse. Fortune favored him, for he was brave. He grabbed a piece of old blanket from a fence and caught a horse by the mane; rapidly twisted the rope from his arm into a halter, flung the blanketing across the horse's back, vaulted aboard, hammered with his heels, and rode, a naked man on a scarcely less naked steed.

He charged recklessly on, through the forest. The branches lashed him fiercely; he did not even feel them. His thoughts all were ahead, ahead, leading to the Scioto River, fifty miles eastward toward the Pennsylvania border.

What a good horse that was! He had chosen the first at hand, but he had chosen the best in the herd. Mile after mile they forged, never slackening. He fancied that he heard pursuit; before this the guards had discovered his absence, the village was aroused and hot in chase. The sun was up, and shining strongly. At this time he might have been "eating fire"; that would not happen now—he would die by bullet, first.

He rode. He pitied the horse, but kept it at the gallop. The sun rose high and higher, and they still were galloping free, up hill and down, through forest, swamp and prairie. If he only might cross the Scioto!

He saw it, before. The time was verging upon noon. He reached the Scioto at eleven o'clock. They had come fifty miles through the trailless wilderness in seven hours! He dared not slacken. Together they plunged into the stream and swam across. He mounted again; they were away. The swim had freshened the good horse, it galloped again.

The sun was past the noon mark. Now the horse breathed heavily; it stumbled, its eyes bulged redly, it had nearly run its course. He forced it on, and it obeyed until it dropped dead under him. It had borne him twenty-five more miles—seventy-five miles in eleven hours, for the time was three o'clock.

A gallant horse, but he could not stop to mourn. He seized the sweat-soaked blanket from its back and ran. The horse had done well, and he had to trust to his own legs. He was not yet safe.

John Slover, naked and carrying the blanket, ran from three in the afternoon until ten o'clock at night. Once he had halted, to sink, breathless, for a rest. He thought that he heard a halloo, behind him. That was a spur. He leaped up and ran on until star-light. Then he rested for two hours; he had not eaten since day before yesterday, and had not slept. At midnight the moon had risen. He stiffly stood, and ran and walked from midnight to morning.

Now he played the Indian. He tried to leave no trail. He changed his course for the southeast, and with a stick bent the grass upright behind him, where he had stepped. This made his progress slower, but more sure. He was getting tired. If the Indians caught him, he would be an easy victim. However, he had no mind to be caught.

Once he was obliged to sit down, sick. He vomited, and this eased him, so he could go on again. His legs and feet were full of nettles and thorns; the gnats and

149

mosquitoes pestered him horribly, for his piece of blanketing did not cover him. He fought them with a leafy branch, and threshing about him, he toiled ahead, cleverly using his crooked stick to conceal his trail.

On the third day, after a sleepless night, he ate a few wild raspberries. He was growing very weak, and every inch of him throbbed and smarted and stung. But he struck another river. It was the Muskingum, in eastern Ohio. He found a place only two hundred yards wide, and swam across. The next day he captured two small crawfish and ate them. The next night he sighted Wheeling, on the other side of the Ohio.

In the morning he yelled and waved from the bank. A man, opposite, saw him, and ventured part way over in a canoe. The man was afraid.

"Who are you? Who do you aim to be?"

"I am John Slover. Take me to Fort Henry."

"You're an Injun. You're no John Slover. He's dead. I've a notion to shoot you, myself."

"I'm Slover. I am Slover. I've escaped from the Shawnees. I'll name you some of the officers who were with Crawford."

So he did. The man took him into the canoe. He was saved. In five days he had eaten only a handful of raspberries and two raw crawfish; in five nights he had not slept a wink; in four days and nights he had traveled across country, by horse and foot, naked except for the piece of blanketing, for a distance of about two hundred miles. He was the true never-say-die kind, and lived for many a year yet, to tell of his adventures and to put them upon paper.

James Paull had reached home before him, and before Doctor Knight also. James was only twenty-two, but he was an old hand at Indian fighting and at scouting. And he was a lad of great spirit, as will now be shown.

When the Indians had fired into the party and then had called upon them to surrender, he had been the one to dodge and run. His foot was very lame from a burn. During the battle his mess had baked bread by spreading the dough upon the back of a spade, scout fashion. Somebody had tossed the hot spade aside, and he had stepped upon it with his bare foot. The burn was a bad one; during the retreat his foot got worse and he could scarcely walk on it.

But now with two Indians chasing him, he paid no attention to his foot. He out-ran them, leaped down the steep bank of a creek, and in landing tore all the skin from his blistered sole. He paid attention to it then. Had to! A man with a flayed foot cannot do much, in the brush.

Luckily for him, the two Indians gave him up. He halted long enough to bind his raw foot with a piece of his trousers. He could not travel fast, but he used his wits. He knew all the tricks of the trail. He hobbled along fallen logs, so as to leave no marks. He back-tracked, in a circle, to cross his own trail and see if he was being followed. He painfully shinned up trees, wormed out to the end of a branch, and dropped as far beyond his trail as he might, so as to break it. This would throw off the dogs, if dogs were used; yes, and it would fool the Indians, too.

That night he slept in a hollow log. By morning his foot had swollen to the size of a bucket. He suffered torment. He had no food with him and was afraid to fire his gun. So this day he ate only a few berries.

To-night he slept like a bear, on a bed of leaves in a crack in a rock. In the morning he sighted a deer. What with his pain and his hunger he was desperate. He shot the deer, cut it open with his gun-flint, and chewed at the bloody flesh.

This evening he came to an old Indian camp. Several empty whiskey-kegs were lying around. That gave him an idea. He could have a fire, to cook with. By building the fire underneath a keg, after dark, there would be no light, and the smoke could not be seen. He tried that, and it worked. After he had cooked and eaten, he slept in the smoke, which kept the mosquitoes off. Assuredly, young James Paull knew how to take care of himself.

In two days more he reached the Ohio River above Wheeling. On account of his foot and his gun he could not swim it. No matter. He made a raft of logs tied together with vines and strips of bark, and paddled over.

There he saw some horses grazing in a bottom. He must have a horse. He fashioned a halter from twisted bark, and hobbled about, trying to catch a mount. He limped and coaxed and sweated for two hours. The horses were frisky and suspicious. Every time he stalked one and was about to lay his hand upon its mane, it tossed its head and with a snort galloped away.

Finally he managed to grab the worst of the lot—an old mare. On her he rode on, down to Short Creek, where he found all the settlers gathered in the little fort there, under Major Sam McColloch, expecting an attack by the Indians who had defeated Colonel Crawford's column.

Other refugees from the battle-field had brought the alarming news. He was asked many questions—about Colonel Crawford, and Doctor Knight, and John Slover, and the score who were missing with them. He could tell little. All he knew, was, that he had escaped, and that he wished to get word to his mother, down in Virginia.

He did not stay. He borrowed a better horse and hastened on—got as far as the cabin of his cousins, and here he had to stay and treat his foot. At first he feared that it ought to be cut off. It was a frightful looking foot, swollen and red and poisoned. However, in about ten days it grew better. He traveled down to his mother. She was in their cabin doorway, peering up the road.

"Jim!"

"Mother!"

She welcomed him as one back from the land of the dead. News was slow, in those days. Nevertheless—

"I knew you'd come—I knew you'd come," she sobbed, gladly, as he held her in his arms. For she was a widow and he was her only boy.

It was different with Mrs. Crawford and many another wife and mother. Mrs. Crawford waited day after day, for word from her husband, the gallant colonel. At last it arrived, with Doctor Knight, and all the border heard.

The brave and courtly Colonel William Crawford had been tortured and burned. So had his gallant young son, John—and others.

Mrs. Crawford never got over that loss. She loved her husband devotedly. Long years afterward, when she was old and wrinkled, she placed a little grandson behind her on her horse and took him far into the forest. She set him down beside a moss-covered log.

"Here is where I parted with your grandfather, when he rode against the Indians," she said. And she cried and cried.

CHAPTER IX

THE BRAVE WOMEN OF BRYANT'S STATION (1782)
AND THE DEFEAT OF THE VILLAIN GIRTY

THE words of John Slover, that the British army had surrendered and that the Americans were victors in the great war, were proved to be true. Now there arose much excitement among the Indians, in their towns and villages beyond the Ohio. Their British father had been laid upon his back, and they did not know exactly what to do.

In June of this year 1782, while Scout Slover was a captive, a grand council of the Northern Confederacy and their allies had been called at the Shawnee town of Wakatomica, to talk matters over. Delegates arrived from the Ottawas, Chippewas, Delawares, the southern Cherokees, Potawatomis, Wyandot Hurons, Mingo Iroquois, and from the other Shawnee towns. They all were alarmed at the unexpected triumph of the Long Knife people, and were fearful lest they had lost their prized hunting-ground, Kentucky.

White men were here: Captain William Caldwell, a trader in the British service; Alexander McKee, George and James Girty, and Simon Girty himself, coming in with a band of the Wyandots.

He made one of the principal speeches. He said that the war between the king and the Long Knives was

155

not yet over; but that, anyway, the Indians did not want a peace in which the British and the Americans should agree to quit fighting. For if they quit fighting, then the Long Knives would be free to turn, all of them, upon the Indians and crush them utterly. (Ugh! Ugh! That is so!) The Indians well knew how the white men were crowding in upon them, from Virginia —were stealing Kentucky and threatening the Ohio country. Without the help from the British father these lands would be swallowed up, the red man would have no hunting-grounds, no food, no furs, no means of getting food, rum and blankets. (Ugh! Ugh! Ugh! That is so!) A peace would be bad for the Indians. Let them join together at once, to wipe out the Americans and clean the hunting-grounds before too late. Now was the time. The American soldiers were still busy, and there were many British soldiers to keep them busy. Strike, strike harder than ever, in full force, and drive the Long Knives back, or peace might come and all Kentucky be over-run by the Long Knife soldiers. (Ugh! Ugh! Ugh! Those are good words. Our white brother speaks well.)

There were more speeches, but none better; and the council had agreed. Runners were sent out to carry the news and bid all Indians to rally for a great blow upon the Long Knives. The meeting-place should be at Pickaway, or Chillicothe as it was also called, after the other towns of Chillicothe. Little Chillocothe had been destroyed two years ago by the gallant General George Rogers Clark.

Two armies were formed: one of about three hundred warriors, to march against West Virginia; the other of about four hundred warriors, to march into Kentucky.

The Kentucky army contained mainly Shawnees and Wyandots, with a sprinkling of British white men from Detroit. It was commanded by Captain William Caldwell, who had for his lieutenants Alexander McKee, Matthew Elliott, and the three Girty brothers, Simon, George and James. And there were many chiefs.

In the night of August 15 they posted themselves around Bryant's (or Bryan's) Station of north central Kentucky about five miles north of little Lexington.

This Bryant's Station was a lonely post, and well exposed to attack. From it north and east to the Ohio River and West Virginia the country lay open and little settled.

Bryant's had been founded in 1779 by the Bryant brothers, from North Carolina. William Bryant was really its father. He had married Daniel Boone's sister, in North Carolina.

The Bryants settled here and formed Bryant's Station. Last year William himself had been killed, not far from the settlement, while he and a party were scouting. The Indians had lured him within reach, by tinkling a horse bell that they had taken. But he and a companion managed to reach home; there he died.

The killing of William Bryant, brother-in-law to Daniel Boone, and a general leader, was a sad blow to the settlement.

Forty log cabins formed Bryant's Station. They were placed in two lines facing inward, and connected by a stout picket fence or palisade. This beautiful morning of August 16 everybody was astir unusually early. An alarm call had issued from the region of the Kentucky River, twenty miles in the south. The Boonesborough country was again being invaded. Estill's Station had been entered—in pursuing the enemy Captain Estill himself and twenty-five men had been cut to pieces by twenty-five Wyandots. From the small Hoy's Station Captain John Holder had sallied in rescue of two captured boys, and he and his party also had been badly defeated.

Hoy's Station was threatened by a siege. Help was needed. The men of Bryant's Station had prepared to march out at daylight this morning to its relief. Captain John Craig commanded.

Bryant's Station did not know that it was surrounded, itself. How could it know? There was nothing to show that death couched amidst the trees and brush close at hand. The night had been unbroken; peace seemed to smile in the sparkle of the early morning dew. But cracking never a twig, with the stealth of creeping panthers the Indian army had arrived and had been posted.

Captain Caldwell divided his force. He stationed one hundred warriors in hiding about rifle-shot from the gate in the northwest end of the fort; told them to shoot and yell and draw the Long Knives out. The three hundred others he stationed in ambush within half rifle-shot of the spring opposite the other end, the southeast end, in readiness for a charge when the Long Knives should have been decoyed.

While Bryant's Station did not know what had happened outside, the Captain Caldwell men did not know what was happening, inside. Had they only waited, they would have seen all the soldier garrison march away, leaving the women and children and a few grandfathers—and the fort would have been seized without trouble except to the defenceless families.

But even when the army had arrived, in the night, the fort seemed to be on the alert: there were lights in the cabins, there were voices, there was bustle to and fro. And before sun-up the drum had beat the assembly, the soldiers were being put under arms—

Captain Caldwell, the Girtys, the chiefs, and all, were disappointed. They thought themselves expected. That was a piece of great fortune for Bryant's Station.

Soon several cabin doors, fronting outside, were cautiously opened, and figures stepped into the clear, as if on hasty errands. The fort gates, at one end, were being unbarred. It was time to try the decoy trick —and with a burst of shrill whoops the Indians posted for a feint fired their guns.

The figures ran, the doors were slammed, the gates closed. The attack had taken Bryant's Station all by surprise, and it wellnigh worked. The men rushed to the pickets, to peer. They saw a score of Indians, at safe distance, capering and gesturing and yelling insults, daring them to come out.

That was not to be borne. The young men were wild to sally and drive the red rascals from the

159

neighborhood. But the older heads smelled a mouse.

"No, boys. Wait a bit. It's a trick. There's something afoot. Those Injuns don't act natteral. They're too anxious. Let's take a good look at the spring, yonder, t' other side. That's where the reel trouble lies in shape o' painted skins, or I miss my guess."

They keenly scanned the coverts near the spring.

"See! Yes, by thunder! In the timber! See the brush shake! See that Shawnee scalp! See that fellow glidin' like a snake! The forest edge is full of 'em. They aim to draw us out at one end, so they can come in at the other. But we'll fool 'em."

"We can't march to Hoy's, this day."

"No. We'll need help, ourselves. Somebody'll have to go for it."

"And water! How about water! The bloody redskins have seized the spring."

For the spring, sixty yards distant, was the nearest water. Bryant's Station had been blindly located. Its water was outside instead of inside.

"First, to send for help. Be firming those loose pickets, too. Who'll slip away and break for Lexington!"

The garrison bustled, strengthening the pickets; the walls were manned; from a spot between cabins, where no Indians had been sighted, Rangers Bell and Tomlinson led out their horses, mounted and were off at a gallop. They were discovered, they broke through, they raced on, down the road for the town of Lexington, to summon reinforcements. It would be a perilous ride. Plainly enough the country was being covered by scouting bands of Indians, bent upon keeping the various forts busy. The disasters to Captain Estill and Captain Holder were a sign.

The two couriers got away. Now for the water. Without water, Bryant's Station would suffer—might be burned.

"The women'll have to go for the water, boys."

"Why so? Women? You'd send the women out, to those tomahawks?"

The women had heard. They gathered, indignant.

"We're as brave as you are, but you can't count on hiding behind our skirits. Shame on you! If you're men, go yourselves. Why send us out? Our skins are no more bullet-proof than yours, and a woman's scalp is the same to an Indian as a man's. Go. Give us rifles and we'll protect you."

"No. Listen here. There are Injuns watchin' the spring, sure enough. They're waitin', in hopes we'll be drawn outside, after those other fellows. They know well that the fetchin' in of water is women's and children's work, and they know well that we'll likely to be needin' that same water. For us men to go out after it would raise suspicion. It would mean sartin death for us and a gen'ral attack before the reinforcements come. If you women go as usual, they'll not harm you. They'll lay close, thinkin' that we're unsuspicious, and that havin' the water we'll chase their other party. That's what they want. Go, every petticoat of you, and every child large enough to tote a piggin. It'll require spunk—we'll be prayin'

161

for you as men never prayed before; but you'll come back safe—that we'll guarantee or we wouldn't send our wives and sisters and children on such a quest. You're Kentucky women and we're Kentucky men."

The women paled.

"I'll go," promptly said one.

"I'll go," said another, and another.

They all seized buckets and gourds; the boys and girls joined eagerly.

"Goodby, brave hearts—and God be with you."

The gate was opened. In a long procession the file proceeded, led by Mrs. Jemima Johnson with ten-year-old Betsy Johnson holding to her hand. There were twelve women and sixteen boys and girls. To see them, nobody would have thought that they feared. Not a foot stumbled, not a figure wavered. Sudden silence fell upon the clearing and the forest. The jabbering Indians in the open stared. Stern faces blanched, peering through the port-holes of the fort; and in the timber beyond the spring the painted visages of the three hundred Shawnees, Wyandots and Mingos and their likewise painted white brothers glared, astonished and puzzled. Captain Caldwell knew not what to do—but he gave no signal. Evidently his ambush was a success, so far, else why had these women come into his very arms, for water?

The procession reached the spring; the women steadily dipped, one after another; the children stoutly grasped the brimming wooden buckets and ladles. It was nervous work. Glancing sidewise, they could glimpse the paint-daubs like scattered autumn leaves;

and they could feel the tenseness of the tigerish forms, itching to leap with knife and tomahawk. Some of the women tried to laugh and joke, but their voices sounded thin and flat.

Still unfaltering, the procession commenced to trudge back, the littlest boy and girl bearing themselves bravely, with lips tight pressed. Could the Indians hold off and see the water enter the fort—see their prey enter, unharmed? It almost passed belief.

Now the head of the procession was at the gate, and in safety. One by one and two by two those in the fore did enter. Those at the rear scarcely could stand the suspense longer; their backs prickled, their feet quickened in spite of their firm resolve to show no fear; they dared not look behind.

Then, at the last, they hastened, fast and faster. At any moment a volley might overtake them; the women clutched their skirts, prepared to run; in low voice they urged the children—"Go ahead of us! Quick! We're almost there, dears. Mother's coming. Don't be afraid."

And they were inside, every one!

The gate swung to, in an instant. A great cheer rang. The women sank here and there, spent with the strain; their knees had given out. The children cheered and laughed and cried. Rough arms hugged loved forms. Trick had met trick; thanks to the brave women of Bryant's Station!

"The men's turn, boys!" That was the shout now. "A dozen of us to give those rascals on the Lexington road a fling. The rest to the spring side of the fort, and be ready for the yellow hides when they come whooping."

The sallying party were cautioned.

"Not too far, but make all the racket you can. Don't spare powder. And when you hear our scrimmage, turn for home."

Thirteen men were told off to pretend a battle with the insulting Indians who to the southeast of the fort were gamboling and challenging on the road which led from the Ohio River to Lexington near the Kentucky River. The thirteen hastened out, as if in earnest for a fight. The Indians fell back, egging them on. Rifles spat smartly, muskets whanged in answer; in a few minutes the sounds were those of a battle—and in the timber opposite the other end of the fort Captain Caldwell the British Ranger lifted his hand in signal.

His three hundred warriors sprang to their feet. Their time had arrived. The garrison had taken the bait—their eyes and guns were busy and the spring end of the fort was undefended.

"Whoo-oo-oop!" The yell burst deafening. With brandished gun and hatchet the three hundred rushed pellmell into the clear and straight for the gate and the flanking palisades. They were within one hundred yards—seventy-five yards—fifty yards—forty—and—

"Crack! Crash!"

Every port-hole spurted smoke and flame. The foremost warriors plunged headlong, dead. The bullets tore on through the crowded ranks. The rifles, quickly handed by the women, spoke again—and again. The van of the charge melted; the rear recoiled; warriors

164

ran right and left, scudding for shelter. "In two minutes not an Indian was to be seen."

At the same time the thirteen scouts pelted in, laughing gaily. The scheme had been a great success.

"Beaten at their own game! Hooray!"

But Captain Caldwell was by no means whipped. His warriors were screeching for revenge. He remembered that the two Bryant couriers had broken through; he knew that they were galloping, galloping to Lexington or Boonesborough for reinforcements. Aid would be coming. So he posted three hundred of his men in ambush where the Lexington road passed between a thick belt of timber and a large field of green corn.

With the others he kept up a hot fire upon the fort. Some of his warriors dashed in near enough to set the roofs of the cabins aflame. There was plenty of water, but before the blaze had been put out several houses had been half burned. Then a change in the wind saved the rest.

Meanwhile Rangers Bell and Tomlinson had raced into Lexington. To their dismay they found the town almost deserted; only women and aged men were there; the able-bodied fighters had left, called to Hoy's Station also. On raced the two couriers, and caught the column at Boonesborough across the Kentucky.

"What's wrong?"

"Bryant's is attacked. The Injuns are there by the hundreds. We're seeking help."

"We'll do the best we can for you."

Sixteen horsemen and thirty men on foot were ordered back with Rangers Bell and Tomlinson. They made a fast march of twenty-three miles, and at two o'clock in the afternoon sighted Bryant's.

The firing had ceased. Captain Caldwell had laid another trap. Every Indian had sunk into forest or weeds or brush, to wait for the expected reinforcements. The garrison saw nothing at which to shoot, and half believed, themselves, that the siege was done.

With a cheer the horsemen galloped up the dusty road, and into the lane between the trees and the cornfield. The men on foot took a short cut through the corn itself, to flank the cavalry and rout out any skulking reds. There was a shot from the timber; another, a score, two score. The horsemen had gone too far to wheel.

"To the fort! To the fort, boys! We're ambushed!

Every man hammered his horse. They thundered on, wreathed in powder smoke and eddying dust. The gate was opened for them; they surged through at full speed, and not a hide had been so much as scratched!

But the men in the corn-field were not so lucky. They heard the volleys; they cared not a whit for numbers, and seeing little they bolted through the tall stalks for the battle, in order to help their comrades. The horsemen had thudded on; out from the timber into the road the Indians, one hundred, two hundred, swarmed and met the footmen with the tomahawk.

The Indians' guns were empty; the thirty Long Knives knew that their own safety lay in the threat of powder and ball. An Indian will think twice before charging a loaded rifle with a tomahawk. There was small chance to reach the fort gate; all the intervening space swarmed with the raging enemy. The thirty dived back into the corn-field. It was desperate hide-and-seek among the nodding stalks, while the Bryant garrison gazed helplessly.

Most of the thirty got away—made a running fight of it, from the corn, and from tree trunks and cane clumps. Six were killed or wounded. But Simon Girty himself was almost bagged. That would have been a victory—and it did indeed put a stop to the fracas. Like any Indian he was hot in chase of a young Kentuckian; at last his quarry turned, leveled on him and fired. Down went Simon Girty, knowing now that he had mistaken his man. The gun had been loaded!

Girty killed! Nothing could have spread greater joy. No! He was up again. The bullet had struck a piece of leather in his shot-pouch and had only bruised him! Pshaw! The young Kentuckian had not dared to pause and finish his job, and ran on until he might reload.

The fall of Simon Girty had created alarm. All the Indians who saw, stopped. When they learned the truth, the pursuit had slackened; they let the few Long Knives go and applied themselves to the siege of the station.

That was now a harder task, for the garrison had been increased by the sixteen horsemen. At sunset the chiefs grew discouraged. They had lost many warriors; reinforcements had arrived, more would be on the way; they wished to draw off and try elsewhere.

Simon Girty addressed them.

"I will talk to the Long Knives. I will make their hearts soft. You have seen that they cannot kill me—I turn their bullets. I will turn their hearts also."

On hands and knees he crawled along to a large stump near a corner of the station. From there he called. They heard.

"What do you want?"

"You are brave men and women. Listen. I bring you terms. You have fought well, and done all that you can do. It is useless to fight farther. We know your numbers. We have six hundred warriors and whites, and cannon are coming. They will be here shortly. They are not like rifles. With them we can blow your walls into the air. Then the Indians will pour in, and nothing can protect you, your women and children. Not a life will be spared. But surrender, and I give you my word of honor that no hair of your heads shall be harmed."

There was a moment of silence. The mention of cannon had had its effect. True enough, cannon had been used, of late, against other stockades, with dire results.

A brave voice answered Simon Girty.

"You lie. Go back to your Injuns before a bullet pierces your coward heart."

"Who says I lie?" Girty demanded, with a show of being much hurt. "Do you know my name, sir? I am Simon Girty."

Aaron Reynolds replied to him. He was a spirited young man, and had noticed that some of his companions were sobered by the word "cannon."

"We know you very well. I have another worthless dog to which I've given the same name—Simon Girty, because he looks like you. If you have either cannon or reinforcements, or both, fetch 'em along. But if you or any of your naked rascals succeed in finding your way into this fort we're ready for you. We'd despise to use guns on you. We have bundles of switches waiting, and we'll switch you out again. As for your reinforcements, there are plenty now coming to our aid likewise. I'll have you know that more are to follow those already here. The whole country is arming; and if you and your gang of murderers linger twenty-four hours longer, your scalps will be drying in the sun on the roofs of these cabins."

Simon Girty made a show of bristling, indignant.

"I spoke to you out of humanity. You answer with insult and the tongue of a boy. Your blood is on your own heads. I grieve at your fate. To-morrow morning you will all be dead."

He crawled back again. But, cheering, the garrison took heart at the bold words of Aaron Reynolds.

The night passed. In the morning the landscape smiled again. A few camp-fires idly smoked. That was all. Not an Indian remained. The whole savage army had gone.

CHAPTER X

BETTY ZANE'S "POWDER EXPLOIT" (1782)

HOW A GIRL SAVED THE DAY

WHEN the column of Indians and British Rangers under Captain Caldwell marched for Bryant's Station, of Kentucky, the other column, planned to invade North-Western Virginia (West Virginia), stayed behind in camp, for a while. They were uncertain just what place to attack first, and finally had almost decided not to attack any place.

But runners came to them, with the news that after the withdrawal from Bryant's the Kentucky column had ambushed a Long Knife army including Daniel Boone men, at the lucky Blue Licks, and defeated it badly. This was true indeed. The victors were homeward bound laden with scalps and booty. There was much excitement.

A vote of the chiefs determined that the march should be continued, for Wheeling. Simon Girty and several others joined. The column numbered three hundred Indians, and fifty "Queen's Rangers" sent by the British father from Detroit. All were under Captain Pratt, of the Rangers, but Simon Girty was head chief. They set onward, through the forest, to the Ohio River.

This was the first week in September, 1782. Scout

170

John Lynn, who was watching the trails in the Indian country northwest of the Ohio, saw them. They seemed in a hurry. At full speed he made for Wheeling, to give the alarm. He swam the river, and arrived with the word just in time. The settlers, excepting those of the Ebenezer Zane cabin, flocked into Fort Henry. While they were still very busy, getting ready, in daylight of September 11, the enemy appeared, strong in savage array and flying their flag.

It was not quite a surprise, although nearly so. The fort contained about twenty men and boys who could handle a rifle, and the same number of women and girls and little children. Before dawn Captain Boggs, the fort commander, had dashed away, to get aid. They hoped that he had escaped. Colonel Silas Zane had been elected in his place. Captain John Sullivan, in a dug-out boat from Fort Pitt, above, loaded with cannon-balls for Louisville, below, had scarcely landed, on a stop-over, and barely made into the fort, wounded. The small garrison were glad to have him. He was an experienced Indian-fighter.

Colonel Ebenezer Zane had grown tired of seeing his house burned. He had declared that never again would he abandon it and take to the fort. It had been rebuilt, on its same site only forty yards north of the fort wall; had been made "Indian proof," and was well under the cover of the fort rifle-fire.

This time, here he stayed. With him there were Andrew Scott, George Green, his own wife Elizabeth McColloch Zane, her sister Miss McColloch, his sister Elizabeth, her friend Molly Scott, and the slaves

171

Sam and wife Kate. That summed three white men
and one black man; four white women and one black
woman. They were going to hold the cabin in spite of
"all the copper skins from Wheeling to Sandusky."
But the program spelled a rude welcome for the young
and lively Elizabeth, who had just arrived from a
fashionable school in Philadelphia, to spend part of her
vacation!

Advancing with the flag and his whooping Indians,
Captain Pratt the British Ranger sent Simon Girty
forward, to demand surrender.

"To all who will give themselves up we promise
you the best protection, in the name of King George,"
called Girty.

"Answer the villain with a bullet," Silas Zane
ordered. "That is what talks for us."

Simon dodged away.

"You may have till to-night," he shouted.

Captain Pratt posted his forces. In the fort and
in the Ebenezer Zane cabin everybody made ready.
The women and girls molded bullets. There were
plenty of rifles; all were loaded and stacked handy to
the loop-holes. Water buckets were filled. Food was
prepared. The fort pickets, many of which had rotted,
were braced and backed. Wheeling had no idea of surrender. It had stood other attacks.

At sunset Girty tried again.

"Your treatment if you surrender shall be that
of—"

"Colonel William Crawford!" old Captain Sullivan
interrupted. "We know you, Girty. We know you

for a dirty dog, too cowardly to be honest, and so filthy a beast that you feel yourself fit to live only among savages. You're such a liar that you couldn't keep your promises if you wanted to. You don't know how to tell the truth. If you think to get us, you'll have to do better fighting than you and your sneaking Injuns have ever done yet. We only hope you'll hang around till our messenger fetches in the reinforcements."

"Yes; and we've got your messenger safe, my crowing buck," Girty yelled. "He'll bring you no help."

"Really got him, have you? We want to know! What kind of a man is he—how did he look?"

"A fine, smart, active young fellow."

"That's another of your lies," laughed Captain Sullivan. "He was an old, gray-headed weazel and far too smart for *you!*"

Haw-haw-haw!

"Laugh while you can," Girty retorted. "We see your wooden cannon-piece mounted on that roof. When you hear our own pieces battering down your walls you'll laugh in a different key. This is the last summons. Refuse, and every soul of you will fall to bullet and hatchet."

"Better to die that way, fighting, than to surrender and be butchered like dogs, the Colonel Crawford way," Silas Zane answered.

The attack was launched furiously. In a howling mob the Indians charged gates and loop-holes. They despised the threat of the little French cannon-piece upon the roof of the headquarters cabin. It looked to be the same "dummy" of seven years ago: a wooden cannon.

Captain Sullivan had climbed up. He stood with a fire-brand over the touch-hole, waiting.

The Indians jeered and gestured.

"Boom! Boom!" they challenged. "Make noise!"

They were massed, capering and mocking. Captain Sullivan lowered the fire-brand. The little "bull-dog" belched smoke.

"Boom!" A hail of grape-shot tore through the painted ranks, leaving a bloody path. Captain Pratt rushed in, waving his sword.

"Stand back! Stand back, you fools!" he bawled. "By Jupiter, there's no wood about *that!*"

And there wasn't. It was the genuine article.

The Indians had wildly scampered for safety. Simon Girty and the other chiefs white and red rallied them and divided them into parties, with due care for the cannon-piece. From every exposed side they volleyed at the fort and the Zane cabin. They charged and fell back and charged again. In fort and cabin the rifles, deftly loaded by the fast-working women and girls, waxed hot.

With darkness the general firing died down. Under the cloak of night an Indian crept to the kitchen end of the cabin, to start a blaze. The cabin had proved a great hindrance to the attack on the fort.

He rose to his knees, to wave his torch for an instant and rekindle it—

"Crack!" This kitchen, added to the cabin, was the fort of Negro Sam and Negress Kate. Sam had eyes and ears that equaled any Indian's, by day or night either.

"Hi yah! How you like that, you Injun man?"

The fire-bug managed to crawl away, but he left his torch and the kitchen too.

Morning dawned. The Indians seemed busy at something. They had ransacked the dug-out and were carrying the cannon-balls in shore, to the hill slope before the fort. Had their cannon come? Yes! No! But look! There it was—they were propping it up, to load it and aim it. A long, dangerous piece, too.

What did it have around it? Chains, by thunder! And hoop-iron! A log, split and hollowed out, and bound together with stuff from Reichart's blacksmith shop! Haw-haw!

Watch, everybody! Could the blamed thing possibly stand fire? Hope not. They were ramming into it powder by the horn full. A ball from their pile followed. They rammed that also, and wadded it. One of them hastened with a smoking stick. They pretended to take good aim. They yelled and shook their guns and hatchets, as they stood aside to make way for the ball from the muzzle.

Now!

"Flash-whang!"

A great cloud of smoke veiled the spot. No ball issued; only shrieks and shouts, and from the edges figures dived into the open and thence into the brush. The smoke cleared. The wooden cannon had disappeared, but the spot was covered with dead and wounded Indians.

"Help yourselves to more cannon-balls," jeered Captain Sullivan. "We wish you a dozen such guns."

Reinforcements had set out from Shepherd's Fort, six miles distant. When they drew near, they saw that they had no hope of entering the fort, so thick and angry were the attackers. They voted to return and get recruits; then try again. But that was not to the mind of the lad Francis Duke—Colonel Shepherd's son-in-law, aged not much over twenty, and rashly brave.

"I've come too far to turn my back on a place that needs help as badly as this does. I'm going in, or die for it."

They could not stop him. He spurred at a mad run, straight as an arrow, hoping to take the enemy by surprise.

"Open the gate! Open the gate!" he shouted, as he neared.

He was seen, and heard. The gate swung for him. Would he make it? He waved his hat and flourished his rifle—hurrah! He was almost there; a few strides more—but to a burst of smoke from the outlying cabins and copse he fell headlong, dead. His horse galloped riderless.

The cannon accident had infuriated the Indians to the last degree. They were especially bent upon taking the Zane cabin, which held them off. Within the cabin matters were tightening up. The powder was getting low. The drain upon it had been constant.

"We must have powder, boys," spoke Colonel Zane.

"The fort will supply us. Who'll go and fetch it on the run?"

There were looks. Betty Zane heard and stepped forward.

"I'll go, brother Eb. You can't spare a man."

"No, you sha'n't, Betty. It's man's work. Besides, you're not fast enough on your feet, child."

Her black eyes flashed. She was a splendid girl, high-spirited and active; had been raised on the frontier and was a pet of her brothers.

"I *shall* go. I can run like a deer, you've often said, and I can't be of any better use. If I get hurt, that'll make no difference; but if you lose a man, you lose a rifle. Tell me what to do."

"Betty!" He really didn't know what to have her do. Everybody pleaded and objected. She stamped her foot.

"I *shall* go. We're wasting time. But first I'll have to take off some of these clothes." So she dropped her skirt and stood in her short petticoat. "There!" And she fastened her hair tighter in a coil.

Her friend Molly Scott sprang forward.

"Betty! Let me go instead! I'm not afraid. Please!"

"No. You can go next time, Molly. I'm the older."

Accounts state that Molly Scott did make such a trip, either first or last. Lydia, the daughter of Captain Boggs, was in the fort, and says that she helped pour the powder into Molly Scott's apron. Whether Molly and Betty both served in this siege, or served

177

separately in two sieges, is still a question. At any rate, the deed was done, and well done.

"All right, Betty. God bless you for a brave lass. You're a true Zane," Colonel Zane uttered chokingly. "Have them pour a keg of powder into this table-cloth. We'll signal them you're coming. We'll do our best to cover you. No red devil shall get near you. Tell the fort we've got to have powder, or my house will fall and the fort'll be hard pressed from the new vantage."

Betty nodded. Her eyes were snapping, her cheeks were red. The cabin was protected in front and on the flanks by a little stockade. Her brother himself opened the gate, in the side, for her. With a bound she was out, her slim ankles twinkling as she ran.

The Indians stared, puzzled. They laughed and jeered.

"Ho! Squaw! Heap run! Squaw heap run!"

And Betty darted in through the gateway of the fort. Five minutes passed, while the cabin garrison waited nervously. Here she came, out again, the table-cloth tied around her waist and baggy with the precious powder.

The enemy guessed. They laughed no longer—they opened fire, the fort and cabin replied rapidly. Betty! Betty! Was she down? Had she been hit? No; not yet. Open the gate! The gate! Let her in—keep those Injuns off! Here she was, plunging breathless, panting, laughing, into the extended arms. Not a ball had touched her.

Now the cabin would hold out. It had to hold out,

after a deed like that, by a girl. Shame on it if it yielded!

The Indians, urged by the white chiefs and by the British Rangers, raged. Twenty times they reached the stockades with bundles of hemp, and tried to fire the pickets. The hemp was damp and refused to burn. They tried with wood. They did not succeed. Under the hail of bullets a portion of the rotted pickets gave way, in a corner; but by great good fortune several peach-trees there concealed the hole.

All this day the hot attacks continued. They lessened only slightly during the night. Toward morning a figure was espied craftily slinking for the fort's sally gate. A rifle bullet stopped it. There were groans and pleadings for water; a weak voice kept asking to be taken in. Two of the men bolted out, grabbed the figure and hustled him inside. He was a negro—claimed that he had just deserted from the Indians.

They hand-cuffed him, and stationed Lydia Boggs, aged seventeen, over him with a tomahawk, to kill him if he tried any tricks. She would have done it, too.

The day dawned; the sun rose. The scene without was fearful. The Indians were shooting the cattle; the settlement cabins were burning. Was it to be another day of stress? Where were the reinforcements? Had Captain Boggs really been captured? If so, he had been killed, or else the enemy would have displayed him, to show the fort that it could not hope for help.

The sun was an hour high, when—listen! An Indian

whoop sounded, in the distance; a long, quavering, peculiar whoop.   In fort and cabin the men cheered.

"The alarm whoop, boys! Hurrah! Their spies have sighted something!"

And—

"Yes! There they go! There the bloody rascals go, hoof and foot! Boggs got through and he's coming back!"

With astonishing speed the enemy had decamped— were streaming for the river. The siege had been lifted. The two garrisons might take breath, and relax, while keenly alert. Were they actually saved! Had the enemy gone in earnest—or might it be a feint, an ambush!

But not an Indian was in sight when, in less than an hour more, sturdy old Captain Boggs, Colonel Andrew Swearingen and Major David Williamson trotted up the hill, leading seventy mounted men.

CHAPTER XI

THE FIVE BOY CAPTIVES (1785)

ADVENTURES OF "LITTLE FAT BEAR" AND ALL

WHEN in 1778 the energetic Colonel George
Rogers Clark marched northwest out of Virginia and descended the Ohio River, to seize the Illinois country bordering the Mississippi, on his way he
camped at the Falls of the Ohio, drilled his men upon
Corn Island, built a block-house and left thirteen families to form a settlement.

The little settlement crossed to the mainland on the
Kentucky side, and the present city of Louisville was
founded.

By 1785 it numbered about 150 persons, on Corn
Island, and on the mainland, living in log cabins upon
clearings amidst the forest.

Among the settlers whose cabins were the farthest
out from the village was Colonel Pope. He and several other men formed a small settlement of their own.
They lived scarcely within shouting distance of one
another, and were independent, like all pioneers.

This winter of 1784–1785 Colonel Pope engaged a
tutor for his two boys, to teach them the three R's—
Reading, 'Riting and 'Rithmetic. He did not wish
them to grow up numbskulls. He invited his neighbors

to send their boys over and be tutored at the same
time. It was a backwoods school.

Of course, on Saturday the school had vacation.
And on a Saturday morning of February, 1785, the
two Linn boys (whose father, Colonel William Linn,
had been killed by Indians), young Brashear, young
William Wells, and a fifth who perhaps was one of the
Pope boys, started out duck-hunting.

The War of the Revolution had ceased by treaty of
peace almost a year and a half before, but the Indians
had not quit. They still were of the belief that the
British had not given up their lands "across the Ohio,"
and that the king their father was "only resting."
So they continued their forays along the Ohio River.
They killed many more Long Knives.[1]

After having been kept at school for most of the
week, frontier boys were not the kind to stay at home
on Saturday for fear of Indians. Not when there was
good hunting, and they could borrow their fathers' or
brothers' guns and skip the chores. A successful
hunter made a successful Indian-fighter. It was the
right training. A fellow who did not know how to
shoot was useless as a soldier, and a fellow who could
not take care of himself in the forest and prairies was
useless as a scout. Besides, the settler had to depend
on his rifle for his meat.

In those days there was wonderful hunting along
the Ohio. The boys knew exactly where to go. For
turkeys, squirrels and deer they need not go far at

[1] See chapter on "Little Turtle of the Miamis," in "Boys' Book of
Indian Warriors."

all. But the prime place for ducks and geese lay about three miles out, at some swampy ponds near the river.

With a couple of fowling-pieces and the ammunition they trudged away. William Wells and the older Linn were fourteen. Boy Brashear was twelve. The other Linn and the fifth boy were nine or ten.

They hunted around the ponds until dusk. Then they decided to stay out all night—which was no trick at all. They made camp like regular scouts, cooked some ducks, and slept in a bough hut that they built. During the night the snow fell, sifting down through the trees, but they did not care a whit.

They had planned to find more ducks in the ponds, in the morning; but the storm interfered.

"Aw, let's go home," said Wells.

"All right. Let's."

After breakfast they gathered their stuff, and were just starting, when with a dash and a whoop the Indians were upon them—likely enough had been watching them since daylight.

"Injuns! Run, boys!"

It was sharp work, but soon over. William Wells, the littler Linn and the fifth boy were grabbed; the larger Linn had a goose and several ducks slung over his shoulder and did not mean to give them up; but he was one of those pudgy, plum-pudding, over-grown boys, and stumbled on his own feet. He was nabbed by a big Indian who patted him on the back and called him "Little Fat Bear."

Brashear, though, nearly got away. He was the best runner at school, and gave the Indians a pretty chase among the trees before they caught him at last. They seemed to think all the more of him for his try, and called him "Buck Elk."

Well, this was a nice how-de-do! Five boys, all captured. Still, the same had happened to other boys, and to trained scouts. Nobody could blame them, but they felt rather sore.

The Indians now began to question them in broken English.

"Where from?"

"Louisville."

"You lie. No from Louisville. Where live?"

"Louisville."

"You lie. Get beatin'. Mebbe get killed. Where live, fat boy?"

"Louisville."

One and all they stuck to the story. They had no notion of betraying the cabins of Colonel Pope and his neighbors.

The Indians grunted in disgust, put the boys in their midst and hustled them to the river.

"Guess we're in for it," remarked William Wells. "We'll keep a stiff upper lip. Who are they? Miamis?"

"Reckon so. Or Potawatomis. Glad they ain't Shawnees," answered Little Fat Bear. "Shucks! If I hadn't tumbled—! Don't you cry, brother," he warned.

"Who's cryin'! Don't you bawl, yourself!"

"I blamed near skinned out. If I'd had a better head start I'd have run clean home; and then the folks would be makin' these Injuns hop, you bet," declared Brashear, the "Buck Elk."

"Aw, the Injuns would have followed you. They'd likely have shot you, so you wouldn't give the alarm," retorted Fat Bear, wisely. "We're all right. Who's afraid of Injuns. If we don't act up they'll treat us well. The Miamis and Potawatomis ain't as bad as the Shawnees."

"Wonder where they'll take us," puffed the fifth boy.

They were being hustled at a trot. The river was crossed on the slushy ice. All that day they traveled northward; and all the next day, and the next, and the next, and on and on. No pursuit was sighted. Probably Colonel Pope and the other families had thought that they were spending Sunday at the ponds, and had not looked for them until Monday morning.

The Indians were Miamis. That promised a journey clear to northern Indiana, perhaps. Whew! But Little Fat Bear and Buck Elk encouraged the fellows to "keep a stiff upper lip," and take whatever came; then the Indians would respect them more. If they put up a "holler" and "bellered," they'd be licked.

This worked out finely. Pluck always does. They and their captors got along splendidly, and they were not tied at night nor made to carry loads. Nevertheless, it was a tremendous journey, straight northward through the wilderness, with never a glimpse of any town, until, after a week or more, they arrived at the Miami village.

"How far've we come, you think?" asked William

Wells, when the village was to be seen and by the preparations they knew that it was the place.

"Upwards of two hundred miles, I'll bet," replied Fat Bear. He was not so fat, now.

That was a shrewd guess. The village was upon the Little Calumet River, near present Valparaiso in northwestern Indiana—a full two hundred and twenty-five miles from Louisville opposite the southern boundary. They had been taken through the whole state.

"The gauntlet! Cracky! We've got to run the gauntlet!"

"Golly! The same as any prisoners!"

"Don't you show the white feather, any of you. Keep together and run like sixty."

"And don't you tumble over again, either," they warned, of Fat Bear. "If you're down once, you'll get licked proper."

"Make for the council house. That's the way to do."

At the "prisoners'" whoop the village people had boiled out of their woven-reed houses. One of the Indians had hurried in advance, to tell the news, and the gauntlet lines were forming. It was to be a gauntlet by boys for other boys! There were only Indian boys in the lines—they were armed with sticks and switches and stones and small tomahawks and handfuls of salt and dirt (for the eyes), the same as warriors and squaws.

The five captives were halted. They had been greeted with yells and screeches; but they set their lips

186

and clenched their hands, and stood ready. What their brothers and fathers and grand-fathers had done, they could do. It was quite an honor, to be made to run the gauntlet, like men.

The littler Linn was shoved forward, to lead the race. He was the smallest, and would hold the other boys back—and he had been the spunkiest, all the way up, because he had a quick temper and was prompt to fight. The Indians had liked to tease him.

"Go!" shouted the chief Indian. "Run!"

They ducked their heads, and ran. How they did run, and dodge, and scoot, in between the two lines which showered them with blows and kicks and stones and dirt! Boys against boys; that was it—and some of the Indian boys were hulking big fellows.

The five white boys did well; they were shifty and butted right on, till young Linn "got his mad up." Two-thirds of the way down a big Indian boy hit him a stunning crack full on the jaw. So what did he do but stop and whirl and with a straight left-hander knock the boy sprawling.

This was contrary to gauntlet rules. Anybody running the gauntlet was fair prey to everybody else, but he couldn't strike back. Now the warriors who were watching the fun doubled over, laughing at the way the small boy had bowled the large boy over. The Indian boy's mother and the other women shrieked angrily.

"Kill him! Kill the little Long Knife demon!"

Young Linn—he burst through the line and ran for life, to the council house. The lines broke, and yelling, chased after. It was to be blood for blood—and more than a mere bloody nose, too.

He got there first. He was a sight. His shock of hair had fallen over his forehead, his eyes glared—he had put his back to the council-house post, planted his foot, his hands were up, and he dared the whole crowd of them. He was so mad he could scarcely see. He looked dangerous for even a ten-year-old.

The largest of the Indian boys rushed him, to down him. Young Linn was left-handed—and a left-hander is a bad proposition, in a fight. "Smack!" Over went the Indian boy; Kentucky Linn was right on top of him in an instant, kicking and pounding and clawing him until he howled.

The warriors were highly pleased. They formed a ring, and danced and cheered and whooped, to see the white boy take care of himself. But the other Indian boys charged in, wild with rage. It might have gone hard with Master Linn had not his four partners joined the fray. Then there was a lively fracas. It was Kentucky against the world. Fat Bear, Buck Elk, William Wells—they all five cleared a circle. The Indian boys large and small toppled right and left—did not know how to use their fists, tried in vain with clubs and rocks, were sent flying every time they dived to grapple, staggered away with bloody noses and swollen eyes; and pretty soon they had enough and to spare.

All this time the men were whooping and yelling, praising the white boys and urging the red boys to thresh them. Now they drove the remaining Indian boys away, and carried the five Kentuckians into the council-house, patting them on the back as heroes.

"We're goin' to be adopted," gasped Little Fat Bear.

"I don't care," wheezed Buck Elk. "Say! Did you see how little Jack uses his left hand?"

"Well, we told him to hold his temper. He'd like to have got killed," complained Fat Bear. "But we licked 'em, anyhow."

"You bet we did!"

They were adopted. All the warriors were eager to have one of the fighting young Long Knives. At last the matter was settled; each boy went into a different family, to be an Indian. But they had to bid goodby to William Wells; his new father lived in another village. He was taken away, and they did not see him again—at least, not for several years. He stayed with the Miamis for eight years; was named Black Snake; grew up with them; lived in Chief Little Turtle's town near the Fort Wayne, Indiana, of to-day; married Chief Little Turtle's sister; and was much thought of by the Miamis. Then in 1793 he left, in the open, saying that he was going back to the white people and help the American army in its fights with the red people. He could not fire upon his own nation.

The four other boys remained here, in this town. They were well treated. They had shown their spunk; they were not cowards. The Indian boys made friends with them. They all played and hunted and fished together, and soon it was hard to tell the white boys from the Indian boys. But the four did not intend to be Indians any longer than they had to. They wanted to go home. It was the kind of vacation they had not figured upon spending—and yet it was fun, if only their folks could know. They learned a lot that they would not have learned in school. Still, they rather preferred school, after all; and home.

The spring passed; and the lively pleasant summer. Indian boys do not work. They are free to loaf or hunt, and train for warriors. Only the girls work, so as to make women who will work.

In the crisp fall all the men except the very old left on a grand hunt, to bring back meat and prepare for winter. The old women and girls and little children remained in the town with the old men. The four young white Indians had not been taken, either. They had to stay. They were thought not to be old enough, yet.

"I reckon this is our best chance to escape," said Buck Elk, when he might.

Little Fat Bear nodded.

"We'll plan and watch sharp. If one goes, all'll have to go, though. No lone trail."

"Of course. We won't desert each other."

"But we've got to wait for a clear field. It's a pesky long way home."

"That's so. Just the same, we can make it if we have a good start."

They told the other boys, and they all lay low, waiting and scheming.

"We're going fishing to-morrow," finally announced Buck Elk, to Fat Bear. "Want to?" And he winked.

"Who?"

"All of us. Old White Eagle and Singing Bird are going with us, to clean the fish. But that doesn't matter."

They were the old father and mother who lived in the same family with Buck Elk.

"Time's getting awful short," Fat Bear mused. "But maybe we can try something."

With wrinkled White Eagle and Singing Bird scuttling close behind, they went fishing in the river below the village. They had not said it to each other, but they hoped never to come back. They must make a break for liberty soon. The warriors might return within a week. The forest beckoned close at hand. And southward, far, far southward, their real home called to them. They had been gone almost eight months, but it felt like an age.

"To-night, huh?" murmured Buck Elk, as he and Little Fat Bear fished together, and the two old Indians drowsed in the shade, or wove baskets of reeds.

"How?"

"Light out from camp while they're asleep. May not get another chance. That's why I told 'em we'd like to stay all night, so as to get plenty fish."

"They'll signal help and trail us. Some of those old men can travel heap fast."

"So can we. We'll have a head start, and I don't believe there's anybody in the village who can catch us."

"All right. They can't do any more than beat us if they do catch us. We'll tell the other fellows."

They sidled along, until they could tell their partners.

"I'll go," Fat Bear's spunky brother agreed at
once. "If they try to catch us we'll fight 'em off with
clubs and rocks. Who's afraid of the old men? We'll
make their tongues hang out."

"I'll go, you bet," agreed the fourth, also. "My
folks need me. I'm sick of playing Injun."

"Well, we'll all lie down to sleep; and in the middle
of the night I'll wake you up," proposed Buck Elk.

"Sure?"

"Sure. Now don't let's talk any more."

At dark the camp went to bed. The two old Indians
were sound sleepers. About midnight Buck Elk softly
turned; he had not slept a wink. He nudged the next
boy, the next boy nudged the next, and the nudge was
passed on. They softly slipped, one after another,
from their blankets. The two old Indians never
stirred. In the star-light the four hastily grabbed
what food they could; and leaving White Eagle and
Singing Bird lying there they tiptoed away, on their
silent moccasins, into the forest.

Fat Bear led. He was a good woodsman. Soon
they ran; and they ran and walked fast until daylight,
traveling with their backs to the North Star. Then
the sun guided them, until about noon, when they had
to stop and rest.

"How far, you think?" panted the fourth boy.

"Twenty-five miles, I guess. We'd better cover our
trail and hide. Come on. Follow me," bade crafty
Fat Bear.

They stepped on rocks and logs, swung from tree to tree, and dropped down among bushes. That was an anxious afternoon. One kept watch while the others slept. They took turns watching and listening. They heard not a sound of the pursuit. Except for the birds and squirrels the forest was quiet. Their hearts beat hopefully. But of course tottering old men on the trail was a different matter from that of swift, crafty warriors.

In the dusk they started on again, to travel all night. After this they traveled by night and slept by day. That was the proper way. They knew how to do, as well as men. They trudged down hill and up, scrambled through ravines, crossed brush and forest and swamps, they waded and swam, they ate the ripe berries and nuts of the October crop, managed to kill a squirrel and rabbit, now and again, with a rock or a club; their buckskin clothes and moccasins were worn to tatters, but they slept warm in sunny nooks: and all the nights they were pushing steadily on southward for the Ohio River and Louisville.

A journey like this, of over two hundred miles afoot, making their own trail, avoiding the Indian villages and hunters and out-pacing the pursuit, and living off the country, getting food by their wits, no boys ever had achieved before.

It took them three weeks. In November they emerged upon the north shore of the Ohio, squarely opposite Louisville. They had struck their goal exactly. They shouted and waved, but nobody would come for them, and the rapids of the falls ran swiftly between the two shores.   They could see people gazing; the people saw them.

"They think us Injuns," Fat Bear gasped, at last. "Blame it, guess we do look some like Injuns, in our rigs."

"Shucks! How'll we get over? We can't swim."

"And Injuns are on our trail. You know we sighted smoke last evening. We don't want to be caught here."

"We'll go up above the rapids and make a raft. Quick! We can manage with this knife."

They hurried. They went up the shore about six miles, and worked hard gathering logs, and cutting brush and vines with their one knife. They feared that they'd hear the Indians any moment. The warriors were hot after them. Whew! And there was home, just across!

The raft, when finished, did not amount to much.

"It won't hold all of us," puffed Fat Bear. "You get on. I'm the heaviest. I'm the best swimmer, too. You-all paddle, and I'll swim alongside."

They tumbled aboard, with branches for oars.   Little Fat Bear shoved off and began to swim and push. They had no time to spare—

"Listen!"

Shrill whoops sounded. The Miamis were on the fresh trail.

"Hurry!"

Fat Bear kicked and pushed mightily; the others dug with their boughs. The clumsy raft moved slowly, and was carried down stream by the current. Would they

194

never get away from shore? Would the Miamis swim after them, or shoot? They made a good target.

"Look! Somebody's coming to meet us!"

That was so. From the opposite shore a boat—two boats had put out. The raft was drifting badly, but the danger shore gradually receded, the rescue boats neared, and the home shore grew plainer. Swimming, Little Fat Bear was getting blue around the mouth, his face was pale and pinched. The November water had chilled him to the bone.

"Can you keep going"

"Yes, I'm all right. You keep paddling."

"There they are!"

The Miamis had burst out upon the shore behind. They yelled furiously, and shook their fists—but they yelled and threatened in vain. Now they dared not follow farther. The boats from the Kentucky shore took the paddlers off the raft; dragged Little Fat Bear from the cold water. His teeth chattered. He could not manage himself. He had not been taken out any too soon.

"Who are you, anyhow? White boys? Where from?"

"We're the boys that the Miamis stole from the Pope settlement last February—all except Billy Wells. He's with 'em still."

"What! How'd you get away? Your folks had give you up. I declare! Made off alone, did you?"

"Clear from the Little Calumet River. Been three weeks."

"Whoopee! Think o' that! Guess we'd better take

you down to Louisville, soon as we can. Colonel Pope's moved into town, 'count o' Injuns. He'll be powerful glad to see you, and so will your other folks."

And that proved true. Colonel Pope met them at the landing. Little Fat Bear was carried ashore, to be rubbed and dosed. And from this time on for many a week there certainly were four boy heroes in the Louisville district, with "tall" stories to be told over and over again.

Sometimes they wondered how William Wells, "Black Snake," was getting along; but they knew that he was all right.

CHAPTER XII

CHIEF LITTLE TURTLE and his brother chiefs of eleven other tribes in the Northern Confederacy signed a treaty of peace with the United States, in August of 1795. This opened the way for the white settlers. They crossed the Ohio and spread westward through southern Ohio, Indiana and Illinois, to the Mississippi River.

But the Indians clung to their old hopes that a portion at least of their lands between the Great Lakes and the Ohio would be left to them. In the beginning of the new century, 1800, there arose among the restless Shawnees a medicine-man styled the Prophet and the Open Door. He aimed to band all the Indians of north, south, east and far west into a vast league that, working like one nation, should some day rule the country. His messengers traveled widely, bearing his instructions. He asserted that he spoke directly from the Great Spirit.

His brother, Tecumseh or Shooting Star, aided him. Open Door counseled peace until the Indians had grown strong by right living. Shooting Star planned for war, as soon as the league had been formed. The United States Government knew the schemes of both,

197

and tried to stop the work. The two brothers refused to obey. Governor William Henry Harrison, of Indiana Territory, struck first.

He marched from Vincennes and destroyed the town of the Prophet. The second war with Great Britain, the War of 1812, was about to break, and Tecumseh went to Canada and joined the British.[1]

A great many Indians enlisted under their red general, Tecumseh. The Potawatomis, Miamis, Ottawas, Winnebagos, Kickapoos, the Sioux of present Minnesota and the Sacs of the Rock River at the Mississippi in Illinois, seized the hatchet and followed him. In the south the Red Sticks war party of the Creeks arose. And on the new frontier of the northwest, from the Ohio to the Mississippi, the American settlers again felt keen alarm.

Tecumseh's star sank, and he with it, at the battle of the Thames, October 5, 1813, when General William Henry Harrison and his three thousand crushed the two thousand British and Indians. The red army was shattered; the chiefs and warriors hastened home as fast as they could, by secret trails; some pretended that they had not dropped their blankets in war, others foraged against the settlements, to get what plunder they might while the whites were fighting.

The Government and the settlers had erected a number of small blockhouses north of the Ohio, through Indiana and Illinois, to keep the Indians off, if possible. One block-house had been located in Bond County, half-

---

[1] For the story of the Prophet and Tecumseh, see "Boys' Book of Indian Warriors."

way down southwestern Illinois, or about eight miles south of present Greenville.

In the summer of 1814 First Lieutenant Nathaniel Jurney and a dozen United States Rangers were stationed here, upon the broad Illinois prairie dotted with timber and cut by streams. Lieutenant Jurney had been captain in the Illinois Rangers raised for service upon the frontier; but a year ago he had been appointed first lieutenant in the Government Rangers, of the army.

The Indians to be feared hereabouts were roving Sacs, Potawatomis and Winnebagos from the north; yes, and the Prairie Kickapoos from the Wabash River on the east.

However, the block-house was not a very stirring place; and when in the evening of August 30 the Lieutenant Jurney men saw a bunch of Indians reconnoitering at a short distance out, they had high hopes of a little "brush" in the morning.

They rode through the gate before daylight, to surprise the Indian camp; but ere sun-up they had been surprised, themselves, on the edge of some timber. At the first volley the lieutenant had been badly wounded, three of the men had fallen, and far out-numbered the six other men, taking the lieutenant, had raced madly for safety in the fort.

The smoke hung so thickly in the still, damp air that they got away without trouble—all except Ranger Higgins.

He had not gone far. Instead of making to the fort he had sprung from his horse and "treed" (the Ken-

tucky way); and in the smoke cover he had stayed for
"one more pull at the redskins." That was rash, but
plucky. He had often said that he did not fear
"trash" like the "beggarly Kickapoos, Saukees, and
such." Kentucky was his home, and he had been
reared on stories of the Shawnees, Wyandots and Miamis.

So he waited, behind his tree, until the smoke thinned.
Soon he glimpsed several Indians; he took aim, fired,
killed one, reloaded, and leaped upon his horse. The
Indians had not seen him; he would reach the fort and
report that he had accomplished a little, anyway.

Just as he tightened rein a voice stopped him. It
seemed to come from underfoot.

"Tom! Say, you aren't going to leave me?"

That was Joe Burgess, a comrade, trying to crawl to
him.

"No, I won't. Come on, Joe. Get aboard. Quick!
We'll make in, double."

"Can't do it, Tom. Leg's busted."

Joe's ankle had been broken by a bullet. Tom, a
fine big fellow, was off in a second, picked Joe up bod-
ily, carried him to the horse—and away the horse
bolted, without either of them. It had smelled Indians.

"By ginger, but that's a mean trick," Tom rapped.
"Never mind. You make a three-legged crawl of it;
keep to the tall grass and hug the ground like a snake.
I'll cover your trail and fight the Injuns off."

A brave man, he let Joe disappear in the tall grass
of the prairie. First he thought that he'd follow. But
that wouldn't do. The smoke was drifting slowly and

clearing; the Indians would see him—would see the trail, anyway, and kill Joe if they didn't kill him, himself.

He dived for a patch of brush, to leave a trail of his own. Hah! Injuns! There was a large fat fellow searching about, on one side, and there were two others between him and the fort. He'd better draw them after him; maybe he could string them out and fight them separately. That would give Joe a good chance. He jumped from the brush patch and ran for the willows of a little creek. The fat Indian saw him and with a whoop ran in pursuit.

Suddenly his leg went bad, almost throwing him down. He had been wounded in the first "scrimmage" and had not known it. Pshaw! He'd never outfoot the Indian, to the willows. He turned, with lifted gun. The fat Indian dodged briskly. That occurred several times. The two other Indians were now coming, also.

"If I don't get shet o' this fat rascal I'm gone 'coon," muttered Tom. "But, dod rat him, he so lively I can't lay bead on his greasy hide! I'll have to draw his fire, Kentucky way."

Daniel Boone and other Long Hunters of Kentucky knew how to dodge Indians' bullets. They would wait for the fall of the hammer and the flash of the priming in the pan, and would spring aside before the ball reached them. It was a great trick, but it took a quick eye and steady nerve.

Ranger Higgins decided to try it. He did not dare to use his own load. He watched the fat Indian, let him take aim—and at the spurt from the hammer he whirled. But he was too slow. The ball struck him in the thigh and knocked him down.

He bounded up. The fat Indian was reloading and the two other Indians were running in. Tom ran, likewise, as fast as he could, which was not very fast, now. The Indians leveled their guns. Over his shoulder he watched; and when he thought their fingers were pressing the triggers he dropped. He dropped too soon! As he staggered up they fired, then; every bullet hit him! Down he went, a second time, with four bullets in his body, and with a bad leg besides.

Up he got. He was a hard man to kill. The three Indians came on with spears and knives, to finish him. But Tom did not propose to be finished. He threatened them with his gun, and they dared not rush in. The fat Indian at last determined to take a chance. Perhaps the white man's gun was not loaded. He charged, with his spear; Ranger Higgins had to shoot, and shoot he did.

That left two Indians for him to face with his crippled leg and an empty gun. He worked hard to reload before they could reach him—but here they were, prodding at him with their lances. He had more than he could do to ward off the darting points. The heads were of thin hoop-iron, and the shafts were of flimsy cane, so that whenever the weapons penetrated to a bone they bent; but he was being slashed to ribbons.

One of the Indians grew tired of such slow killing, and stepping back a pace threw his tomahawk. That was more quickly done, and resulted, as Ranger Higgins afterward said, "in a close shave!" The whirlling blade sliced off his ear, and part of his cheek clear beyond the point of his jaw.

Down went Tom Higgins. The other Indian jumped him, to prod again. Doubled on his back, in a ball, Tom fought with hands and feet, like a 'coon indeed. He got a grip on the lance; he hung on, the Indian tugged, and dragged him to his feet. Tom let go, so that the Indian staggered back; picked up his musket, smashed the Indian's head—and broke the gun at the grasp between stock and barrel! Was there ever such luck!

The third Indian rushed, with a knife. He was only one, but Tom was weak from loss of blood, and other Indians might arrive at any moment. Ranger Higgins parried with his rifle-barrel, found it too heavy, drew his own knife, and gallantly closed. They locked and swayed and panted and stabbed.

The Indian proved much the stronger, but he had no liking for this knife work. He hurled Tom sprawling, and hastened to a rifle. After all, a bullet was the surest weapon against this kind of a white man.

Up rose Ranger Higgins, once more—gory but not defeated. He was chopped and gashed from head to foot, had three balls in his thighs and one in another part of his body, and a crippled lower leg. Now he, too, sought for a gun, and hoped that he might load first.

All this amazing lop-sided duel had occupied but little time—just long enough for Joe Burgess to escape into the safety zone of the block-house. The smoky fog had been split by the first beams of the sun, and much of the struggle had taken place in full view of Ranger Higgins' comrades inside the fort gate.

They were six men and one woman—Mrs. Pursley, the wife of Ranger Pursley. What could they few do? Tom! Hurrah for Tom! See! He was still on his feet —he was still at it! The brave fellow! But how could they help him? The main band of Indians were in sight; the block-house, and the wounded lieutenant, must not be left unprotected—

Mrs. Pursley stormed.

"Out with you? Are you men, to let a comrade be butchered?" She appealed to her husband: "Are you a coward, too? Did I marry a coward?"

"We'd save Tom if we could, but the Injuns are ten to one. We don't dare leave."

A cry welled.

"Tom's down again! He's fainted. There's the end to him."

"No, it isn't." Mrs. Pursley tore the gun from her husband's hand. "The more shame on you, to let a defenceless man lie. But I'll not see so fine a fellow as Tom Higgins lost for lack of a little help."

And before they could stop her she was galloping through the gate and into the prairie.

"After her, boys! That's too much to stand. Never mind the fort."

They raced in pursuit. The one Indian was searching for his gun; the other Indians, coming in, halted, confused. Mrs. Pursley was there first—already on the ground and bending over Ranger Tom, trying to lift him to her saddle. They had no time to waste.

One helped her—slung Tom across in front of a saddle; and fighting a rear action they gained the block-house without a wound.

Tom Higgins was the hero, but Mrs. Pursley was the heroine.

Two of his bullets were taken out, and he got well, except for a limp and considerable "botheration" from a third bullet. After the war he made a day's ride to find a doctor and have the ball extracted.

"What's your fee, Doc?"

"It'll be fifty dollars."

"What! Not much, by golly! That's more than half a year's pension. For less I'll fetch it out, myself."

He wrathfully rode home again; the ball seemed to have worked toward the surface—yes, he could see it, away in.

"Old woman, hand me my razor, will you?" he bade. "And jest put your fingers on this hole and stretch it."

Without a quiver he cut into his thigh, put in his two thumbs, "and," he said, "I flirted that ball out as slick as a whistle, at the cost of nary a cent!"

In his later years Veteran Ranger Tom Higgins was assistant doorkeeper for the Illinois legislature. His sturdy form and the story of his fight with the three Indians when he covered the escape of Comrade Burgess made him a famous character.

CHAPTER XIII

JOHN COLTER'S RACE FOR LIFE (1808)

THE TRAPPER AND THE BLACKFEET

IN all the planning for possession of the country north and west of the Ohio River the Indians were far out-stripped by the white men. By the treaty of peace with England, in 1783, at the close of the Revolution, the United States obtained the lands west to the Mississippi River. When beginning in 1805 the Shawnee Prophet, or Open Door, tried to league the red people together, the Long Knife nation of the Thirteen Fires had extended clear to the Rocky Mountains. There was no stopping them. In the spring of 1803 President Thomas Jefferson, for the United States, had succeeded in buying the great Louisiana Territory from France. This Province of Louisiana covered from the Mississippi to the summits of the Rocky Mountains, and from Texas to Canada.

The messengers sent out by Open Door traveled even to the Blackfeet Indians of present Montana; but messengers sent out by President Jefferson had traveled farther. Starting from near St. Louis, in June, 1804, they had carried the new flag and the new peace word clear up the Missouri River, through Sioux country, through Blackfoot country and through Snake country, and had explored on to the Pacific Ocean at the

206

mouth of the Columbia River in present Washington. They had beaten the Open Door by several years.

These messengers of the United States were true Long Knives: young Captain Meriwether Lewis of Virginia and Lieutenant William Clark, his friend and a brother of the famed General George Rogers Clark, of Kentucky. They were to report upon the nature of the northern Louisiana Purchase, talk friendship with the strange Indians, and find a way by water across the Oregon Country beyond, to the mouth of the Columbia.

They took a company of thirty-one men enlisted as soldiers and boatmen and interpreters. Among them there were nine of the Kentucky Long Hunters. It is said that Lewis Wetzel joined, but he dropped out. John Colter, of Maysville on the Ohio River at the mouth of Limestone Creek, opposite West Virginia, was another. He went through.

Ten years before, Daniel Boone had moved west, into Louisiana Province while it was owned by Spain. He had settled in central Missouri, on the Missouri River above St. Louis; wanted "elbow room," he said —and the Spanish governor gave him eight thousand five hundred acres of land. Colonel Boone the Big Turtle was the first of the American dead-shots in the new West. When the Lewis and Clark men toiled up-river here he still was, living among the French in the very last white settlement.

He was not to be alone long. Many another Kentuckian and Carolinan and Tennesseean and Virginian had been thinking of a try at Boone's latest hunting-grounds; they remembered that he had made a good choice when he picked Kentucky: and now that the country yonder was being opened by Americans for Americans they pressed after Lewis and Clark—their own kind. There were furs to be found, under American protection, and sold at St. Louis, an American city.

So when in the summer of 1806 the Lewis and Clark men were on the down-river trail, bound for St. Louis again, on the Missouri below the mouth of the Yellowstone River away up in North Dakota they met two American trappers, Forest Hancock and Joseph Dickson, hailing last from Illinois.

John Colter, of the nine Kentuckians, thought that this was a good chance for him. The two free-trappers had been in here for two years—had set out right on the heels of the exploring party; they had caught many beaver and were doing well. They turned back, for fifty miles, with the company. On the way down John Colter arranged to become their partner. Captain Lewis gave him his discharge; and instead of going home he stayed, to be a trapper.

This land of high bare plains and snow-tipped, rock-ribbed, pine-clad mountains was very different from the forests of the Ohio region; but he had learned a great deal during his two years' trip. He was no greenhorn. He could take care of himself—he had been farther than Hancock and Dickson, felt no more fear of the Western Indians than he did of the Eastern Indians. After all, an Indian was an Indian, although these plains Indians like the Sioux and Black-

208

feet numbered thousands and seemed to think themselves much better than the white man.

In the fall his partners went "out," to take their furs to St. Louis. He remained in, and spent the winter alone, up the Yellowstone River of Montana, which was Blackfoot country. Captain Lewis had had trouble with the Blackfeet. They had tried to rob him, and two had been killed. But the Blackfoot head chief announced that this had served his young men right, and that the other Blackfeet bore the Americans no ill will.

Therefore Trapper Colter passed the winter in peace. The Crows, who also claimed the Yellowstone, did not molest him, either. In the spring he was taking the lone trail for St. Louis, when he met a company of American and French fur-hunters under Manuel Lisa, a swarthy Spaniard. They were coming in to build a trading post among the Blackfeet or Crows.

Trapper Colter had reached the mouth of the Platte River, in Nebraska—was almost "home," to the States, after an absence of three years; but he cared little. Trader Lisa wished him to be their scout to the Yellowstone and help them with the Indians; so he promptly turned around and took the back trail. He loved the trapper's life.

They built the post, named Manuel's Fort, beside the Yellowstone at the mouth of the Big Horn River in southeastern Montana. Trader Lisa found out that the Blackfeet were friendly; but their trade was not enough for him. He coveted the furs of the Crows and other Indians. John Colter was the man to carry the word that a trading post had been "brought" to the Yellow-

stone, and that all Indians were invited to visit it. He
.set out with the news.

This part of the Yellowstone was really Crow country; they ranged in southern Montana, the Blackfeet
ranged in northern Montana, but they fought each other
whenever they met in south or north, or in the mountains west. The Blackfeet were the stronger; they
were eating the Crows, year after year. Trader Lisa
should have known better than to invite them both
to trade with him.

John Colter shouldered a pack of thirty pounds
weight, containing presents, and with his rifle and ammunition started to hunt the Crows in the southwest.
He paddled his canoe up the Big Horn into northern
Wyoming, and finally discovered the Crows in their
summer quarters of the Wind River Valley, to the westward.

With them he traveled westward still, across the
Wind River Mountains and the Teton Mountains into
northeastern Idaho. For the first time the eyes of a
white American saw this wild and grandly beautiful
scenery of a hunter's paradise.

He had traveled by canoe and foot and horse about
five hundred miles. Here he met the Flathead Indians,
with whom he had made friends when with Captain
Lewis and Lieutenant Clark. Here he met the Blackfeet, too—fifteen hundred of them on a horse-stealing
expedition. But he met them in battle. He was with
the Crows and Flatheads, and of course had to aid his
own party. It was do or die, because the Crows and
Flatheads numbered only eight hundred.

He showed them how a white man could fight; he was wounded in the leg, the Blackfeet were driven off, they had seen him as a leader in the ranks of their enemies, they refused to forget, and ever after that they were the sworn foes of the whites.

There was no use now in his trying to talk with the Blackfeet. If they caught him they'd kill him. He'd better avoid them. The Crows were afraid to guide him far, and he struck out alone for Manuel's Fort, and made his own trail. Possibly the Crows had told him of a "big-medicine" country—a region of bad and good spirits, lying between him and the Big Horn, and into which few Indians ventured. It promised to be a safe trail, he was not afraid of "spirits"—preferred "spirits" to the Blackfeet; he struck out, and plunged into the wonders of the Yellowstone Park.

He arrived at Lisa's Fort (which was another of its names) without trouble, and full of stories about hot geysers and boiling mud and strange colorings. For many years nobody believed his stories; they were only "trapper yarns;" but there he had been, in this year 1807, and had had the place all to himself.

Trader Lisa was not satisfied. He wished furs, and more furs; he wished the Blackfeet furs, as well as the Crow and Flathead and Sioux furs. In the spring of the next year he sent Trapper Colter out again, to seek the Blackfeet, make peace with them, and urge them to come in Fort Manuel. By this time they probably would have forgiven the one white man who had been in a tight fix and obliged to fight whether or no.

John Potts agreed to go with John Colter. They

were comrades of old. John Potts was another of the
Lewis and Clark men: had served as a soldier enlisted
at Carlisle Barracks, Pennsylvania, by Captain Lewis
himself. He had joined the Trader Lisa company at
St. Louis, a year ago, and on the way up-river had been
glad to meet John Colter. It was a reunion.

Now from Lisa's Fort they paddled up the Yellowstone again, down which they had come in 1806 with
Lieutenant Clark, and crossed westward over the divide between the Yellowstone and the heads of the
Missouri. This was the Three Forks country, of present southwestern Montana, where the Missouri split
into three branches named by Captain Lewis the Madison, the Gallatin and the Jefferson. They knew it
well; had they not worked hard here, when bound for
the Columbia in the summer of 1805?

Likely enough they were not at all anxious to find
the Blackfeet or to have the Blackfeet find them. The
Blackfeet sometimes roamed here; so did the timid
Snakes, descending from the mountains to hunt buffalo
on the Missouri River plains in the east; so did the
Crows. While spying around, they two built a canoe
apiece and trapped beaver in the Jefferson River, over
toward the mountains.

The beaver were as abundant as ever. To keep out
of sight of Indians, they set their traps after dusk, ran
them very early in the morning, and lay hidden all day.
It certainly was not pleasant, to live like 'coons and
owls, but so many furs were worth the trouble.

One early morning they were in their canoes, deep
between the high banks, down toward the mouth of the

river where it united with the Madison, when they heard a dull tramping in the valley.

"Harkee!" spoke John. "D'ye hear, Jack? That sounds like Injuns. We'd better drop our traps an' câche (hide) ourselves."

"Injuns nothin'!" John Potts laughed. "Them's buff'ler. Seems like every time the wind blows you're thinkin' 'Injuns.' Can't you tell buff'ler from reds? Or are you gettin' skeered out?"

"Jest as you say, then," the other John replied. "But if anything happens, don't blame me. I've a notion we ought to climb up an' spy 'round."

"If they're Injuns, our heads would give us away. We'll keep where we are, snug under the banks, an' they'll pass us by. But those are buff'ler, I tell you."

They worked along, lifting their beaver traps. The dull tramping increased, as if the buffalo were about to cross the river. Suddenly, above them, on the edge of the east bank, there appeared dark figures, with blankets and feathered crowns and guns and bows.

"Blackfeet!" John Colter gasped. "Watch out. Stop paddling. Drop your traps." His own he let slide over the side of his canoe farthest from the Indians.

The Blackfeet instantly covered the two canoes with bended bows and leveled muskets. The whole bank was bristling with their fierce array, so that the narrow river seemed shadowed.

A chief called sternly, and gestured, bidding the two canoes to land where the bank had washed in a little cove.

"We're in for it," remarked John Colter. "Come on, and I'll talk with 'em."

"Not I," the other John growled. "Let's talk from here."

"That's pure folly." And knowing Indians better than his comrade did, John Colter paddled in with a few strokes.

One of the Blackfoot warriors seized his canoe at once; hands rudely hauled him out, and upon the bank, wrenched his gun from him and tore off all his clothes. It was an alarming welcome.

John Potts was still in his own canoe, in mid-stream. The Indians again called to him, and the chief beckoned.

"Come ashore, or they'll kill you where you are," urged John Colter. There were eight hundred of them!

But Trapper Potts shook his head.

"I'll not. I might as well be killed here and now, as be robbed and beaten first. You—"

A bow twanged angrily. Down he fell, in the bottom of his canoe. John Colter could scarcely see, by reason of the dancing, shouting Blackfeet. Then he heard.

"Colter! They've got me! I'm wounded!"

"Bad hurt?"

Trapper Potts was standing, rifle in hand and an arrow jutting from his hip.

"Yes. I can't make off. Get away if you can. I meant to kill one at least."

He aimed and fired; shot a Blackfoot dead. That

was his last act. The smoke had no more than cleared the muzzle of his gun, ere a hundred arrows and bullets "made a riddle of him." Thus he died, also; a brave no-surrender man.

Yelling furiously, the Blackfeet, in a jostling mob, rushed into the stream, pulled the canoe ashore, dragged the body out upon the bank, and hacked it to pieces. They threw the pieces into John Colter's face, the slain warrior's relatives fought to get at him with their tomahawks, while the other Blackfeet formed about him and thrust them aside.

It was a doubtful moment. The air quivered to threat and insult. Trapper Colter expected to be killed at once. His friend had sealed the doom of both of them; had destroyed the one chance, for if no blood had been shed the Blackfeet might only have robbed them and let them go.

The tumult gradually lessened. The chiefs squatted in a circle, and while all scowled at the prisoner a council was held. The only point to be discussed was, how should he die?

They appeared to have decided. The head chief arose, and stalking to John motioned to him to go farther out into the open.

"Go! Go away!" he ordered, in the Crow tongue. Evidently they recognized John Colter as the white man who had fought against them among the Crows. That made matters worse.

John guessed that they were using him for a practice target. As soon as he was out a little way, they would shoot at him—see how many times they could hit him

215

before killing him. That would be great sport as well as good practice. He slowly walked, to the east, upon the open plain, expecting with every step to feel the first arrow or bullet. This was a nervous stroll for a naked man. He heartily wished that he never had seen the Crows, or John Potts either.

He was not moving fast enough to suit the Blackfeet. An old fellow commenced to shout at him, and motion for him to go faster. But he didn't wish to go faster; the ground was thickly grown to prickly-pear cactus, and he had to pick his path amidst the spines.

Then the old Indian scuttled after him, very impatient. Told him to go faster yet—hurry, hurry! Even gave him a shove, or two.

From about one hundred yards out he looked again, and saw that the younger warriors were casting off their blankets and leggins; were stripping as if for a race!

What? A race it was to be, with his scalp the prize? A wave of hope and determination surged into his throat, and his heart beat madly. After all, the Blackfeet were treating him like a man. He was one among eight hundred; they had given him a chance!

He drew long breath. He was in his prime, aged about thirty-five; was five feet ten inches in height, stout-limbed, broad chested—strongly built after the Daniel Boone type of hunter. And he was a swift runner; few men that he knew were his equal.

With a leap, he launched himself full-speed across the bare plain, aiming for the Madison River, five miles before. A burst of yells and whoops reached his ears.

He glanced behind and saw some one hundred young braves, naked, the most of them, to their breech-clouts, careering after with spears.

He had made good time in other races, but he never had run like this. His strength and stride astonished him. The ground fairly whizzed from under him, the wind whined in his ears, almost drowning the cries of the pursuit. He wasted no moments now in picking his way through the prickly-pears; had to step on them with his bare soles, whether or no; and he gathered the stinging spines as a pin-cushion gathers pins.

He wasted no moments, either, in looking back. He bent all his energy upon reaching the Madison River. Soon he had run a mile, without slackening; could hear no feet except his own, had felt no lunge of spear. He kept on for another mile, and had not dared to relax. His lungs were sore, his throat dry, his breath wheezed, and his eyes were dizzy. But he was half way to the Madison. Was he going to escape? He did not know. The yells were fainter.

But what was that? Blood began to gush from his nose, choking him. He had burst a blood-vessel. It frightened him and weakened him, and he rather despaired. For the first time he glanced over his shoulder, to measure distance. Hurrah! He had dropped all the Blackfeet except one; but that one was overhauling him, and was within the hundred yards: a tall, fast young warrior, with a spear in his right hand and his blanket streaming from his left arm and shoulder.

Exhausted, Trapper Colter about decided to give up.

He had done his best. So he ran more slowly; and when he thought that the Indian was about to spear him he turned abruptly, and spread both his arms, in surrender, and gasped, in Crow language:

"Do not kill."

He took the Indian quite by surprise, for a gory, frightful sight he was. But the Indian's mind had been made up. He saw the scalp, his hard-won prize; and poising his spear in both hands he charged on, to lunge. He, too, was wellnigh all in, and stumbled as he tried to thrust. John managed to grab the spear near the head, and hold it off, and they swayed and tugged. The spear broke, and the Indian fell flat. Trapper Colter stabbed him with the point, snatched the blanket, and leaving him lying there was away again.

A tremendous yell echoed from the Indians who had been watching; but now filled with hope once more he ran, he said, "as if he had not run a mile." Ahorse and afoot the whole Blackfoot band were tearing after.

He reached the Madison in the lead. He had run his five miles, but he had not won his life. There was to be no mercy for him, now that he had killed a warrior. Would the Madison save him? Beyond, there was only another open stretch, to be crossed, and a high mountain to be climbed.

He did not know exactly what to do, as he crashed through the willows bordering the little river. Then he saw a very large beaver-house, like a small haystack rising ten feet above the water, in a dammed pond. He plunged for it, and commenced to swim. If

218

he might manage to get into that beaver-house before he was sighted—! He had quick wit, did John Colter.

The water was some ten feet deep, at the house. He held his breath and took a deep, deep dive. Luck was with him, to reward him. He groped, near the bottom, and struck the entrance; got his head through, and his body, and wriggled on—perhaps to stick fast inside and drown! No! As he had wildly hoped, the house was of two stories and big enough for him. The second floor was high and dry, for the beavers to lie upon; and the hole up through it was wide enough so that he could support his shoulders and breathe. Here he panted and waited, in the darkness.

Presently he could hear the Blackfeet, plashing about, and talking. In a moment or so they were upon the beaver-house itself. Their moccasins crunched the brittle sticks and mud; they thrust with their spears, and seemed uncertain what to do, themselves.

Another fear thrilled him. Supposing they guessed that he was under them, and set the house on fire! It would burn; the fire would eat down, and he would be roasted or smothered. He listened intently, for the crackling; even fancied that he could smell the smoke; let himself down as far as he might, so as to dodge the spear points.

After a long, long time the voices and the plashing grew less, as the Blackfeet appeared to be giving up the search. Then they all collected again. Then they went away. Then they came back. Would they never quit? He was chilled stiff, soaked with the icy water. But he hung on.

Finally silence reigned. They had gone; or hadn't they? Maybe they were hidden, near, waiting for him. He grimly waited, too. At last he could stand the place no more. By the blackness, and the feel of the air, night had arrived. He drew another breath, let go, and dived from under. He cautiously rose to the surface; all was darkness. So he swam upstream and landed on the east side.

He did not dare to linger, though. A mountain range enclosed the valley, and he had to make it before daylight. He traveled on as fast as possible, with his blistered feet and his sodden blanket and his spearhead, for thirty miles, to a pass that he knew of.

However, the Blackfeet doubtless were before him, to cut him off in the pass. There was nothing for him, but to climb the mountain here instead of taking to the regular trail. Up he climbed, in the dark, by such a steep route that he had to haul himself by grasping at the rocks and brush and branches. Soon he was into snow. And when, at dawn, he gained the crest of the ridge, he could go no farther. He might yet be seen, and captured.

He lay here all day, aching and shivering and starved, with his wet blanket wrapped around his naked shoulders; managed to chew on some sappy bark, and swallow some tender tips; but that was poor fare. At dusk he started down, to try for Manuel's Fort, northeast three hundred miles across the open plain again.

That was a terrible journey, for a man in his shape. He had nothing except his blanket and his spear-head;

so he had to eat roots and bark. He found enough *pommes blanches* (white apples) or Indian turnips to keep him alive. They were starchy, and ought to be cooked, but he ate them raw.

When, on the eleventh day, he staggered into the fort, he was so thin and haggard in face and body, and his legs and feet were so puffed, that he scarcely looked like a man, and nobody recognized him. But he was a man indeed, and had out-matched the Blackfeet and the rigors of mountain and plain.

After all, the white American is a hard fighter to down.

While getting away from the Blackfeet, Trapper Colter had vowed that if he escaped this time he'd go straight to St. Louis. He had had enough. When he grew strong at Fort Lisa, he changed his mind; he thought he'd better stay through another season; go back for his beaver-traps, at any rate. First-class beaver-traps cost fifteen dollars apiece.

It took him until winter to grow strong. Then he set out alone, to find his traps in the Jefferson River. He hoped that the Blackfeet would be in their winter villages, and not ranging about.

Well, he crossed the same mountain, into the valley, and was in camp, at night, in the Three Forks country not far from where he had run his race—yes, was not far from the very beaver-house in which he had hidden, when while cooking his supper of buffalo-meat he heard the cracking of brush behind him. He pricked up his ears, and did not stir. But when he heard the sharp click of gun-locks, out there in the dark-

221

ness, at one jump he had leaped over his fire and dived for safety.

A volley scattered the fire and spurted the sod under his flying feet. He had been none too prompt. Away he ran, as before, only this time he was better clothed. Again he climbed straight up the mountain; again he lay on top; and again he traveled by night for the Manuel Lisa post. And again he declared that if he might only escape, he surely would quit such a region forever.

Did he do it? Not he. Early in April, 1810, he was once more at the perilous Three Forks, but now with a company of other trappers. The deadly Blackfeet attacked, on the Jefferson, killed or captured five—and John Colter roundly asserted:

"That's three times for me, boys. I daren't risk a fourth time. I'm going to pull out for the States. Goodby."

He arrived in St. Louis in thirty days, having traveled three thousand miles, mainly by canoe. His stories of his fights and of the marvels he had discovered in the Yellowstone Park caused much talk in the newspapers and among the people. His fights were believed, but not his Yellowstone "yarns." He married, the next winter, and settled at Dundee, on the Missouri River in Franklin County, west of St. Louis. It was a tame life.

When the fur-traders and the beaver-trappers passed up, bound for the plains and mountains and the Blackfeet country, he eyed their "fixin's" wistfully, and longed to go. But he would not leave his wife. He postponed his next hunt until in November, 1813, he died of the jaundice while still an able-bodied man with his thoughts turned westward to the land of the fierce Blackfeet.

CHAPTER XIV

HUGH GLASS AND THE GRIZZLY BEAR (1823)
"AS SLICK AS A PEELED ONION"

THE Blackfeet remained firm enemies of the invading trappers and fur-hunters. John Colter's adventures were the beginning of a long and bitter war. The Crows made friends with the white men, and only stole their horses and traps and other "plunder;" but to a Crow this was no crime. The Sioux and Cheyennes and Arapahos and Utes frequently declared that their hearts were good. The Blackfeet never softened. They were many in number, and proud and scornful, and did not stoop even to pretend friendship.

The Three Forks region became known as one of the most dangerous places in the beaver country. All the Upper Missouri River, from the Yellowstone River on, was dangerous by reason of the widely roaming Blackfeet.

Of course, the American trapper and trader did not stay away, on this account. Manuel Lisa and others had formed the Missouri Fur Company, in 1809. In 1822 the Rocky Mountain Fur Company was organized, at St. Louis, and advertised for "one hundred young men to ascend the Missouri River to its source, there to be employed for one, two, or three years," trapping.

It proved to be a famous company. It had on its

224

rolls Jim Bridger, Kit Carson, Jedediah Smith the Knight in Buckskin, the Sublette brothers, Jim Beckwourth the French mulatto who lived with the Crows as chief, and scores of others, mainly young men, genuine Americans of both French and Anglo-Saxon blood. Its career did not cease until the summer of 1834.

The two men who organized the company were General William Henry Ashley of the Missouri militia, and first lieutenant-governor of the State; and Major Andrew Henry who had helped to found the Missouri Fur Company and now was mining for lead in Washington County southwest of St. Louis.

Major Henry already had served in the Blackfeet country. He was there at the Three Forks in the spring of 1810, when five trappers had been killed or captured and John Colter had decided to pull out. Next, George Drouillard, who had been a hunter with the Lewis and Clark party (another of John Colter's old companions), and whose father Pierre Drouillard had rescued Simon Kenton from the Shawnees, was killed while fighting bravely. Finally the Blackfeet had driven all the trappers from that region. Major Henry led his remaining men west across the mountains, to the Snake River in Idaho. There on Henry Fork he built a trading-post. It was the first American post west of the Rocky Mountains.

Major Henry returned to St. Louis in 1811. He had met with bad luck in the fur-hunt business, so he went into mining. But the beaver country kept calling to him. He was not yet beaten by the Indians, the snows, the freshets and the hunger.

Therefore in 1822 he started again, for the mouth of the Yellowstone and the Great Falls of the Missouri, farther up. The Assiniboines stole all his horses. He stayed at the mouth of the Yellowstone until he had traded for more, from the Crows; went on to the Great Falls—and the Blackfeet again smashed him and sent him back down-river, minus four good men.

General Ashley was to follow him, with reinforcements of another one hundred young men. He was met by a courier from his partner, asking for horses, horses, horses. He stopped to trade with the Arikaras, in present South Dakota; they suddenly attacked him, rolled him up, and stopped him completely.

He had to drop back, fortify, and call for volunteers to take word to Major Henry that nothing could be done this season until the way had been opened. Jedediah Smith, aged twenty-five, stepped forward. He was of New York State, and had been in the West only two years; had never been farther from St. Louis than this, into the Indian country. But his voice rang true; he wished to learn. General Ashley gave him a French-Canadian of St. Louis as a scout companion, and together they crossed the six hundred miles of vast lonely plains infested by the Arikaras and Sioux and Assiniboines, to Major Henry at the mouth of the Yellowstone.

Major Henry's party returned with them, to General Ashley at the mouth of the Cheyenne River in South Dakota. From the United States post at the Lewis and Clark's Council Bluffs, western Iowa of to-day, Lieutenant-Colonel Henry Leavenworth (Fort Leavenworth of

Kansas is named for him) of the Sixth United States Infantry, hastened up with six companies of regulars, several cannon and three keel-boats. Joshua Pilcher, president of the Missouri Fur Company, joined him; General Ashley and Major Henry met him with other men; four or five hundred Sioux enlisted—the Sioux hated the Arikaras. And all together (except that the Sioux soon quit, disgusted with the way the white soldiers fought) they battered at the Arikara village from a distance until the enemy announced that it was time to make peace.

Now Major Henry took eighty men and once again set out, with horses and packs, for the Yellowstone, to finish the season. He had a fine company—the pick of the rank and file: Jedediah Smith, Jim Bridger, William ("Billy") Sublette whom the Indians were to name "Cut Face" and "Left Hand," Davy Jackson, old "Cut Nose" Edward Rose who was half white, one quarter Cherokee and one quarter negro and had been a chief of the Crows, "old" Hugh Glass, and others.

Major Henry, of the dark hair, blue eyes, and fondness for the violin, had only fair luck on this trip. Trapper Hugh Glass had much worse, at the beginning, although he ended well.

He was from Pennsylvania, but was no greenhorn on the beaver trail, or else they would not have called him "old." The title "old" announced that a man was "beaver wise" and "Injun wise." So "old" Hugh Glass was a leather-faced, leather-clad, whiskered veteran of probably not over forty years but of the right experience as a *"hivernan"* or "winterer."

The route taken left the Missouri River, to cut across country more to the westward, for the Yellowstone direct. Near evening of the fifth day out they all had turned up the Grand River, still in present South Dakota, and the hunters were riding widely or trudging through the river thickets, looking for meat.

This was elk, deer and buffalo country—also bear country. Those were days when the grizzly bear ranged the plains as far east as the Upper Missouri; and he posed as the monarch of all he surveyed. The Lewis and Clark men had discovered him on their outward trip in 1804–1805; they had brought back astonishing reports of him. He stood almost nine feet tall, on his hind legs; his fore paws were nine inches across; his claws were over four inches long; his tusks were prodigious; his nose as large as that of an ox; and two men could scarcely carry his hide. Eight and ten balls were sometimes required, to kill him; he would run a mile and more, after being shot through the heart; he feared nothing. Captain Lewis declared that he would rather fight two Indians at once, than one "white bear." No such an animal was known in Kentucky.

The great grizzly usually lurked in the willows, wild-plum trees and other brush of the stream courses. Here he made his bed, and from here he charged without warning—afraid not at all of the two-legged enemy and their single-shot, muzzle-loading flint-lock rifles. In spite of his size, he was marvelously quick. Besides, he had a short temper.

Hugh Glass was making his way, this August evening, amidst the tangle of wild plums, berry bushes, and willows along the bank of the Grand. Suddenly he had burst out into a small clearing—a bear's "nest" made by crushing the brush in a circle: and the bear was at home, had heard him coming.

More than that, it was an old she-bear, and a mother bear, lying with her two cubs upon the twigs and sand. Hugh Glass, a careless though a skilled hunter, had met with a surprise. Before he had time to spring back or even to set the hair-trigger of his rifle, she was towering over him: a huge yellowish bulk whose deep-set piggish little eyes glowed greenish with rage, whose white tusks gleamed in a snarling, dripping red mouth, whose stout arms (thicker than his calves) reached for him with their long curved claws.

This alarming sight he saw—and then she grabbed him, with a stroke that nearly scalped him; drew him in to her, lifted him off the ground to hug him, bit him in the throat, and hurling him flat tore a mouthful of flesh from him and gave it to her cubs!

Horrible! Was he to be eaten alive, like a deer? Evidently she looked upon him as a species of animal that might be a tidbit for her family. When she turned to call her cubs and give them the meat she slightly removed her weight from him. With a writhe he scrambled to get away. No use. She was after him at once; so were the cubs, as eager as she. They did not mean that their supper should escape. The whole family commenced to maul him. The mother seized him by the shoulder and straddled him; she bit, the two cubs bit and raked. He was only a toy to them, and being rapidly gashed to ribbons he would have died then and there had not his shouts and the growling of the bears brought help.

First, his hunting partner arrived, hot-foot, with rifle ready. One cub drove him waist deep into the river before a ball finished that young battler. The other men hastened in, summoned by the redoubled cries for help. The old mother grizzly was standing upon Hugh Glass and bellowing defiance. The second cub ran. By several volleys they killed the mother grizzly; then they rolled her off from Trapper Glass and inspected him, to see what they could do.

"Poor old Hugh! He's a goner—he's nigh et up." That was the verdict. He certainly looked like a "goner"—all bloody and mangled, with scarcely an inch of sound skin on his face, body and limbs. He could not see, he was past speaking, he was unable to stand; he only lay and dismally groaned.

They washed him and patched him and bound him as best they might, and took counsel together. They couldn't carry him on; they couldn't send him back; and they couldn't camp here, waiting for him to get well or to die; they had to reach the Henry fort at the mouth of the Yellowstone, with their horses and supplies, before winter.

"If two of you men will stay and nurse Glass, we'll make up a purse to pay for the loss of your fall hunt," Major Henry proposed.

Trapper Fitzgerald, and a seventeen-year-old who is said to have been Jim Bridger, agreed to stay with Hugh Glass and nurse him or bury him. They were given eighty dollars, to cover the beaver fur that they might miss out on. Major Henry left them and the groaning Hugh, and hastened with his other men for the Yellowstone.

It was a dangerous and lonely job. They were two (one of them only seventeen and rather of a greenhorn yet); this was Arikara and Sioux country; the Arikaras had shown bad hearts; they fought the Sioux and all friends of the Sioux, the Sioux fought them and all friends of them; and caught by one band or another, white hunters might fare ill. Forty dollars was small pay for risking one's scalp. As for risking it to save a comrade, of course no pay at all was asked. So the money did not figure.

Old Hugh did not grow better; on the contrary, he seemed to grow worse. He was a frightful sight. The teeth and claws of the bears had poisoned him and he was one mass of gaping wounds; lay moaning and raving until his fever weakened him so that he had no strength—couldn't swallow nourishment to keep alive and the men had to sit beside him constantly to brush away the flies.

On the fifth day they gave him up.

"He'll not live the night."

"No. He's goin' fast. It's a wonder he's held out this long, poor Hugh. I never did see a human bein' hang on like him."

"What'll we do, then?"

"Wall, youngster, thar's only one thing to do. That's to pull out while we kin, 'fore we lose our ha'r. 'Tis a wonder the Injuns ain't diskivvered us already. Glass is as good as dead, now; but we'll wait till dark."

"I don't feel jest right about leavin' him, Tom,"
young Jim objected. " 'Tain't natteral to desart a
man, that way, an' we said we'd stay."

"We said we'd stay to nurse him or bury him, but
he's past nursin' an' he ain't quite ripe for buryin',
son. He will be, by mornin'; but what difference to
him whether he's layin' atop the ground or under
the ground? An' that's a matter o' twelve hours to
us, an' twelve hours counts a heap, on the Injun trail.
The Injuns can't do him any harm. They kin harm us
a lot. No; it's time we kin light out, an' if we say he's
dead we'll not be lyin', for dead he'll be long 'fore we
get to t'other end. Two live men are wuth more'n one
dead man, in this country; an' we've done our duty to
old Hugh, sech as he is. We'd best take his gun an'
fixin's, too; he won't need 'em an' you kin be sartin
he wouldn't want the Injuns to have 'em."

When they left, that night, Trapper Glass appeared
to be scarcely breathing. He could not possibly last
through till morning; and by morning they might be
well upon their way. They rode off. It was a mean
thing to do—not at all like Jim Bridger if that was
young Jim Bridger; but he could not stay alone and
they neither of them had any idea that Hugh Glass
would be otherwise than dead within a few hours.

When, early in a morning several days afterward,
Trapper Hugh opened his tired eyes and gazed weakly
around him, he saw nothing astir except the birds and
rabbits. He heard nothing. He had faint memory
of two companions—knew their names, or thought that
he did; but where were they? The camp-fire ashes

232

were cold; no breakfast smoke arose. He saw no packs, no bedding; the bones of the she-bear were scattered and white and dry.

He called feebly.

"Tom! Jim! Hello! Whar be ye?"

Nobody answered. He tried to sit up; looked for his rifle, felt for his shot-pouch and powder-horn. His two nurses were gone; so were his gun, horn, pouch that held his knife and flint and steel. He had been abandoned; and such a blaze of wrath surged through him that he determined now to live if only to trail those fellows and kill them.

Yes, by thunder, he'd crawl clear to Fort Henry at the Yellowstone and shoot the two in their tracks!

He was too weak to sit or stand, but he managed to draw himself along and find a spring. There he lay, day and night, picking the fruit from the low wild-cherry and buffalo-berry bushes as far as he might reach, and dozing and bathing his wounds; and he got stronger. The tide of life crept higher and higher. Trapper Hugh knew that he was going to live. But he was scarred redly from head to foot, had lost part of his whiskers and part of his hair; was peeled to the bone, in places. What a face he had, although he could not see it!

In about ten days he was ready to travel. The nearest trading-post that he knew of was fully one hundred miles southeast, on the Missouri. That looked like a long, long distance for a man who could not walk straight and had not even a knife. But he was bound to go, get patched up, and find those two villains who had abandoned him—who had left him as dead when he wasn't dead at all!

He managed to find roots, and more berries. At last, on his staggering, slow way, he sighted a late buffalo-calf surrounded by wolves. The wolves killed the calf. He waited until they had dulled their appetites; then waving his arms and shouting he staggered in upon them. He was enough to put almost anything to flight. The wolves dropped their bushy tails and slunk off; and Hugh Glass thankfully "chawed" the raw, warm meat.

He stayed here a short time. He went on, stronger. He came to a deserted Indian village. A few Indian dogs were prowling around. He was very hungry again. He spent two days in coaxing the dogs to him, in order to get his hands upon one. Then he killed it and partly ate it. Living thus, by his wits, like a wild animal or a wild man, he arrived at the trading post near the mouth of the Teton or Mad River, central South Dakota.

But he did not stay long—not even to get patched up. A party of trappers arrived, in a boat from down-river; they were going above, to the Yellowstone— the very spot for which he hankered and where his revenge waited. He embarked. The Arikaras ambushed the boat and killed all the party except Hugh Glass.

They did not get the scalp of old Hugh; no, indeed. He bore a charmed life. He had left the boat, the day before, to make a short cut to Fort Tilton, which lay around a bend. The Arikaras only chased him into the arms of two Mandans; the Mandans took him into

Fort Tilton—and that same night, such was his hurry,
he set out alone again, on foot, for the Yellowstone
and the Andrew Henry fort at the mouth of the Big
Horn in Crow and the Blackfoot country.

He did not fear; he believed that nothing could kill
him. Nothing had been able to kill him, yet! Thirty-
eight days later, or near the close of October, Trapper
Glass strode to the gate of the Henry fort at the mouth
of the Big Horn, up the Yellowstone.

The sentry stared, agape.

"Who are you?"

"How, yoreself, young feller. Whoopee! Tell
'em hyar's old Hugh Glass, who war et by a grizzly
b'ar an' is slick as a peeled onion; an' he wants his
gun an' fixin's. Whar's the rascals that stole all my
plunder?"

Hugh Glass! A miracle! But he it was.

"We thought you were dead and buried, man!"

"Wall, I ain't, not by a jugful. An' I wants my
plunder an' the scalps o' them two villains."

"They aren't here. They're down at Atkinson."

What! Fort Atkinson was the Council Bluffs, on
the lower Missouri one thousand miles away.

"I'll git 'em yit," vowed old Hugh. "If I'd only
have knowed! I warn't very fur from Atkinson."

In February he started for Atkinson, with four other
men. They traveled across country, through central
Wyoming, and struck the Platte; paddled down the
Platte in hide boats that they made—and ran right into
the Arikaras. By night-fall old Hugh found himself
again alone; he had lost all four of his comrades (two

had been killed before his eyes), and most of his new
outfit. But, he said:

"I felt quite rich when I found my knife and steel
in my shot pouch. These little fixin's make a man feel
right peart when he is three or four hundred miles
away from anybody or anywhere—all alone among
the painters (panthers) and the wild varmints."

In the early spring the buffalo calves are young
and senseless. He easily caught them, cut them up,
made a fire and cooked the meat; and in June he was
at Fort Atkinson.

By this time he had forgiven the youngster. He was
willing to believe that the "young feller" wasn't used
to trapper ways, and hadn't known any better. But
he still bore a grudge against Fitzgerald.

Fitzgerald was at Atkinson, enlisted in the army.
Old Hugh raged and stormed, but did not dare to
touch him. They talked it over; Fitz explained why
he had left the grizzly bear camp—had stayed five days,
at the risk of his own life, until there wasn't any
nursing to be done; and when he had gone on Hugh
Glass was the same as dead and he ought to have
stayed dead. Wasn't that reasonable?

Hugh scratched his scarred head and half agreed.
The commanding officer ordered that he be given a
brand new outfit; whatever he needed. This squared
matters, and Trapper Hugh proceeded to entertain the
garrison with his tall stories of how he had been "et by
a b'ar," and had been chasin' his plunder for ten
months, between the lower Missouri and the Yellowstone.

HUGH GLASS AND THE GRIZZLY BEAR

This bear adventure made "Old Glass" a celebrated figure among the traders and trappers of beaver days on the Upper Missouri. As seemed to him, he had earned the right to live forever, in defiance of Injuns and "varmints." But in the winter of 1832–1833 the Arikaras killed him, on the ice of the Yellowstone River, hard by the mouth of the same Big Horn where he had so astonished the Andrew Henry fort nine years before.

CHAPTER XV

A FRACAS ON THE SANTA FE TRAIL (1829)

AND THE BUILDING OF BENT'S FORT

THE United States east of the Upper Mississippi River was opened to the white race by the settlers, who fought to locate their homes in the country of the Shawnees, the Mingos, the Delawares, the Potawatomis, and all.

The newer United States of the vast Louisiana Territory, west of the Upper Mississippi River, was for a long time thought to be of little value as a home land. Its value seemed to lie in furs and in trade with the natives.

After the exploration by Captain Meriwether Lewis and his friend Lieutenant Clark, the fur-hunters were the Americans who opened the trails into the country of the Sioux, the Arikaras, the Blackfeet, the Crows and all. They did not make permanent homes; they built only rude forts, as store-houses, and when outside lived in camps like Indian camps. They did not till the ground. When they left, the country was about the same as before, given up to the wild men and the wild animals.

This, during fifty years, was the principal use made of the Missouri River portion of the Louisiana Terri-

238

tory, in the northwest. And in the southwest portion little more was done, but the American merchants were the ones who opened that.

Young Lieutenant Zebulon Montgomery Pike first explored it, sent out by the commander-in-chief of the army, in 1806, while Lewis and Clark were still homeward bound from the other direction. He traveled up the Arkansas River and into the Rocky Mountains of Colorado, and landed as a prisoner in Santa Fe of New Mexico.

The news that he brought back, of New Mexico and the way to get there (an easier way than his own roundabout tour) encouraged the merchants and capitalists of St. Louis to hope that a trading route, back and forth, might be opened with Mexico. Calico, cotton, shoes, tobacco, trinkets and the like were to be sold for gold and silver, or exchanged for buffalo-robes, beaver-furs, blankets, and wool—all at one hundred per cent. profit over the original cost. Mexico manufactured very little, and was eager for American goods.

As the result, through the country of the Kiowas and the Comanches there was opened the great Santa Fe Trail of the merchants and traders. From the Missouri River at the Kansas border it struck out into present central Kansas, headed southwest to the Arkansas River, and passing on across the desert into northeastern New Mexico arrived at old Santa Fe, seven hundred and seventy miles.

The other great national trail, the Oregon Trail of the fur-hunters, was long a pack trail, until the wagons of the emigrants and gold-seekers to California began to throng it. The Santa Fe Trail soon became mainly a wagon trail, for the Santa Fe caravans.

From the Missouri River the traders set out, twenty, thirty, forty wagons in a train—huge canvas-covered Conestogas, thirty feet in length with boxes six feet in depth, carrying three tons of freight and drawn by eight span of oxen or mules. From the lead span's noses to the end-gate of the wagon the length over all was thirty yards. These Santa Fe wagons were not prairie schooners; they were prairie frigates.

Thus they lumbered on, at not better than fifteen miles a day; and during their fifty or sixty days' trips out, loaded, and their forty days' trips back, partly empty, the Kiowas and Comanches, the storms and the hot dry desert, saw to it that they did not have easy sailing.

Among the early Santa Fe traders were the Bent brothers, Charles, William and George, of a large and well-known American family. Their grandfather Silas Bent had been captain of the Boston patriots who in 1773 dumped overboard the English tea on which the Colonists refused to pay a tax; their father Silas Bent, Jr., was first judge of Common Pleas in St. Louis; their younger brother Silas III became a naval officer and discovered and chartered the warm-water flow or Japanese Current of the Pacific Ocean; and they themselves aided civilization by building the massive Bent's Fort of the Plains, on the Arkansas River in southeastern Colorado—for many years the only trading-post and supply depot that could be depended upon, in all the Southwest.

There had been a few traders killed, almost every year, by the Indians; but in 1828 matters grew so bad that the St. Louis merchants asked help from the Government. This year 1828 not only were several traders killed; a party of Comanches who knew nothing of the killings were invited into camp and were shot, except one, out of revenge. The one escaped, to tell his friends. Of course, after this nothing but war could be expected from the southwest Indians, who would be only too glad of an excuse to capture the white man's goods and teams.

William Bent, and perhaps George, already were looking up a site for the fort. They had been attacked, and almost wiped out in a fierce battle. Charles Bent, who was older than they, had made the round trip to Santa Fe. In the spring of 1829 he started again.

The caravan numbered thirty-five wagons and seventy men. He was captain in charge. Under him there were Traders Samuel C. Lamme, William Waldo, and other wagon owners, determined upon making the trip as usual. It would never do to let the Indians close the trail.

Besides, President Andrew Jackson, "Old Rough and Ready," the hero of the battle of New Orleans in 1815, had directed that a soldier escort be furnished as far as the Arkansas River. The Arkansas was the boundary line agreed upon between the United States and Mexico. It was about half way. The Mexican government promised to meet the caravans there, with other soldiers, and escort them the rest of the way, and bring them back to the United States frontier. That was the arrangement.

Fort Leavenworth, up the Missouri, had been located two years before. Troops were ordered from there, to join the caravan. They were four companies of the Sixth United States Infantry commanded by Captain (brevet Major) Bennet Riley, after whom Fort Riley of Kansas is named. Major Riley had fought as a young officer in the War of 1812. He had just gained his brevet of major for having served as captain for ten years. Promotion was very slow.

The caravan owners and its hunters and adventurers were glad to see the sturdy infantry. Infantry is poor stuff with which to catch Indians quickly; cavalry was more used, in a chase: but after a time the Indians grew to fear the infantry more than the cavalry.

"Pony soldiers run; walk-a-heaps no can run, must fight," they said.

So while the caravan might have preferred dragoons or mounted riflemen, to scour on either side and ride in front and rear, it must have taken comfort in the presence of the plodding solid "walk-a-heaps," the unbeatable dough-boys.

Now for the first time since the Lieutenant Pike expedition of 1806 a detachment of American regular soldiers marched into the Southwest between the Missouri River and the Arkansas.

The march of a Santa Fe caravan was a noble sight: the enormous hooded wagons, flaring like poke bonnets, each drawn by twelve and sixteen oxen or mules, lumbering on in a long double file or sometimes four abreast; the booted teamsters trudging beside the fore-wheels, cracking their eighteen-foot lashes; the armed out-riders guarding the flanks—galloping here and there in quest of Indians and game; the captain and his aides spying the country ahead; and the *caballada* or herd of loose extra animals bringing up the rear.

The gait was only two or two and a half miles an hour, so the Major Riley infantry easily kept pace.

When the Arkansas River had been reached, at the crossing or ford Major Riley made camp, to wait until the caravan returned. The teams were doubled and trebled—twenty, thirty, forty animals to a wagon; and with them all straining and snorting, a dozen teamsters cracking whips and shouting, and the heavy Conestogas careening to their hubs in the quick-sand, the crossing was won.

No Mexican escort had appeared. Captain Bent boldly led on, into Mexico.

This portion of the Santa Fe Trail was especially perilous. Between the Arkansas River and the Cimarron River (which through most of the year was no river at all) there was no water for fifty and sixty miles, except right after rains. The stretch was called the "water scrape." All the five-gallon kegs hanging under the wagons had to be filled, and the teams were hustled day and night in order to get across as quickly as possible.

It was a hot country, of soft sand hub-deep and of wind-swept tracts so hard that the wagon wheels left no trace. Caravans traveled by compass; and even then were likely to toil and wander miserably, with their mules and oxen dying from thirst. The Indians loved to catch a caravan in here. The Kiowas and Comanches frequently lay in wait among the billowy sand-hills.

Thus it came about that the Bent caravan, this July of 1829, was attacked on the very first day out from the Arkansas. It had marched only nine or ten miles. The going was very bad, in the hot, flowing sand. All around arose the sand-hills, shimmering yellow, with the sun beating down out of a blue sky. The wagons were strung in a long straggling line, while mules and oxen, their tongues hanging, tugged hard. The teamsters, their feet blistering in their cowhide boots, their beards and flannel shirts caked with dust, urged manfully.

The sand-hills, fifty feet high, formed a complete circle around this sandy basin here. The caravan had entered by a narrow passage, and was stringing across, for another narrow passage. Whether the passage opened into the country beyond, nobody knew. Trader Lamme and two companions spurred ahead, to find out: a foolish thing to do.

They disappeared among the hollows; were gone not half an hour, when on a sudden, distant gun-shots sounded thinly, and back into sight galloped two of the men, racing full tilt, bare-headed. Following fast there came a drove of other figures—and as if from the very ground, on right and left of the leading wagons, still more figures up-sprung. A chorus of wild whoops echoed.

Injuns!

244

All the caravan was in confusion. Horsemen rode, teamsters shouted as they grabbed their guns from the seats and swung their whips. Oxen bellowed and jumbled, mules snorted and balked, the herders of the caballada shrieked for help.

"Close up! Close up!"

"Corral!"

"Charge 'em! Meet the beggars!"

"No! Under yore wagon, everybody!"

"Get out o' my way! Yip! Gee, Buck!"

"Haw, Spot! Haw, Whity! Haw with you!"

"Durn these mules! We'll all be wolf meat."

"Look! There's nigh a thousand of 'em!"

The out-rider guards had lined, on either hand, to stand the enemy off while the wagons bunched. A rear guard sped to protect the caballada. Captain Charles Bent tore back from the advance. He was bare-headed. His long black hair streamed in the breeze that he made. He was mounted on a rangy, raw-boned black mule, with split ears—Comanche brand. No man more fearless ever ranged the plains. A host in himself, was Charles Bent.

His voice fairly thundered as he sped along the struggling line of wagons and teams.

"Bring on those wagons! Corral! Don't lose your senses, men! We're all right. But corral, corral!"

The two fugitives arrived, breathless, their animals sweat-covered and blown. Alas, neither of them was Samuel Lamme, and Samuel Lamme had not appeared.

"We've lost Lamme!" they shouted. "The Injuns got him, first fire."

"Fetch up that cannon. Unlimber," Captain Bent was shouting.

It was a small brass cannon, but had been so wrapped to protect it from the sand that the men could scarcely untie the knots. Away galloped Captain Bent, on his split-ear mule, to encourage the skirmishers' line. He had to be everywhere at once.

Out yonder the rifles and shot-guns were volleying, as the skirmishers, slowly retreating, held the Indians off. The leading wagons had turned broadside to the trail; one by one, or two by two, the other wagons lurched on—they also turning right and left, their teams inside, and their fore wheels almost touching the rear wheels of the wagons already halted. In this way a corral was being formed, in shape of an oval, with an opening at the end, for the caballada to enter.

That was desperate work. Around and around scurried the Indians, lying low upon their ponies' backs or hanging to the farther side, whooping, shaking their blankets, and launching their arrows and balls. They were Kiowas and Comanches both; and had the caravan just about where they wanted it.

The corral was completed; the caballada jostled in; the teamsters crawled here and there, to poke their guns through the wheels; in rode the skirmishers, Captain Bent last. The circling Indians pressed closer, and the cannon piece was yet useless, although the men yanked and slashed.

But the rifles and muskets kept the enemy off. When finally the cannon was unlimbered, aimed, and fired, it only broke the circle. The Indians scattered; and yelling angrily settled down to a siege.

The sun of mid-afternoon was scorching. The wagons on the west end of the corral furnished a little shade, but even in the shade the sand burned the skin. The men, lying flat, shifted wearily. The animals dropped their heads, and panted. The bare yellow hills around quivered. All the little basin was like a furnace. There was not a drop of water except in the casks, and this water would not last long—the air would suck up what men and beasts did not soon drink. The Indians need only wait.

What a fix! The attack could not have been made in a worse place, were it not for the soldiers.

Captain Bent called a council. The Major Riley escort, scarce ten miles back, was the main hope. Some way must be found to summon them.

"But we're in Mexico. It's ag'in the law of nations for soldiers from one country to march in time o' peace into another country."

"Never mind. They're Americans and they'll not stop to figure on boundary lines," Captain Bent answered. "They'll come, I'll wager, even if it brings on war with a dozen nations. Who'll take the back trail? There ought to be enough to make a running fight."

Nine men volunteered. They had a slim chance, but some of them might break loose. They rode away, in the full open. The Indians could not fail to see them.

Rifle-pits had been dug for the out-posts. In the

pits and in the corral the merchants, teamsters, and hunters sweltered, while they anxiously gazed. Scattered in squads among the dips and hollows, the Indians uttered never a sound. Then they burst into a yell. They saw the nine horsemen bolting for the north.

Aha! Several of the Indians had swooped in chase. No! They turned again. What did they fear? The cannon? Or a trap? Or didn't they care? They preferred waiting for bigger booty. Evidently they did not know about the soldiers at the river. The nine riders had got away! Now if the Indians only would hold off for a few hours, the caravan was saved. There seemed to be more than a thousand of the Kiowas and Comanches—in one grand charge they could ride right over the corral; but they knew that they would lose many a warrior, and they planned to get the victory more easily.

The Major Riley command were loafing in their tents and in the shade of the few cottonwoods, until the sun should set. Everything was peaceful—and plaguey hot. Then a sentry's musket gave the alarm signal; he shouted and pointed; the sergeant of the guard ran; from the tents officers and soldiers boiled out, or sprang to their feet, in the shade; bathers in the river plashed for their clothes; and the men on herd commenced to gather their oxen, mules and saddle animals.

A squad of horsemen were galloping in from the south; as they approached they called and waved, and pointed backward. They were a part of the traders who had left the camp only a few hours before. Something had happened, and that could be only Indians. Major Riley did not delay to ask.

"Sound the general," he bade, buckling on his saber at the door of his tent; and the chief bugler sent the notes rollicking through the waves of heat.

Officers ran hither-thither; the men ran; the teamsters ran; the herd swung in, for the parked wagons. The "general" was the first signal to form ranks.

The leading horsemen of the nine couriers galloped into the water and surged across. By the time the last had arrived, the second signal, the "assembly," had been sounded; the tents were being struck, baggage tied, and the oxen driven to their yokes. The companies were about to form.

All these preparations took some time. Two hundred men cannot break camp in an instant and march with bag and baggage into Indian country. And when "To the color," as the final call was known, had been sounded, the sun was set, and the first purple was flowing into the hollows of the vast, lonely land.

The major was going, with his whole force. The couriers had reported one thousand Indians, at the least; the sand-hills were full of them; all the Kiowa and Comanche nations were rallied to close the trail. It would not do to leave an unprotected camp, and no men were to be spared.

In the twilight they forded the shallow Arkansas— the army oxen straining in their yokes, a squad of soldiers pushing each wagon. They entered Mexico; all were liable to arrest, but who cared?

The couriers guided into the sand-hills. The major and his staff followed on their mules. The column of footmen and wagons toiled after.

They could hear no sounds of fighting, before. The twilight deepened. They must move cautiously. The Indians had seen the couriers ride out, they might be laying an ambush. A file of skirmishers fringed either flank, well out; scouts examined the country, ahead. Every ear was pricked, every eye searched right and left.

The silence was very mysterious. The couriers had reported that the Indians' circle was wide, to avoid the cannon. When the stars read midnight, the major thought that he surely had arrived at the scene. The word was passed that every wheel and hoof and foot should be muffled as much as possible, and the infantry were halted, to await the baggage train.

They proceeded. About one o'clock their advance struck the wagon corral itself. The Indians had not discovered them; the caravan out-posts had not discovered them: either side might have surprised the other side, evidently, but neither side knew. In fact, they had not been expected before morning. No one had dreamed that Major Riley would risk a night march through the sand-hills, infested with a thousand and more Indians.

Now the corral and the soldiers waited for morning. At first daylight the reveille was sounded in the army camp. This was military regulations, but gave the Indians warning.

The shrill notes pealed far among the slumberous

dunes. The Kiowas and Comanches, leaping to their feet, stared amazed. Down there, at the wagon corral, two hundred blue-coated American soldiers had grown over-night! Musket barrels faintly gleamed, two score fresh wagon-tops glimmered, figures hastened to and fro, there was clatter of arms.

Wah! These were no traders. They were warriors—American warriors. That made a different proposition. How had they come, and from where?

"We will go," the chiefs decided. "The Mexican soldiers may be coming, too, and we shall be caught between."

So they all rode away.

Major Riley determined that the whole party must march on. To stay here, in this little basin surrounded by the hills, was dangerous. It was no place in which to fight. He would escort the caravan at least a day's stint farther, into more open country.

First, Trader Lamme's body was found, and buried. He had been arrow-shot and lanced; scalped, stripped, and his head cut off. So he was left under the desert sand, and later his bones were dug up and reburied in St. Louis. Then the long column wended for the narrow pass out. It was reconnoitered and found to be undefended. They hastened through, while occupying the high ground on both flanks, and after a short but hard march halted, to camp.

Major Riley was still game. He agreed to advance another day's stint, in order to see the caravan well started into safer regions. With the rise of the sun, a gale also arose. The wind blew hot and hotter, driving the sand in clouds and almost smothering the men and animals. Therefore little could be done. The mules and oxen had to be unyoked—they stood with tongues out and tails to the gale; the wagon covers lashed and bellied; the men sheltered themselves as best they might from the stinging storm out of a clear sky.

By four o'clock in the afternoon the wind died. Every vestige of a trail had been wiped clean; but in ten miles the column luckily blundered upon sign of water, in a dry creek-bed. Hurrah! The scouts searching about found water itself: a pool, in the midst of an acre or two of grass!

The surface of the pool was covered with dead fish, killed by the heat of the sun. That made no difference. The pool was wet.

Major Riley and his soldiers turned back the next morning. Captain Bent took the caravan on, to Santa Fe.

From here, he and his brothers that fall located their trading post. The place was two hundred and sixty miles north of Santa Fe, on the north bank of the Arkansas River, fourteen miles above the mouth of the Purgatory River, or about half way between the towns of La Junta and Las Animas in present southeastern Colorado.

One branch, the Mountain Branch, of the Santa Fe Trail, led up the Arkansas, to it, and on, to turn south across the Raton Mountain for Santa Fe. The Cheyennes gathered near-by, every fall, for their great winter camp. The Utes from the Rocky Mountains, one hundred and thirty miles west, sometimes came down. A traders' and trappers' trail between Santa Fe and the Platte River passed this way. It was a sort of a cross-roads, in the wilderness.

Bent's Fort, called also Fort William after William Bent, was built of adobe or clay bricks. It was one hundred and fifty feet long and one hundred feet wide. Its walls were eighteen feet high, and six or seven feet thick at the base. The tops formed a parapet or walk. In two diagonally opposite corners were bastions of round towers, thirty feet high, swelling out so as to command the walls. The main gateway was thirty feet wide and closed by a pair of huge plank doors. Over the gateway there was a sentry box, floating the United States flag. The six-pounder brass cannon of the caravan was mounted upon a wall, on a swivel, to fire in all directions; other cannon were added.

Bent's Fort became famous. Soon all the Indians for leagues around knew of it. The Arapahos and the Southern Cheyennes traded in their buffalo robes here; the mountain Utes, and the Red River Comanches of northern Texas came in. At one time, in the late fall and in the winter, twenty thousand Indians would be camped within sight of it.

Trappers from north, west and south made it their market and headquarters. Traders trailed in, from the States and from New Mexico. In 1846 General Stephen Watts Kearny's army from Leavenworth for Santa Fe and California halted here, to refit.

So Bent's Fort prospered. It had the only ice-house on the plains; the pumpkin pies of its negress cook,

Charlotte, spread its fame wider; the rank and file of the Indians and the trappers and traders, and the army officers themselves, swore by Bent's Fort.

The Indians called William Bent "Hook-Nose Man" or "Roman Nose." He married a Cheyenne girl. He was the governor of the fort. His brother George helped. Charles Bent was largely at Santa Fe, at Taos, midway, and on the trail, until in 1846 he was appointed first American governor of New Mexico.

The next year the Mexicans and Pueblo Indians revolted against the American government, and killed him at his home in Taos.

Bent's Fort lasted through more than twenty years. Then William Bent offered to sell it to the Government for an army post. He asked $16,000; the Government proposed $12,000. They dickered. Colonel Bent would not yield one penny. He had a short stock of patience in dealing with white men or red men either. So in the summer of 1852 he blew up the fort with powder and marched away, to build another post, for Indian trade, thirty miles down-river.

This became Fort Wise, of the army, but was known to the settlers as "old" Fort Lyon.

Ten years after selling it to the Government, this time at his own price, in 1869 William Bent died, aged sixty, near the ranch that he owned only a few miles from the ruins of his celebrated Bent's Fort.

CHAPTER XVI

A SEARCH FOR A SILVER MINE (1831)
AND THE "BOWIE INDIAN FIGHT"

WHILE the American traders were bent upon opening a trail through the desert country of the Southwest Indians—the Kiowas, Comanches and Apaches—into northern Mexico, American settlers had entered Mexico itself.

Moses Austin, born in Connecticut, but lastly a lead merchant in those same mines of Washington County, Missouri, where Major Andrew Henry the fur-hunter also was working, heard of the rich lands of the Spanish province of Texas. Major Henry thought mainly of beaver-fur—a get-rich-quick business that took what it might out of a country and left little in exchange. Moses Austin was a merchant and a manufacturer—in Missouri he turned his lead into shot, bars and sheets, and shipped his product to New Orleans. Now in 1820 he determined to settle Texas with American farmers.

Toward the close of the year he obtained from the Spanish governor, at San Antonio the capital of Texas, a grant of land. He died before he had removed there, himself; but his son Stephen Fuller Austin led the first settlers, gathered at New Orleans, in December,

255

1821. They located up the Brazos River in southeastern Texas.

The government of Mexico was glad to have the sturdy Americans upon its frontier, to act as a bulwark against the Indians. All Texas, like the Ohio Valley, was the favorite range of hard-fighting tribes; from the cannibal Karankawas (six feet tall, and wielding long-bows that no white man could draw) on the Gulf coast in the south, to the widely riding Comanches and Apaches in the north, with the Wacos, the Tawakonis, the Caddos, and others, in between.

The Spanish soldiery had made little progress against them. The Mexican settlements were few, the missions built by the Spanish priests had been destroyed; from San Antonio in the west to Nacogdoches in the east the country still belonged to the red warriors.

They began to pillage and kill the Americans. Texas was another Kentucky. But as in Kentucky and the Ohio Valley the Americans pushed on and on. They were not the kind to quit.

Among the early Americans to make their homes in Texas were the Bowie brothers: James, Rezin and Stephen. They were Georgians, but raised in Louisiana. The United States claimed Texas as a part of the Louisiana Territory that had been bought from France. Before ever Moses Austin had obtained his grant of land, parties of American adventurers were constantly invading, to seize the country which as yet seemed to belong to nobody.

In 1819 James Bowie had landed, in just such a company, near Galveston; and although the company was driven out he chose Texas for his home. He traveled through it, lived at old San Antonio, entered into business, at Saltillo, south of the Rio Grande on the present Mexican border, was naturalized as a Mexican citizen, and in 1830 married the daughter of Juan Veramendi, the vice-governor of the State of Coahuila and Texas.

His brother Rezin also was now a Texan; Stephen came in a little later.

The two, Jim and Rezin, were famous for their bowie-knife, as well as for their bold fighting qualities. The knife was an accident. The first one had been invented by Rezin from a finely-tempered blacksmith's file, for a hunting-knife, in Louisana. When hammered and drawn into shape it had a blade five and one-quarter inches long and one and one-half inches wide; was so nicely balanced that it was proved to be both a useful tool and a terrible weapon.

Rezin gave this first knife to his brother Jim, and ordered another for himself. "Bowie's knife" gained much favor from those who tried it; and speedily the "bowie-knife" was being adopted by the hunters, backwoodsmen, desperadoes and all. Some wore it in their belts; some wore it in their boots.

The Spanish from the south had been in Texas long before the Americans were admitted; the Spanish military post of San Antonio de Bejar was founded in 1718, to protect the Catholic missionaries there. Two hundred miles to the northwest of San Antonio the Spanish priests had started the mission of San Saba, in 1857, among the Lipan Apaches; but that had been destroyed in the spring of the next year by the Comanches, Wichitas, Tawehash, and other Indians who hated the Apaches and the Spaniards both.

They had other reason, than revenge upon the Lipan mission Indians and the Spanish who were helping their enemies. Along the San Saba River there were rich veins of silver which the Tawehash owned. Miners from the mining district of Amalgres, Mexico, came to the mission and worked the veins, and sent the precious metal away. The Indians did not wish to have their silver taken; and they set out to close the mines. This they achieved in one stroke—wiped the mission and the pupils and the miners from the face of the valley.

For almost seventy-five years the "New Amalgres" mines, as they were known, of the San Saba, remained only as a secret to the Indians. No outsider could get near them; no Indian would show them to the stranger: and of course the longer they were hidden from view, the richer they grew in story and guess.

About the time that he was married to the lovely daughter of Vice-Governor Juan Veramendi, Jim Bowie himself, with a party of thirty other fearless bordermen, started from San Antonio to prospect, and discover the storied Amalgres mines, which would make their fortunes.

Before swinging north they traveled one hundred miles west, to the Frio River country; here they came upon an outcrop of silver and sunk a shaft; at the same time they built a rock fort near a spring on a ridge between the forks of the Frio, so as to stand off the Indians.

The Indians found them very promptly; in the early morning drove them from their shaft to the rock fort, and besieged them hotly all the day. These Texans were good shots; they were Texan Ranger stuff—and the Texan Rangers have been unmatched as frontier fighters. But though the Indians could not get in, they themselves were out-numbered and could not get out; could not even get to the spring, and what with the thirst from sun and powder-smoke they at last had drained their canteens.

Doubtless the Indians were counting on this; but they had not reckoned the nerve of the men behind the walls.

Jim Bowie was the commander there. He figured the situation over. They had to have water; already thirst was torturing, and making his men reckless. There were twenty-nine white men, and one negro slave, Jim—his own servant. Jim was the poorest shot and could be the most easily spared. He turned to Jim, by his side.

"See here, Jim. I want you to take the canteens and fetch us water from that spring.'

It may be readily believed that Jim's eyes popped.

"Out among dem Injuns? No, sar, Marse Jim! Dem Injuns is layin' dare in dem rocks an' bushes by de t'ousand, an' all dey gotto do is rare up an' kill dis nigger 'foh he could say 'Scat!' at 'em twice! No, sar; I cain't fill dem cainteens. Dey won't let me. No, sar!"

The white Jim looked for a moment at the black Jim, with those steady gray eyes that never wavered even when, six years later, they gazed from a sick-bed and waited the attack of a hundred Mexicans in the tragic Alamo.

"Jim!" he said, "Which are you most afraid of: me, or those Indians?"

Black Jim's knees shook, and he scratched his woolly thatch.

"Well, now, Marse Jim, if de boys got to have water 'foh dey kin lick dem Injun, an' you 'sist on me goin,' 'cose den I'll volunteer. Jes' gimme dem cainteens."

"All right, Jim." And white Jim smiled grimly. "You'll be safe. We'll cover every head with our guns and you sha'n't be hurt. The spring's in short range. Just fill the canteens, and come back with them."

Out went Negro Jim, as brave as the bravest. Sure enough, he made the spring and not a shot was fired at him; he filled the canteens, and started back with his load—and no Indian had managed to get sight of him. But the canteens clinked, a warrior peeked and saw, and the whoop of alarm rang.

The Indians' guns spoke; the fort replied briskly; dark forms sprang from shelter, to cut the water-carrier off, and through the whizz of balls black Jim legged for the fort, with the canteens bouncing on his back and shanks.

One warrior gained rapidly on him—tomahawk raised to strike. Jim's voice rose in a panting wail.

"Marse Jim! Oh, Marse Jim! Shoot dis hyar Injun, quick! He's gwine to hurt somebody d'rec'ly!"

That looked likely. Most of the guns in the fort had been emptied, white Jim himself was madly reloading for a shot in time, if possible; the tomahawk was poised over poor black Jim's bobbing wool; when a report sounded smartly, and the "Indian fell back so suddenly his feet flew up in the air."

Negro Jim's voice changed.

"Never mind now, Marse Jim. Marse Bob done knock his heels higher'n his haid. Oh, glory!"

And puffing and sweating he dived into the fort with all the canteens. He had brought the water. But—

"Marse Jim, please, sar, make dis water go fur as possible," he pleaded. " 'Twon't take much mo' dat kind o' work 'foh dar'll be one nigger less in dis world. No, sar! If Marse Bob hadn't kep' him load back an' make de bullet come straight dat big Injun'd put his hatchet squar' into my haid! Har! har! He suht'inly did grunt when dat piece ob lead hit him 'kerchug'! But mebbe next time dar wouldn't be no piece ob lead."

Robert Armstrong was the man who had fired the shot. Black Jim had recognized the rifle-crack. He knew all the men well, and they all knew him. Although he ranked as only a slave, they were free to admit that whatever his color he had done well; and Marse Jim Bowie was proud of his faithful servant boy.

This evening the Indians withdrew, discouraged.

The Texan treasure-seekers went home while they had
the chance. Negro Jim found himself quite a hero in
San Antonio; he lived long after his master perished
in the historic Alamo fight, there, and was called
"Black Jim Bowie" until his own death.

As for the other Jim Bowie, he did not give up his
search for the Amalgres mines. They filled his
dreams. Almost immediately he left his bride and
went out again, into the San Saba country; this time
was more successful; discovered an old shaft eight feet
deep, and at the bottom chopped out some ore with
his hatchet; had it assayed at New Orleans. It tested
rich indeed. He decided to take another party in.
The result was not wealth, but glory; for "Bowie's
Indian Fight" has never been forgotten.

There were eleven in the little company: Jim Bowie
and Rezin Bowie, David Buchanan, Robert Armstrong
again, Jesse Wallace, Matt Doyle, Tom McCaslin,
James Coryell, Cæphus Ham, black boy Charles
("Black Jim" stayed at home, this time), and Mexican
boy Gonzales. They rode out of old San Antonio on
September 2, 1831; everybody knew where: to open
up the lost Amalgres silver mines in the San Saba
hills. Many a hand had grasped their hands, to bid
good luck; but sundry hearts rather doubted whether
even the two Bowies could hold the country against
the redskins.

"Hang tight to yore scalps, boys, and keep a weather
eye out for sign."

"We shore will."

They clattered away. Nothing especial happened

on two weeks of trail; by the nineteenth they were almost at the San Saba—the ruins of the ancient mission lay close ahead, and the mines were not far beyond. This noon they sighted Indians bearing down upon them. A fight? No. These were Comanches, and the Comanches had turned friendly; had announced that they did not war with the Texans, but with the Spanish.

Besides, Cæphus Ham was a Comanche, himself; that is, he had gone out with a band of Comanches, from San Antonio; had been adopted in a chief's family; and had lived and traded among them for five months. They had treated him well. But Jim Bowie had sent word to him to return; that the Mexicans were preparing to attack the Texas Indians, and in the fighting he might be killed. Twenty-five warriors escorted him back to San Antonio, and he joined the Bowie excursion to the San Saba.

The Comanches who now arrived were sixteen, under a chief, and acted friendly. They brought news. They said that over one hundred and fifty angry Indians—Tawakonis, Wacos and Caddos—were on the same trail, to kill every Texan that they found. No stranger should be permitted in the San Saba country.

"But if you will turn back," added the Comanche chief, "I and my men will go with you and we all will fight them, together."

"No," Jim Bowie replied. "You are our brothers; your hearts are strong; we thank you but we cannot accept. If they are so many, you would only die with us. We do not wish to fight. If we travel fast we shall reach the old mission and the walls will protect us. Adios."

He and his Texans rode one way, the Comanches rode the other.

They had hoped to arrive at the old mission or Spanish fort by night. And they might have done so had the trail not become so rocky that their horses' feet gave out; therefore they made camp in a small prairie island of live-oaks. The clump was bounded on the west by a stream; on the north by a thick growth of mesquite trees and prickly-pear cactus about ten feet high.

"That's where we'll 'fort,' boys, in case we have to hunt a hole," Jim Bowie said.

So they posted a look-out; cut a crooked lane into the midst of the mesquite and cactus; cleared a fighting space there, hobbled their horses among the live-oaks, ate supper, refilled their canteens, and with night guards on watch they rolled in their blankets, until morning. They still had hopes of getting to the San Saba ruins.

That was not to be. They were just cooking breakfast by the first gray of daylight, when the guard called:

"Whoopee! They're a-comin', boys."

"Get your guns and lie low, boys," rapped Jim Bowie, the captain. "See that your horses are tied short."

The guards ran in, to join the line.

"How many?"

264

"One buck afoot, with his nose to the ground, followin' the trail. But plenty more behind."

The camp had been discovered. A dozen Indians, horseback, had ridden forward, reconnoitering. There were shouts, a shrill chorus of glad whoops; the back trail looked alive with warriors. One hundred, one hundred and fifty—one hundred and sixty-four!

"Well," Captain Bowie remarked, "that's a big mouthful for eleven men. I reckon we'd better try a talk, and see what they want. If we can come to terms, so as to pull out with what we have, all right. Otherwise, we'll fight. Who'll go with me?"

They all trusted Jim Bowie. He was not a large man; he was of medium height, small-boned and wiry. He never blustered; had a quiet way and a soft voice— but it could cut like steel when the case demanded. He was a fighter, in defence of his rights or the rights of others; but his bravery did not depend upon "bowie-knife" or such weapon.

"No; you stay here, Jim, and boss matters. I'll go," spoke his brother Rezin. Rezin Bowie was like him in manner, but of slightly heavier build.

"I'm with you," said Dave Buchanan.

"Go ahead, then. We'll cover you. Give them the peace sign and ask them what they want."

Rezin and Dave stood, and walked boldly out of the live-oaks, into the open; advanced on to within forty yards of the waiting Indians. Rezin could be heard calling to them in Spanish.

"Cómo 'stá (How are you)? Where is your capitan (chief)? I want to talk."

"How do? How do?" they answered, from all quarters—and drowned their voices with their guns.

Down lurched Dave.

"Got me in the leg," he gasped.

"I'll take you in." Rezin spread two barrels of buck-shot among the howling ranks, hoisted Dave upon his back, and with shot-gun in one hand and pistol in the other staggered for the trees.

There was another volley.

"Got me twice more," Dave gasped. "Drop me if you can't make in."

Rezin Bowie had no thought of dropping him, but eight of the Indians were hot after, with tomahawks. Led by Jim, out charged the Texans, firing; they killed four of the Indians, scattered the others, and rescued Rezin and Dave. Dave was badly hurt, but not fatally. Rezin's hunting-shirt was cut in several places; he himself was unharmed.

The Texans formed a half circle, fronting the enemy. The most of the Indians had disappeared, in the grass and chaparral. For about five minutes there was no shooting. Then, on a sudden, the yells burst forth from a new quarter. A little hill to the northwest, across the creek, was "red with Indians." The Texans shifted front slightly, to meet the attack; the bullets and arrows pelted in and the Texan ball and buck-shot replied.

A chief upon a horse was riding back and forth, urging his warriors to charge. His words sounded plainly.

"Who's loaded?" cried Jim Bowie, as he rammed

266

the powder into his gun, and most of the men seemed to be doing likewise.

"I am." That was Cæphus Ham.

"Then shoot that chief yonder."

Cæphus drew careful bead, and fired. It was long range, but the chief's pony fell kicking and the chief hopped wildly about on one leg. The ball had passed through his other leg and killed the pony. He tried to cover himself with his shield and his struggling horse; four Texan rifles spoke together—every ball plumped into the shield, he crumpled in a heap, his warriors hustled to bear off his body and other bullets caught some of them, also.

So far the honors of war were with the Bowie men. The Indians scampered to the safe side of the hill. What next? On a sudden, led by another chief, the Indians again swarmed into sight, at the same place. The chief was yelling:

"Forward! Forward! Kill the Texans!"

"I'll stop your gab," muttered Jim Bowie. He aimed, touched trigger, killed this second chief.

That infuriated the Indians. They dared not charge the grove, but they deluged it with lead and arrows; the few white men answered rapidly. Without warning, bullets and shafts spattered in from another angle.

"Look out! They're flanking us!" Captain Bowie shouted. "They're in the creek bed."

So they were; a party of them had gained the banks of the creek, on the west. The men at that end of the line turned, and ran, stooping, to face the attack. Matt Doyle was fatally shot, through the breast. Tom

McCaslin, springing to drag him to cover, and get sight of his slayer, if possible, received a ball through the body.

"Into the chaparral," ordered Jim Bowie. "We'll stand 'em off from there. Never mind the horses."

Carrying their wounded, they dived for the lane into the mesquite and cactus. From here they raked the creek bed, and cleared it. That was better. They had good view of the hill and prairie, too. They fought cunningly. The Indians could locate them only by the powder smoke from the gun muzzles; but the instant that they fired, the Texans squirmed aside for six or eight feet, and the answering bullets were wasted.

The Indians were still getting the worst of it. A large number were lying dead or wounded. The sun was high.

"What they up to, next, I wonder?"

"They're goin' to smoke us out! I see a fellow crawlin' through the grass to windward."

"Can't you get him?" demanded Captain Jim.

"No. He's foxy."

"Whereabouts?"

Bob Armstrong's heavy rifle interrupted.

"I fetched him, boys! Plumb through the head. Dead center."

Bob had scored at two hundred and fifty yards, with a snap-shot. He was one of the best rifle-shots on the border.

The grass was fired, nevertheless, in several spots. It was dry, and caught like tinder; the flames crackled and leaped, and raced down upon the thicket. The smoke rose densely. The Indians might be dimly seen, running about in the drifting veil and carrying off their killed and wounded.

Jim Bowie's voice pealed like a trumpet.

"We're not dead yet. Clean away the brush and leaves as far as you can reach, some of you. The rest of us pile up rocks and dirt for a breastworks for the wounded."

They labored madly. The horses tore loose and bolted. The Indians whooped, gleeful, and shot briskly. But the wind changed, into the north, and the fire surged past, just grazing the thicket; the slowly creeping back-fire was easily smothered with blankets.

Had they been saved? No! The Indians started another fire, on the north. The dried grass was even higher here. The flames roared in a front ten feet in air; the pungent smoke drifted chokingly.

"Put the wounded and baggage in the center," were the orders. "Then every man clear his own space. When it comes, lay on with blankets, robes, anything. We may be roasted here, but it's sure death for us outside."

The heat and smoke became terrific. "The Indians," said Rezin Bowie, "fired about twenty shots a minute," riddling the thicket. "The sparks were flying about so thickly that no man could open his powder horn without running the risk of being blown up." If the Indians charged in after the fire, under cover of the smoke, the Texans could only empty their guns and meet the charge with knives and hatchets.

Now the flames were upon them. The branches and the cactus twisted and popped. Cowering and shielding their wounded, the men "lay to" with whatever came to hand—blankets, buffalo robes, bear-skins, coats, shirts—and beat out the ground-fire. Their hair, beards and eye-brows were singed; they could scarcely see. And leaping overhead, or splitting, the storm passed on.

It left the thicket bare to the blackened branches and shriveled cactus-lobes. Every inch fumed with the acrid smoke.

"Raise that breastworks. It's all we've got, boys. We'll have to fight from inside it."

"Dat Jim nigger 'lowed he was in a toler'ble fight, but 'twa'n't nothin' 'side ob dis," chattered boy Charles.

They toiled, piling their rampart ring higher, while they constantly peered right, left, before, behind, expecting a charge.

Bob Armstrong cheered.

"The reds are going! They've had enough!"

That seemed true. The Indians had taken away their dead and wounded; they were commencing to follow, but some of them remained in sight.

The sun set. It had been a short day. In the dusk the Texans got fresh water, at the creek. Soon they were ready for the morrow. All that night the Indian death chants sounded. Morning came. There was silence, while inside their little circle of rocks and sod amidst the scorched brush the five able-bodied white men and two boys waited.

No Indians appeared near. They were somewhere, burying their dead. It was found out afterward that they were in a cave, not far off.

This night Bob Armstrong and Cæphus Ham stole away, and examined the other side of the hill.

"Forty-eight blood signs we counted," Bob reported, "where Injuns had been laid."

"I reckon we'd best stay here awhile, just the same," Captain Jim Bowie counseled. "And we've got a man or two who ought not to be moved yet."

On the ninth morning after the fight they started home, with their three wounded and their baggage on horses, but themselves mainly afoot; traveled ten days, and reached San Antonio in early night.

They met with a great reception. The Comanches had been there, to tell of the danger and to say that the Bowie party were surely doomed. Stephen Bowie had heard and had hastened in; was forming a company to set out and avenge Jim, Rezin and the rest. But now a shout arose—

"Here they are! The Bowies are back! The whole party's in!"

Men and women rushed out of the adobe houses, for the plaza. All San Antonio rejoiced. The escape was looked upon as a miracle.

One killed, three wounded, was the list; "but we fought fire as well as Injuns." Of the one hundred and sixty-four Indians over eighty had fallen—fifty-two of them never to rise again.

Such was "Bowie's Indian Fight," in the San Saba country of central Texas, September 20, 1831.

The Bowie brothers did not give up. James was certain that the mine was there, in the San Saba; it only waited to be reclaimed by brave men. He organized another party; they were ready, and feared not, when Texas rebelled against the unjust laws of the Mexican government. For the next three years all was in confusion. On October 2, 1835, the American settlers, collected at Gonzales, east of San Antonio, defied the Mexican troops in the skirmish called the Lexington of Texas.

The noted Sam Houston was appointed commander-in-chief of the Texan army, to fight for State rights. These were not times in which the Bowie brothers or any other true man would search for a mere mine. On March 2, 1836, Texas declared independence, as a republic. On Sunday, March 6, General Santa Anna of the Mexican army stormed the old Alamo mission of San Antonio with two thousand five hundred soldiers supported by cannon.

Colonel Jim Bowie was among the defenders, but sick in bed. Of the one hundred and eighty only three women, a baby, a little girl and a negro boy were spared; and in bed Jim Bowie died, pistols in hand, face to the doorway through which the Mexican soldiers crowded and shot him—they were afraid to use their bayonets.

After the war Rezin Bowie went back to Louisiana. The "Bowie Mine," of the old Amalgres workings in the dangerous San Saba country remained unopened, for the secret of it perished with Jim Bowie himself.

CHAPTER XVII

THROUGH THE ENEMY'S LINES (1846)

THE THREE KIT CARSON COURIERS

ON December 8, 1846, one hundred and twenty-five United States dragoons, rangers and scouts were being closely besieged upon a bare hill in Southern California by one hundred and fifty Mexican California cavalry. The place was thirty miles northeast of San Diego, near the Indian village of San Bernardo.

Texas, for which Jim Bowie and many another brave man fought and died, had won independence ten years back. Last year it had been admitted into the United States, and the boundaries of the United States had been extended to the Rio Grande River at last.

To this boundary Mexico objected; she said that it had not been the boundary of the Louisiana Territory nor of Texas. Now she was prepared to hold Texas and the Rio Grande. War neared and in March of 1846 the United States troops under General Zachary Taylor had marched across Texas to the north bank of the river.

An American column from Fort Leavenworth on the Kansas side of the Missouri River had marched eight hundred miles through the southwest desert, and captured Santa Fe and the province of New Mexico. From Santa Fe the First Dragoons had set out upon a

273

desert trail of one thousand miles more, to capture California.

Here they were, less then one hundred of them "fit for service," reinforced by a detachment sent by Commodore Robert Stockton of the navy, who had seized San Diego; all commanded by General Stephen Watts Kearny of the army, and their advance stopped short. The "Horse-Chief of the Long Knives," as the Plains Indians called him, had met with misfortune.

There had been a battle. After their long, toiling march of close to the thousand miles the California irregular cavalry under Captain Andres Pico had attacked them among the California hills; had caught them at disadvantage; killed eighteen, wounded fifteen including General Kearny himself; and driven them to refuge upon this other hill. Indians could not have been more swift and wary than those light-riding Californians armed with lances.

Rain had been falling. The ground, cold and wet, was so rocky and cactus-covered that even the wounded could not be placed comfortably. The morning following the battle had "dawned on the most tattered and ill-fed detachment of men that ever the United States mustered under her colors"—"provisions were exhausted, horses dead, mules on their last legs, men, reduced to one-third of their number, were ragged, worn and emaciated."

On this second day, here upon the hill, there was no water except that which gathered in holes. For the dragoon mules no water at all, and no forage except the stiff brush. The fattest mule was killed, as food, but he proved very tough. The wounded could not be moved save in rude travois or litters of blankets slung between poles, the ends of which dragged along the ground. The hill was open, and exposed to weather and the enemy's view. Although San Diego and Commodore Stockton were only thirty miles distant (yet far out of sight beyond the high, brushy hills), the camp was completely cut off by the nimble riders of Captain Pico, and without doubt reinforcements for him were spurring in.

Altogether, General Kearny was in a fix: a fix both mortifying and perilous. He himself had been lanced twice, and was not a young man.

Commodore Stockton must be notified, to send relief of men, ambulances and food, at once. After the battle, and before the siege, the scout Alexander Godey and three other trappers had set out on foot, using their best skill, to take the word to San Diego; but they had been captured by the Pico videttes, and nobody upon the hill knew whether the Stockton relief was coming. A second try should be made.

With the General Kearny dragoons there was the famous Kit Carson. He had been met by the general at the Rio Grande River in New Mexico south of Santa Fe, and had turned back to act as guide to California. He was a veteran on the long trail: had been traveling mountains and deserts for over twenty years, or ever since he was sixteen.

There was a greenhorn, much younger than he, but just as brave: Acting-Lieutenant Edward Fitzgerald Beale of the navy, aged twenty-four and commissioned midshipman only sixteen months ago. He came of a stanch navy family; his grandfather and his father had been navy officers before him; the spirit of service to his country was in his blood.

The boyish Lieutenant Beale had joined the Kearny column before the battle, with the little force that brought dispatches to the general from San Diego. He was a sailor; had not been trained in scouting upon land; but that made no difference, for when this afternoon General Kearny called a council, to discuss means again of reaching Commodore Stockton, the first scout volunteer was Lieutenant Beale.

He said that he had come out; he thought that he could find his way back. He offered himself and his Indian boy servant, who would be able to guide him. The boy was a native of this country, and knew the trails.

Kit Carson heard, and lost no time in volunteering also. That was good. Everybody had confidence in the bravery of young Lieutenant Beale, but felt more dependence upon the training of Kit Carson. He had performed such trips, through watchful Indians themselves, many a time before.

They three, the scout, the sailor and the California Indian, proceeded to get ready, in order to start at nightfall. Each was supplied with a rifle, a pistol, knife and a canteen; but food seemed a question.

General Kearny had saved a handful of mouldy flour. This was baked into a loaf and given to Lieutenant Beale, with the general's compliments.

"It's the last of everything, sir," said the soldier

who brought it. "The general'll have to do without breakfast, but you're welcome to it, sir."

"Take it back to General Kearny," Lieutenant Beale directed. "Tell him that I thank him heartily, and will provide for myself."

So he scraped in the ashes where some baggage had been burned; managed to find a little charred corn and dried peas; stowed that in his pocket. Kit Carson and the Indian provisioned themselves with a small piece, each, of half-cooked mule beef.

Of all Kit Carson's dangerous scouts in enemy country this turned out to be the most ticklish. For young Lieutenant Beale, the tenderfoot, it was hair-raising. Captain Pico had known that the celebrated Kit Carson was with the Americans upon the hill, and feared him. He had placed three lines of mounted patrols around the base of the hill, and instructed them to keep riding so as to leave no intervals.

"Se escapara el lobo (The wolf will escape)," he warned.

And the wolf did escape.

Naturally, Lieutenant Beale let Kit Carson take the lead, for "Kit" knew best what to do. They had to crawl on their hands and knees, and stomachs, through the brush, down the hill, for if they stood up they might be seen against the sky.

"Wait," Kit Carson whispered back. "Take off yore shoes, lieutenant. They make too much noise. Stow them in yore belt."

They tucked their shoes in their belts. Twigs had been cracking alarmingly. Presently their feet, knees and hands were afire with the cactus spines. Now twigs rasped along the canteens. Kit Carson paused and laid his canteen aside. Lieutenant Beale did the same; so did the cautious Indian.

They reached the base of the hill; waited here for a sentinel in the first line to pass; and crawled silently across almost at his horse's heels.

Foot by foot, wellnigh inch by inch, they snaked on, listening and peering for other patrols. Suddenly they encountered a second outpost, and crouched low, flattening themselves, scarcely daring to breathe. A Californian horseman leisurely rode by. Kit instantly squirmed forward, and they crossed this line also.

It was nervous work, in the thick, dark brush, and amidst the barbed prickly-pears that filled their flesh with sharp needles, all the worse because they struck unexpectedly.

Lieutenant Beale was hoping that now an open way lay before. They had avoided two outposts; were there others, still?

Ah! Kit Carson again flattened, motionless except that he kicked behind him and with touch of his bare foot signaled danger. Lieutenant Beale flattened; the Indian, third in the file, had flattened. The brush cracked; a horseman, dimly seen, was right upon them. He was another of the patrols. His figure towered huge as he halted, at Kit Carson's very head. He got off his horse; and shielding himself from the chill, damp breeze, stood there.

What was the matter? Was he searching? Should he be killed? And what then? Young Lieutenant

Beale's heart pounded so that Kit Carson afterward said he had heard it beating "like a maul."

The sentry struck flint and steel. As some tinder in his hands caught, they might see that he was lighting a cigarette. The glow revealed his olive face, his flashing eyes, and the blanket shrouding him to his chin; it momentarily revealed the brush under which the two *Americanos* and the Indian were lying.

Whether they had been seen, who might tell? The sentry remounted, in careless manner, and slowly rode on—but perhaps to give the alarm and bring reinforcements to beat the brush. Lieutenant Beale broke. He could stand the suspense no longer. He was not used to so many close calls without action. They are the hardest of all to bear. And to crawl on and on, in this way, over rocks and cactus, made his heart sick. He would rather stand up and challenge the enemy.

He crawled ahead to Kit.

"Kit, we're gone. We can't escape. Let's jump and fight it out."

Kit Carson laid hand upon his arm, and steadied him.

"No, no, boy. I've been in worse places before and got through."

Those were good words. Kit Carson knew, if anybody did. It was fortunate that he had come! The Indian might have got through, but Lieutenant Beale, never. Even Alex Godey, who had a great reputation as a scout and path-finder, had been captured.

They kept on, Kit Carson leading; narrowly dodged other patrols—for the outskirts of the hill seemed alive with them. They finally met no more, and Kit announced that they were through, he thought, at last.

But they found disappointment. Their route was cut by a wide, open valley covered only with stones and cactus. They dared not stand up; they might yet be seen. It was two miles across, and they hitched along, on their knees and on hands and knees, every foot of the way, while the rocks and cactus tortured them.

Here, where the brush grew high, Kit stopped and appeared to be relieved.

"Put on yore shoes, boy. We're out of the trap and we can make better time."

Hurrah! Lieutenant Beale laid his hand to his belt. What!

"I've lost my shoes, Kit."

"So've I. That's mean, but we can't help it. Come on. We've a long way yit; we daren't line in direct. Thar'll be more o' those patrols watchin' the trails into San Diego."

They hastened as best they might, on a circuit to avoid the trails. The country was rough and rolling. When day dawned, they left the mesas and kept to the dense brush of the canyons; were almost lost, so crooked their path; but the Indian guided them, and constantly sniffed for the salty air from the ocean. In the middle of the day they rested; their soles, knees, and hands were raw, and body and limb burned with the cactus; their throats were parched for lack of water.

At evening they smelled the ocean. The Indian said

that they were within twelve miles of San Diego. From a high point they might have seen the glimmer of the Pacific. Kit Carson spoke.

"We'd better divide up, I think. Then one of us will get through. That's safer than travelin' together. Lieutenant, you head off to south'ard; amigo (that to the Indian boy, in Spanish), you go on straight; I'll take around north'ard, whar the *Mexicanos* probably are thickest to close the Los Angeles trail. Whoever gets in fust will report without wastin' any time."

"All right, sir," agreed the lieutenant.

"Bueno (Good)," muttered the Indian, nodding.

It was understood. The lieutenant and Kit shook hands; and they three separated, to steal swiftly away in the waning twilight.

At San Diego, Commodore Stockton had landed sailors and marines to reinforce the American Riflemen in San Diego. He was building Fort Stockton, to command the town. The frigate *Congress* and the sloop-of-war *Portsmouth* swung at anchor in the narrow channel of the harbor.

He had learned of the plight of General Kearny, and was just starting a relief column upon a night march for the hill, when at nine o'clock one of his sentries challenged a dark figure laboring in.

"Halt! Who goes there?"

"Amigo, amigo (Friend, friend)!"

'Twas the Indian boy. He had arrived first. The sentry called the sergeant of the guard, the sergeant of the guard took the boy to the officer of the guard, and the officer took him at once to the commodore.

The Indian was still telling his story in breathless Spanish, when another of the couriers arrived—carried by two marines. He was Lieutenant Beale, unable to walk.

Away trudged the relief party; the Indian and the lieutenant were placed in bed and the surgeon was summoned. The lieutenant had grown delirious—babbled and tossed and moaned. His boy lay twitching with pain and weariness, but uttered never a sound.

Where was Kit Carson? He staggered in about three o'clock in the morning. Had been obliged to wander and hide before he struck a way through. He had chosen for himself the longest and the hardest route. That was like him, and that was proper for the oldest and the most experienced. Now he, too, needed a surgeon. The bandy-legged, long-bodied, toughly-sinewed little Kit Carson who had faced many a scrape and "scrimmage" on plains and mountains, was "all in."

After this night we do not know what became of the Indian. His name never was recorded; he has been forgotten; all of which is a pity, because he risked his life to serve a new people and a new flag.

In the morning Lieutenant Beale was transferred abroad the *Congress,* and placed in the sick-bay. He was invalided for more than a year—did not really recover until after he resigned from the navy in 1852; he rose to be brigadier general in the Civil War, was United States minister to Vienna in 1876, and while ranching on two hundred and seventy-six thousand acres of land in California died, aged seventy-one, in 1893.

Through several days the surgeon thought that he would have to cut off Kit Carson's feet. But he saved them, and the plucky Kit marched north to Los Angeles with the rescued Kearny column.

CHAPTER XVIII

THE HOTTEST CHASE ON RECORD (1864)

TWO IN AN ARMY WAGON

WHEN in the eastern part of the United States the Civil War flamed up, another war broke out in the western part. The Indians of the Plains saw their chance. While the white men, who had been busy forcing peace upon the red men, were foolishly killing each other, the red men saw themselves free to strike, and clean the buffalo country.

So the Sioux, the Cheyennes, the Kiowas and many of the Arapahos arose, to close the wagon trails, plunder the stage stations, drive out the settlers, and save the buffalo.

The result was the great Indian war of 1864. The Government hastily sent what troops it could—mainly Volunteer cavalry and infantry, assigned to fight the Western Indians instead of the Southern soldiers. Thus two wars were being waged at once.

The white Americans had extended their towns and ranches clear across the continent. Through Kansas and Nebraska there were ranches scattered clear to the Colorado mountains. Denver was growing into a city. Beyond the mountains the Mormons had built another city at the Great Salt Lake. The Overland

Stage was making daily trips over the trail between the Missouri River and California. Another well-traveled stage and emigrant trail ran from the Missouri River through central Kansas, south of the Overland Trail, to Denver. And the freight wagons for New Mexico plied between Leavenworth and Kansas City, and Santa Fe, over the old Santa Fe Trail.

There were yet no railroads across the plains. But the Union Pacific of the Government's Pacific Railway was surveyed out of Omaha, for Salt Lake City and beyond; and its Kansas Division, known as the Kansas Pacific, was starting up the Kansas River, for Denver.

To protect the wagon route through Kansas, and the advance of the railroad (which was following the stage road), the Government located a line of military posts; the same as upon the Overland Trail farther north, in Nebraska and westward.

The first was Fort Riley, just outside of Junction City, where the Republican River joined the Kansas River. Beyond, there was Salina; and Ellsworth on the Smoky Hill River; and southward, to guard the Santa Fe Trail over which huge quantities of Government supplies for the Southwest were being hauled, there were Camp Zarah at Walnut Creek of the Arkansas River, Fort Larned up the Arkansas, and so forth.

Many of the posts were only camps or cantonments, and received their fort name later.

In November, 1864, Captain Henry Booth started from Fort Riley to inspect the posts south to the Arkansas River in Colorado. Lieutenant Hallowell was his companion. They had planned to travel comfortably in Lieutenant Hallowell's light spring wagon instead of in a heavy jouncing army ambulance—a hack arrangement with seats along the sides and a stiff oiled-cloth top.

Lieutenant Hallowell had a canvas or wagon-sheet cover fitted over his wagon: stretched tightly upon bows and puckered to enclose the rear end with the exception of a hole in the middle there about the size of one's head. Now the spring wagon looked like a small prairie-schooner or emigrant outfit.

Captain Booth obtained from the quarter-master department the best span of Missouri mules at the fort. He and the lieutenant would do their own driving, and be independent. Whereupon, provisioned for the trip, they gaily set out, in the frosty morning, escorted by a mounted detachment of Kansas United States Volunteers under Lieutenant Van Antwerp.

This was particularly Kiowa and Cheyenne country, as soon as they left the Kansas River; and if any Indians were more dreaded than the boldly riding, hard fighting Cheyennes, those were the never quitting Kiowas.[1]

They and their allies the Comanches were the guardians of the Santa Fe Trail. The Kiowas ranged the farthest north and fought the soldiers on the Leavenworth cut-off or Government road which entered from the Kansas River.

Going down, on this road, Captain Booth and Lieutenant Hallowell had no trouble at all. They arrived

[1] See "Boys' Book of Indian Warriors."

safely at Camp Zarah, without having sighted a sign of Indians. The captain inspected the post. The next morning he directed his escort to ride on; he and Lieutenant Hallowell would catch them in about half an hour.

But it was nearer three hours later when the wagon rattled over the log corduroy bridge across Walnut Creek, on the road for the Arkansas River and Fort Larned, west up-stream.

They had the road all to themselves. The escort were out of sight, but probably would wait for them; and anyway they felt no fear as they jounced over the rutty, frozen road. They rather looked forward to shooting buffalo from the wagon with their revolvers. The mules were lively; Lieutenant Hallowell drove (he was an expert with the "ribbons"); the captain helped him with the whip; and they caroled songs together.

After a time the lieutenant changed his tune, to remark:

"What's the matter with the buffalo? They're grazing wide of the road to-day. That looks as though Injuns were about."

This was Captain Booth's first season on the plains, so he only laughed easily.

"Oh, pshaw! They say back at Zarah that there hasn't been an Injun seen from the trail in ten days. I fancy our escort scared the buffalo. Now like as not we won't get a shot."

"Just the same, it's queer the buffalo are all out yonder in the open instead of grazing on the river bot-

toms. If any Injuns are at hand, they'd be hiding
along the river.''

"Oh, pshaw!" laughed the captain. "We're safe
enough. I'll get you back to Lizzie. Don't you worry
yourself.''

"Lizzie" was the lieutenant's bride, at Fort Riley.
He had left her for the first time since they were married.

Drawn by its rapidly trotting mules the wagon
trundled about three miles farther—and the captain
had a glimpse of something new, moving over the low
brush ahead and toward the river. It seemed to be a
flock of wild turkeys bobbing along, now above the
brush, now settling into it. N-no! What, then!
Men on horses.

He clutched the lieutenant's arm.

"Look there, Hallowell. What is it?"

The lieutenant looked only once.

"Injuns, by Jiminy! We're in for it.''

He whirled his team around and with voice and shake
of lines quickened them to a gallop on the back trail
for Zarah, six miles.

The captain objected.

"Wait! Hold on, Hallowell. They may be part of
the escort.''

Lieutenant Hallowell was wiser. This was his second year in Indian country.

"No, no! I know Injuns when I see 'em. Gid-dap!
Yip!''

"Well, by thunder, I'll see for myself.''

So the captain clambered from the seat to the side

step, and hanging hard to the front wagon-bow, took a good look.

"Indians, aren't they?" asked the lieutenant, braced to the lines.

"Yes; and coming like blazes!"

That they were. The objects that had resembled turkeys were their feathered heads rising from a ravine. They were fully out now; had dropped their buffalo-robes, and all exposed in the open were tearing for the road.

"How many, Cap?"

"About thirty."

"Oh, dear!" sighed young Lieutenant Hallowell, "I'll never see Lizzie again."

"Never mind Lizzie. Let's get ourselves out of here, first."

"All right, Cap," replied Lieutenant Hallowell, briskly. "You do the shooting and I'll do the driving."

He snatched the whip, slipped from his seat to the very front end of the box; and letting the lines lie lax began to lash and yell. The mules bolted free, twitching the wagon over the ruts.

Captain Booth sprawled inside; grabbed the lieutenant's one navy revolver, and with his own two tumbled over the seat and dived to the pucker-hole at the rear end, to fight the Indians off.

There were thirty-four of them, racing on up the road at top speed.

"How far now, Cap?" called the lieutenant, while he yelled and lashed.

"Still coming fast, and getting closer."

"Yip! Yip! Gwan with you!" Pretty soon—

"How far now, Cap?" The lieutenant could see nothing, behind, and the Indians had not uttered a sound.

"Still coming. 'Most within shooting distance."

"Yip! Hi! Yip! Yip!" And—"Whack! Whack!"

The captain, sitting upon a cracker-box and peering out through the hole, was tossed from side to side. He could see the Indians very plainly. They were paint-daubed Kiowas, and well mounted—armed with bows and lances and a couple of guns. Their striped faces grinned gleefully as their quirts rose and fell and their heels hammered their ponies' sides. The captain almost believed that he was dreaming a bad dream. But here they were, and how he and the lieutenant were going to escape he did not yet know.

"What they doing now, Cap?"

"Getting ready—" and he didn't need to report. The two guns of the Indians spoke, the whole band screeched horridly, the bullets passed diagonally through the wagon-cover between the passengers, Lieutenant Hallowell yelled louder and threshed faster, Captain Booth yelled, the mules lengthened a little, the wagon bounced higher, the Indians had reached it, they divided right and left and swooped past on either side while their arrows whisked and thudded, Captain Booth frantically fired his pistol and heard the lieutenant call:

"I'm hit, Cap!"

He turned quickly. Horrors! Lieutenant Hallowell had an arrow stuck in his head above his right ear!

But he was whipping and yelling, regardless. The captain tumbled forward, to help him; grasped hold of the shaft.

"Hurt much?"

"No. Pull ahead. Hi! Yip! Gwan with you!"

Out came the arrow. Its point had lodged only under the skin.

The Indians had charged beyond the mules, in delivering their arrows. They wheeled, and back they came. The captain fired, but he was being jounced so, that he could not aim. He started rearward, to receive them at that end—

"I'm hit again, Cap!" called Lieutenant Hallowell, a second time.

So he was. This time an arrow had stuck over his left ear and was hanging down his shoulder. Whew! The captain had to pause and pull it out.

"Hurt, Hallowell?"

"No, not much. Hi! Yip! Gwan with you!" And—"Whack! Whack!"

The lieutenant had said: "You do the shooting and I'll do the driving;" and he had not changed his mind about it. But driving was no joke.

The captain hustled to rear. The Indians were about to make a third charge. They appeared to be having great sport, chasing this mule-wagon. There was one withered old warrior close behind now, following in the middle of the road, on a black pony, and shooting arrows at the pucker-hole. The captain ducked from the hole just in time. The arrow whizzed through, struck the walnut back of the seat and split it.

291

The arrow point came out on the other side! That was a powerful bow.

The arrow shaft hummed so, as it quivered, that the captain killed it as he would a wasp; he jumped for a shot at the old warrior—missed him—another arrow, from the left, grazed his pistol-arm crazy-bone and his pistol fell into the road. He grabbed to catch it, the mules lurched and out he pitched, half through the pucker-hole, so that he hung doubled on his stomach, over the end-gate, clutching at nothing.

A fraction more, and he'd have been in the road, too. The Indians whooped gladly, ready to pick him up. He barely managed to reach for the wagon-bow, and haul himself back. Wh-whew!

There was no time for cogitating. He plucked a second revolver from his holsters—

"Right off to the right, Cap! Quick!" called the lieutenant, sharply.

It was an appeal. To the front end scrambled Captain Booth. An Indian was just loosing an arrow at Hallowell; the captain let loose at the Indian; both missed—the arrow stuck in the side of the wagon, and the Indian himself veered away in a hurry, frightened if not hurt.

That was poor shooting, all around. But to shoot from galloping pony or from bouncing wagon is uncertain work.

Back scrambled the captain. He had a great deal to do. He found another warrior—a young fellow—keeping pace with the wagon, in the foot-trail where the wagon teamsters walked when traveling with their freighting outfits.

The pony's head was actually within arm's length from the pucker-hole. The captain struck at it with his revolver; the Indian, hanging low, kept whipping the pony and forcing him in again. The Indian began to notch an arrow upon the bow-string; he was going to shoot. As the captain leaned, to get a shot in first, the arrow point threatened not three feet from his breast!

He could not see the Indian's body; could see only half his leg, hooked over the pony's back. All that he might do was to strike at the arrow; then he dodged back. Up rose the Indian; out popped the captain. Down sank the Indian; back dodged the captain. Up rose the Indian; out popped the captain. Down sank the Indian—up he rose and "Bang!!" spoke the captain's navy six-shooter. It was a chance shot, but the bullet tore through the Indian's heart, and dropping the halter, he toppled, dead.

"I've killed one of 'em, Hallowell!" cheered the captain, excitedly.

"Hurrah! Bully for you! Hi! Yip! Yip!" And —"Whack! Whack!"

He never quit driving, not Lieutenant Hallowell!

The Indians had halted, to examine their dead warrior, and yell over him.

"What they doing now, Cap?"

"Holding a funeral."

"Gwan! Yip! Gwan with you!" urged the lieutenant, trying to squeeze more speed out of the lathered mules.

Captain Booth sat on the cracker-box, watching through the pucker-hole. Had the Indians given up?

"Cap! Quick! Here! Right off to the left!" That was the lieutenant. The captain whirled about; he saw a lone Indian racing close to the fore end of the wagon, aiming an arrow at Lieutenant Hallowell. There was no time to change position for a clear shot.

"Hit him with your whip! Hurry up! Hit him!"

The lieutenant flung the lash sideways, instead of over the mules. The knot of the cracker must have caught the Indian in an eye, for he lost his bow, clapped both hands to his face and scurried away, howling.

"Good shot! Hi! Yip! Betty! Joe! Gwan with you!"

The Indians behind were yelling louder.

"What's the matter, Cap?"

"They're coming again like Sam Hill!"

"All right. Guess we'll make it. Hi! Yip!" And —"Whack! Whack!"

Yes, the Indians were coming. In a minute they had overhauled the wagon, bombarding it with arrows as they passed on both sides. Captain Booth turned around on his box, to watch them through the front end. He did not know that his body bulged the wagon-sheet cover.

"Hit again, Cap!" called the lieutenant.

"Where now?"

"In the back."

The captain started to rise; could not get up. He

was pinned fast to the canvas, by an arrow. But he wrenched free—never felt his wound and hurried to the lieutenant.

"Right in the back, Cap."

Sure enough. The feathered tip of an arrow was sticking out from under the slat of the seat-back behind the lieutenant. The captain pulled at it, the lieutenant squirmed.

"Hurt you much, Hallowell?"

"Some. No matter. Pull it out. Hi! Gwan! Yip!"

The arrow was red with blood for six inches, but the lieutenant did not even glance at it. He kept driving.

The captain scuttled for the rear. He did not get far. The lieutenant called.

"Off to the left, Cap! Right off to the left! Quick!"

Another Indian was there in the favorite position, scarcely three yards from the driver, and aiming his arrow. The captain sprang for the front, leveled his revolver—it was empty! So:

"Hey! Bang!" he shouted.

Ha, ha! Down lay the Indian, low upon his pony's neck; he hammered hard with his heels and away he scoured.

The captain sprawled for the rear once more, and tried to load. How those mules ran! How the lieutenant yelled and whipped! How that wagon jolted! And his powder spilled when he poured it into his old-style cap-and-ball pistol.

He had not succeeded in loading a single chamber

when the lieutenant again called. He was constantly in trouble, poor Lieutenant Hallowell. The Indians knew that he couldn't shoot.

"Off to the left, Cap! Hurry!"

Still another Indian, making ready; occupying the same old spot. The captain hurried; leveled the revolver; shouted "Bang!"

But the trick did not work. This Indian was wiser. He only grinned and notched his arrow, and took his time for a sure shot. Something had to be done to get rid of him. Angry clear through, the captain leaned as far as he dared and hurled the revolver. Good! The heavy barrel landed full upon the Indian's ribs, cut a long gash—and much astonished the Indian veered off for repairs.

Only one revolver was left, and it had been emptied. But the captain was given no pause, to load.

"I'm hit again, Cap!" the lieutenant called.

"Whereabouts now?"

"In the hand."

An arrow was fastened to the base of the thumb of his whip hand. Its shaft waggled, but its head remained firm.

"Shall I pull it out?"

"No. Can't stop. Hi! Gwan! Yip! Yip with you!"

The lieutenant's hand did not falter, as he plied the whip. Presently the arrow flopped free and was gone, taking some of the flesh with it.

The Indians seemed to have shot most of their arrows, but were not done. Now one of them rode to the head of the left mule and commenced poking with his lance, to force the team into the hedge of tall, stiff sun-flowers that lined the trail.

Lieutenant Hallowell hauled with all his might on the rein; Captain Booth climbed forward to the step opposite the Indian and kicked the nearest mule. He threw his revolver. It did not strike the Indian, but it struck the pony, and the pony ran away.

Other Indians promptly came up. The captain threw both sabers, and both scabbards. Wagon and mules were being surrounded, and still more Indians were pursuing and closing in rapidly.

The captain had an idea. He tossed out his suit-case. The Indians behind stopped, to inspect. They slit the suit-case open. In a moment one was wearing the officer's sash tied around his head; another was wearing the captain's dress-coat, another his best shirt, another his undershirt and another his drawers! It was a funny sight. But others came on.

"What they doing?" gasped the lieutenant.

"Wearing the clothes from my valise. Out goes yours, next."

"All right. Anything to gain time."

Camp Zarah was only a mile and a half before.

The clothes delayed the Indians behind; those already here were still prodding at the mules. The lances proved too slow. A warrior fitted an arrow, drew to the point, and let go. He had intended to kill a mule, but he only wounded it in the fore leg. The blood spurted—ah! Look out! Great Cæsar! That was a lucky shot, for the wagon. The other mule saw the blood, and smelled it. He bolted at such a gait

297

that he actually out-ran the Indians while he dragg&d the wagon and the disabled mule!

Camp Zarah was in sight. Would they make it? Alas! The mules were stumbling; were near spent. They had run a great race, but they could not hold to it forever. The Indians were gaining rapidly.

"If we're taken, Cap, we'll fight; we'll kick, scratch, bite, till they kill us. We won't stand for torture," panted the lieutenant.

"I agree."

The lieutenant yelled and whipped; the captain yelled and kicked the wounded mule in the flanks; the Indians arrived, and prodded; the mules dodged the lances— they seemed to know. Only a few yards from the bridge did the last Indian pursuer give up the chase; and as the wagon rattled over the corduroy the carbine of a sentry at the post sounded the alarm.

"No need to drive so fast now, Hallowell," spoke the captain. The jolting was terrific.

"I sha'n't stop till we're clear across," rapped the lieutenant.

The staggering mules white with lather and crimsoned with blood, the wagon as full of holes as a sieve, they pulled in to the commanding officer's tent. They were safe.

Lieutenant Hallowell could not stand up. Was he fatally hurt?

"What is it, Hallowell, old fellow?"

"I dunno. Can't move only so far."

"No wonder! It's your coat-tails, man!"

The tails of his overcoat had worked outside and

were pinned fast to the wagon box by four arrows. He could not use his right arm, either. The steady threshing with the whip had almost paralyzed it.

He was helped into the surgeon's office. His right hand was badly torn, and the wound in his back serious. Captain Booth watched the wounds being dressed; didn't feel very comfortable, himself, somehow.

"What makes you shrug your shoulders so, captain?"

"I don't know. There's a curious smarting."

"I should say there was! Why, you're wearing an arrow-head, man!"

So he was. When he had wrenched free from the wagon-sheet cover he had taken an arrow-head with him. It had to be cut out.

They both got well. Twenty-two arrows were found in the wagon box; the whole vehicle was a sight! As for the plucky little mules, they never amounted to much for service, after that, but they managed to hobble around in their pasture and enjoy their reward as veterans, on a pension of the best grass and water.

CHAPTER XIX

RELIEF FOR BEECHER'S ISLAND (1868)

AND A RATTLE-SNAKE IN THE WAY

THE Plains Indians—the Sioux, the Cheyennes, the Arapahos, the Kiowas, the Comanches—had fought hard, during the war of the white men in the East, to clear their hunting grounds; but when in 1866 the Civil War had ended they found that the Americans were pressing forward more strongly than ever.

Two iron roads were being surveyed through the buffalo country; new gold fields, in Montana, were being opened and a white man's wagon-road, protected by forts, was being laid out to reach them by a short cut through Wyoming.

With two thousand of his Oglala Sioux, Chief Red Cloud undertook to close this wagon-road; and close it he did. He beleaguered new Fort Phil Kearney in northern Wyoming, wiped out one detachment of eighty-one men, attacked other detachments, cut off the supplies from all the forts, stood firmly in the path; and in 1868 the United States Government agreed to withdraw all soldiers and leave the country to the Sioux.[1]

But the iron trails continued. There were the Union

[1] See "Red Cloud Stands in the Way," in "Boys' Book of Indian Warriors."

300

Pacific in the north, the Kansas Pacific on the south. The first drove its stakes and laid its rails along the great white wagon-road of the Oregon Trail and the Overland Trail, which already had split the buffalo herds. The Sioux and the Northern Cheyennes fought it in Nebraska, they fought it in Wyoming; until in 1868 it still had not been stopped, it was lunging on straight for the mountains, and in the treaty that promised him the hunting grounds north of it Chief Red Cloud also promised to let it alone.

The Cheyennes, their allies from the Sioux and the Arapahos, made no such promise regarding the Kansas Pacific. The Union Pacific "thunder wagons" had divided the buffalo into the northern and the southern herds; now the southern herd was to be divided again. A line of forts was creeping on; the soldiers were increasing; and the "thunder wagons" were to travel back and forth between the Missouri River and Denver, frightening the buffalo that grazed in central Kansas, and bringing in hunters to kill them.

"If the road does not stop," said Chief Roman Nose of the Cheyennes, "I shall be the white man's enemy forever."

By the fall of 1868 the rails had reached four hundred and twelve miles, almost clear across northern Kansas, to Fort Wallace near the border of Colorado. Every mile of the last two hundred and more had been a fight; wellnigh every mile of these same had been stained red; all western Kansas was a battle ground, upon which settlers, soldiers, surveyors and track-builders gave up their lives. The Cheyennes lost

301

heavily, but they showed no signs of quitting. They were getting worse.

At the end of August General Phil Sheridan, who commanded the Military Division of the Missouri, directed Major George A. Forsythe of the Ninth Cavalry to enlist fifty scouts and ride against the Indians— fight them in their own way. He left Fort Wallace on the morning of August 29; struck a broad Indian trail leading northward; early in the morning of September 17 was surprised by six hundred Cheyennes, Sioux and Arapahos, and was forced to entrench upon a little island in the Arikaree River of eastern Colorado not far from the Nebraska line; and here he stood off the charges of the Indian horsemen—five hundred at once.

All that day the fight was waged. Major Forsythe was wounded three times; Lieutenant Beecher was killed; Surgeon Mooers was dying; all the horses were dead; horse-flesh was the only food and the enemy had ringed the island with rifle-fire.

This evening volunteers were called for, to steal through the deadly circle and carry messages to Fort Wallace, one hundred miles south. There was no lack of men eager to try; Scouts "Pet" Trudeau and "Jack" Stillwell were chosen.

Scout Trudeau was a grown man, but Jack Stillwell was only nineteen, and boyish looking. Nevertheless, he, too, was a man. He knew Indians and he knew the plains; he was able to give a good account of himself. Scout Trudeau asked no better comrade on the danger trail.

302

They prepared to leave in the dark. At midnight they shook hands with their officer and their nearest fellows. With a piece of horse-flesh for food, with revolvers at belts and carbines in hand, and their boots slung from their necks, in their stockinged feet they quietly vanished, wrapped in their blankets so as to look as much like Indians as possible.

At first Trudeau led, because he was the older; toward the end Jack Stillwell led, because he proved to be the stronger. As they crossed from the little island to the dry bottom of the river-bed, they turned and walked backward. On the sand their stockinged feet made tracks like moccasin tracks, all pointing for the island. The Indians would not know that anybody had escaped.

Quiet reigned all around, except for the yapping of the coyotes. But they two were well aware that the camps of six hundred warriors were scattered everywhere, resting only until daylight.

Having entered the dry channel of the river, they did another wise thing. They crossed it, instead of keeping on down; and crawling, they stuck to the high ground, even the tops of the bare ridges, instead of taking to the ravines and washes.

"Never do what the enemy expects you to do," is a military maxim, although rather hard to follow in modern fighting. The natural trail for scouts through the lines would be by the river bottom, and by other low ground out of sight. The Indians, Scout Stillwell learned afterward from chiefs themselves, were watching all the river channel and all the ravines, this night.

The two scouts fooled them, and found the ridge trails thinly guarded. Those Indians not on guard were sleeping out of the breeze.

Through every yard of their crawl the hearts of the two scouts were in their throats. To creep amidst the dark, this way, with Indians before, behind, on right, on left—who knew where?—was nerve-racking. When the stars began to pale only two miles had been covered. Slow work, careful work, fearful work! Now for a hiding-place. They would be seen instantly by daylight.

They cautiously slipped on, for a little arroyo or dried wash, bordered by brittle weeds. Even this might be occupied ahead of them. If it was, then that meant death or capture—and capture meant death also, by torture in revenge for warriors slain. They had agreed to fight to the last cartridge, and then to use their last cartridge on themselves after destroying their message.

Cautiously, cautiously they harked and peered; they gently parted the weeds and wormed in, closing the weeds behind them again. The arroyo was empty. In the first tinge of gray they crouched under the high bank overhung by the weeds, to wait.

The night had passed, and here they were, abroad in the very thick of the Indians, to face a day of unknown perils. It was to be a long, long day.

The stars faded; the sky brightened; squads of Indians galloped by, to the fight. The sun rose, flooding the world above the arroyo. Gun-shots spatted dully—fast and faster; the fight at the island was on.

304

From hour to hour they listened, hoping that the shots would not cease. While the firing continued, the island was holding out. The firing did continue, and that nerved their hearts afresh. Their comrades were bravely battling while depending upon them.

The arroyo grew stifling hot. They had no water, and saved their horse-beef for an emergency. They had been tired when they started—already had fought one whole day through, on slim rations. But they dared not move on. When they ventured to peep over the edge of the arroyo, they saw an Indian camp of women and old men in plain view—could catch the voices, now and then. The country was an open country; nothing could stir above its surface without being sighted.

Finally the sun set, the dusk gathered, and in darkness again they crept out. A full day gone, only two miles gained in a day and half a night—two miles in one hundred! But the island was still held by their comrades.

They put on their boots, and to-night they made better headway. Twice they had to flatten and muffle their breathing, for parties of Indians rode almost upon them. The country seemed to be alarmed; Indians were riding back and forth constantly. All the landmarks were shrouded and changed; they headed south and easterly by the stars—and at daybreak were obliged to hide in a hurry, for they somehow were running right into the main village of the Cheyennes!

They had come ten miles from their arroyo, and were at the South Republican River in western Kansas.

This time they crawled along under the river bank, and into the tall coarse grass of a bayou that bordered the river. They could see the village; they could hear the squaws chanting the mourning songs for dead warriors, and might watch them carrying bodies to the scaffolds.

Had that village known two white scouts were so near—! Why, once during the day a party of warriors watered their horses not thirty feet from where Scouts Trudeau and Stillwell were lying; and time after time other war parties crossed and recrossed the river here. It was a ford.

The second long day passed. In the darkness of the third night out they crossed the river themselves, and side-stepping the village and its wolfish dogs struck south once more. They had to dodge night-roving Indians, as before, but they traveled steadily; there was no sign, by any of the Indians they met, that the island had been taken. This gave hope, still.

"We're getting through, Jack," spoke Scout Trudeau, toward morning. "But we'll have to do better. Will you risk day travel with me, so we can finish up. There are anxious hearts, back yonder; and by this time the boys are suffering something fearful."

"I'm game, 'Pet.'"

So they did not stop, with daylight. Keeping to the coulees or washes, and the draws, and the stream beds, they zigzagged on. They had counted upon the Indians all being attracted in to the island, by this time; but they had counted too soon.

About eight o'clock, while they were crossing a high

rolling prairie, Scout Trudeau suddenly dropped. Scout Stillwell imitated—did not hesitate an instant.

"Don't move! Don't breathe! Look yonder!"

A long file of mounted Indians had emerged around the base of a low hill not a mile away, off to the north-west, and were coming on.

"We'll have to câche ourselves in a hurry."

The table-land was bare and level. For a moment their hearts sank. Then they noted a patch of tall, stiff yellowed weeds growing from an old buffalo wallow. In the wet season the buffalo had rolled in the mud here, until they had scooped a little hollow; the hollow had formed a shallow water-hole; the rains had collected and sunk in, and provided moisture for the weeds long after the surrounding soil had dried.

It was the only cover in sight, and for it they crawled.

The Indians came straight on. Had they seen? If so, goodby to life and to the message.

The two scouts had intended to break the weeds and cloak themselves with the stems—a camouflage of old days and new. The screen was very thin, for con-cealment on all sides. But the Indians granted no time. Trudeau and young Jack might only squirm into the very middle. An old buffalo carcass was here. It had not been disturbed. Scraps of brittle hide still clung to its frame-work of ribs. All that they might do was to crawl close to the frame-work and lie beside it.

The Indians halted before reaching the wallow; they

could see that it contained no water. But presently one of their young men rode forward, surveying the landscape; posted himself not one hundred yards from the wallow, and there he sat, on his horse, like a sentry.

The two scouts hugged the ground; it was white with alkali, and as seemed to them they were clearly outlined, through the yellow weeds. Then an alarming thing happened. The buffalo carcass had not been the only occupant of the wallow. Jack nudged Scout Trudeau, and pointed with his thumb. A king rattle-snake, over four feet long and as thick as their arm, was gliding for them, and the carcass.

His head was up, his tongue shot in and out; possibly the carcass was his tipi—at any rate, they had annoyed him, and he was declaring war.

Now what to do! If they waited, he would keep on coming! Horrors! If they moved, he would coil, and rattle. They dared not shoot; they dared not wait—could not stand having him crawl under them or over them, and perhaps strike; they dared not let him *rattle*.

A rattle-snake does not rattle for nothing. The Indian sentinel would hear, would gaze, would be curious, would suspect, would approach; and then— death to two scouts, despair for the island.

Fascinated, they watched the great, yellowish blotched snake. He loitered, basked, his tongue played, his fangs showed, he came on, little by little. Oh, if he would only veer off! But he was determined. What an ugly, obstinate brute! What an abominable trick! And yonder, still sat the vigilant Indian.

They waited until the snake was within six feet. They could fairly smell his musky odor, and he was growing angrier and angrier—was likely to coil and rattle, any moment. They were at their wits' end, their nerve almost breaking, what with the menace of the snake and the menace of the Indian look-out, at the same time.

Jack Stillwell solved the problem. He was chewing tobacco.

"Sh! I'll fix him," he whispered.

He slightly raised—at the movement the snake coiled, rattle sticking up in the center, head poised, tongue licking wickedly. And aiming his best, Jack spat.

The stream spurted truly. It drenched the beady-eyed, flat-iron head, flooded the swaying neck and spattered the thick scaly coils. With a writhe and a hiss the blinded snake threshed to one side and burrowed for shelter. Jack chuckled and shook. He had cleared the decks of one enemy.

Nearly at the same time the Indian look-out rode away, following the retiring band. That was a great relief. Between the snake and the Indian scout Trudeau and Stillwell had experienced, as the record says, the most terrible half-hour of their lives.

The collapse of the danger left them both weak. They now had found out that it was not yet safe to travel by day; so they stayed here in the wallow, with the buffalo carcass for company, till evening.

In this next night's journey poor Trudeau broke. The strain was proving too much. They had eaten nothing since leaving the island, they had crawled for miles, had traveled by night, through the midst of the Indians, for fifty miles; had escaped again and again only by the sheerest good fortune. He broke, and young Jack had all that he could do, for a time, to keep him from seeing imaginary forms and running amuck over the plain, or else killing himself.

Toward morning he succeeded in quieting him, making him drink heartily from a stream and swallow some of the horse-beef. They pushed on. It was a foggy day, and they did not stop. Jack now had to furnish the brains and the strength, and do the bracing. But he was equal to it; he selected the trail and helped his staggering partner. Neither was braver than the other, but one had more reserve power.

At noon they were within twenty miles of Fort Wallace. That fourth evening after dusk they were challenged by the post sentry, and tottered on in with their message from the island in the Arikaree, one hundred miles to the northward.

Jack Stillwell went with the relief column from the fort. Scout Trudeau could not; he was exhausted. He never did recover, and the next spring he died; he had given his life to save the lives of others. Scout Stillwell followed many another danger trail, until the Indian wars upon his plains were over; then he became a lawyer and a judge, and in 1902 answered the last roll-call.

CHAPTER XX

THE DEFENSE OF THE BUFFALO-HUNTERS (1874)

WHEN THE COMANCHE MEDICINE FAILED

THE Plains Indians were losing out. They saw their buffalo grounds growing smaller and smaller. The Sioux and Northern Cheyennes had not stopped the Union Pacific Railroad. It had cut the northern herd in two. The Cheyennes and Arapahos and Dog Soldiers from other tribes had not stopped the Kansas Pacific Railroad. In their last great raid they had been defeated at the battle of Beecher's Island, as the fight by Major Forsythe, at the Arikaree in September, 1868, was known. The Kansas Pacific had cut the southern herd in two. It was bringing swarms of white hunters into the Kansas buffalo range; they were slaughterng the game and wasting the meat.

Then, in 1872, still another iron road, the Atchison, Topeka & Santa Fe, pushed out, south of the Kansas Pacific, and took possession of the old Santa Fe Trail, the wagon-road up the Arkansas River. The wagon-road itself had been bad enough; for the emigrants were gathering all the fuel and killing and frightening the buffalo. The snorting engines and swift trains were worse. The buffalo were again split. From southern Kansas north into central Nebraska there was no place for the buffalo, and the Indian.

311

This year, 1872, the white hunters commenced to kill for the hides. They skinned the carcasses, and let the meat lie and rot, except the small portion that they ate. Many of the buffalo were only wounded; they staggered away, and died untouched. Many of the hides were spoiled. For each hide sent to market, and sold for maybe only $1.50, four other buffalo were wasted.

In 1873 the slaughter was increased. Regularly organized parties took the field. By trains and wagons the buffalo were easily and quickly found; the Atchison, Topeka & Santa Fe Railroad shipped out over two hundred and fifty thousand hides; the Kansas and Pacific and the Union Pacific twice as many. At the plains stations the bales of hides were piled as high as houses. In order to save time, the hides were yanked off by a rope and tackle and a team of horses. Almost five million pounds of meat were saved, and over three million pounds of bones for fertilizer; but the meat averaged only about seven pounds to each hide taken—and that was trifling. Evidently an enormous quantity of buffalo were still being wasted.

It was considered nothing at all to shoot a buffalo. So-called sportsmen bombarded right and left, and kept tally to see who should kill the most. Passengers and train-crews peppered away from coach, caboose and engine, and the trains did not even halt.

In 1874 there was a great difference to be noted among the herds. They were getting wild; the hunters laid in wait at the water-holes, and killed the buffalo that finally had to come in, to drink. In the three years, 1872–1873–1874, no less than 3,158,730 were killed by the white hunters; all the Indians together killed perhaps 1,215,000—but they used these for food, clothing, and in trade for other goods. A full million more of buffalo were taken out by wagon and pack horse. So this sums up over five million. The plains were white with skeletons; in places the air was foul with the odor of decaying meat.

The buffalo had two refuges from the white killer: one far in the north, in the Sioux country; the other far in the south, in the Comanche and Kiowa country of present Oklahoma and Texas.

By a treaty made in 1867 the United States had promised that white men should not hunt south of the Arkansas River. But in 1874, when the buffalo in Kansas and Nebraska had become scarcer, and the price of hides was so low that long chases and waits did not pay out, the hunters gave no attention to the treaty, and located their camps south of the river, in forbidden territory.

The Indians awakened to the fact that soon there would be no buffalo left for them. For years they had depended upon the buffalo, as food, and glue, and clothing and lodge covers. They had believed that the buffalo were the gift of the Great Spirit, who every spring brought fresh numbers out of holes in the Staked Plain of western Texas, to fill the ranks. Now the bad medicine of the whites was about to close these holes; the buffalo would come north no more.

In the spring of 1874 the Kiowas, Comanches,

Cheyennes and Arapahos held a council in Indian Territory, to discuss what was to be done. They decided to make one more stand against the white hunters, especially those south of the Arkansas.

It was arranged. The Comanches had sent a peace pipe to the council; all the chiefs smoked, and agreed to peace among themselves and war against the Americans who were destroying the buffalo reserves. I-sa-tai, a Comanche medicine-man, announced that he had a medicine that would make the guns of the whites useless. Many of the Cheyennes and Apaches and others believed him.

The first point of attack should be the white hunters' camp at Adobe Walls, in the Pan-handle of northern Texas. That was the nearest camp, and was one of the most annoying.

"Those men shall not fire a shot; we shall kill them all," I-sa-tai promised. "We shall ride up to them and knock them on the head. My medicine says so."

A war party of seven hundred Red River Comanches, Southern Cheyennes, Arapahos, Kiowas and Apaches were formed, to wipe out Adobe Walls.

Quana Parker, chief of the Kwahadi band of Comanches, became the leader. The Kwahadi Comanches had not signed the treaty of 1867, by which the other tribes sold their lands and settled upon places assigned them by the Government. They continued to roam freely, and hunt where they chose. They always had been wild, independent Indians of Texas.

Chief Quana Parker himself was a young man of

thirty years, but a noted warrior. Like his name, he was half Indian, half white—although all Comanche. In 1835 the Comanches had captured a small settlement in east Texas, known as Parker's Fort; had carried off little John Parker, aged six, and little Cynthia Ann Parker, aged nine. Cynthia grew up with the Comanches, and married Peta Nokoni or Wanderer, a fine young brave who was elected head chief of the Kwahadis. Their baby was named Quana, and now in 1874 was called Quana Parker.

In 1860, or when he was fifteen years old, his mother had been retaken by the Texas Rangers. She lived with her brother, Colonel Dan Parker, four years. Then she died. Boy Quana was Indian; he stayed with the Comanches. He won his chiefship by running away with a girl that he loved, whom a more wealthy warrior tried to take from him. Many young men joined him in the hills, until his rival and the girl's father were afraid of him, and the tribe elected him head chief.

The Texans feared him, if they feared any Indian; all Indians respected him; in June, this 1874, he marshalled his allied chiefs and warriors for the raid upon the buffalo hunters. He had more faith in bullets and arrows than in I-sa-tai's medicine, but I-sa-tai went along.

There were two Adobe Walls, on the south branch of the Canadian River, in Hutchinson County, Texas Pan-handle. The first had been built in 1845 by William Bent and his partners of Bent's Fort, as another trading-post, to deal with the Red River Comanches.

315

William Bent had sent one of his clerks, named by the Cheyennes Wrinkled Neck, to build it.

After it had been abandoned, in 1864 General Kit Carson had attacked the winter villages of three thousand Comanche, Kiowa, Apache and Arapaho warriors and their families, here. He was just able to get his four hundred men safely away.

The second Adobe Walls had been built only a year or two ago. It was down-river from the old Adobe Walls, and formed a small settlement where the buffalo-hunters came in, from their outside camps, to store their hides and get supplies, and so forth. There were Hanrahan's saloon, and Rath's general store, and several sheds and shacks, mainly of adobe or dried clay, and a large horse and mule corral, of adobe and palisades, with a plank gate. Such was Adobe Walls of 1874, squatted amidst the dun bunch-grass landscape broken only by the shallow South Canadian and a rounded hill or two.

The Rath store was the principal building. It was forty feet long, and contained two rooms—the store room, and a room where persons might sleep. It looked not unlike a fort; the thick walls had bastions at the corners, the deep window casings were embrasured or sloped outward, so that guns might be aimed at an angle, from within.

In the night of June 24 twenty-eight men and one woman were at Adobe Walls. Excepting Mrs. Rath, and her husband, and Saloon-keeper Hanrahan, and two or three Mexican clerks and roustabouts, they mainly were buffalo-hunters. Billy Dixon, government scout, was in with his wagon and outfit; he expected to start.for his camp, twenty-five miles south, in the morning. The Shadley brothers and their freighter outfit were here. And likewise some twenty others.

It was not to be expected that Indians would attack Adobe Walls itself; they were more likely to raid the camps: but the general store seemed to be a great prize—the Comanches and Kiowas and Apaches and Arapahos and Cheyennes counted upon plunder of clothes and flour and ammunition, and I-sa-tai's medicine had told him to try Adobe Walls first.

The night was warm. Scout Dixon slept out-doors, in his wagon; the Shadley brothers slept in their wagon; several men slept upon buffalo-robes, on the ground; others were in the Rath store and in the saloon.

Shortly after midnight the men in the saloon were awakened by the cracking of the roof ridge-pole. They were afraid that the roof might be falling, so they piled out to fix it. Their noise aroused the men in the wagons and on the ground; and all together they worked. By the time they were done, sunrise was showing in the east, and Billy Dixon thought that it was not worth while to go to bed again.

He prepared to set out for his buffalo-camp. Pretty soon he sent one of his men down to the creek bottoms, to bring in the horses. The man came running back, shouting and pointing.

"Injuns!"

A solid line of feathered heads, sharply sketched against the reddening sky, was charging in across the bottoms, directly for the store and saloon and corral. The drum of galloping hoofs began to beat in a long roll, and a tremendous war-whoop shattered the still air.

"Look out for the horses!" Scout Dixon yelled. He tied his own saddle-horse short to the wagon and grabbed his Sharp's buffalo-gun. He thought that this was a raid for a stampede. But instead of scattering to round up the grazing stock the Indians rode straight on—in all his experience as scout and hunter they were the boldest, best-armed "bunch" that he had ever seen; and they meant business. They were here to wipe out the whole place; had warriors enough to do it, too.

From one hundred yards bullets spattered. Without waiting longer he dived for the saloon and shelter. There were six other men in the saloon, mostly jerked from slumber in all kinds of undress. Firing right and left and whooping, the Indians poured through among the buildings like a torrent; from the saloon windows the white men and Mexicans replied.

Chief Quana Parker's cavalry had high hopes. He led. Last night I-sa-tai's medicine had been strong. This morning a foolish Cheyenne had killed a skunk —a reckless thing to do, for a skunk was a medicine animal. Whether this broke the medicine, I-sa-tai did not say. They were to find out.

Had the ridge-pole not cracked and got the hunters up; or had the Indians arrived only fifteen minutes earlier, while the hunters were busy with the ridge-pole, they truly would have captured Adobe Walls and killed everybody in it. The medicine almost worked, but not quite. Just the killing of the skunk had broken it.

For a brief space the seven men in the saloon were hard beset. They appeared to be the only defenders of the settlement. The heavy sleepers in the store and the house were not yet enough awake to know what had occurred. On their rapid ponies the Indians flashed past between the saloon and Rath's, darted here and there around the corners, flung to earth and ran to pry at windows and doors.

Horses were down and kicking, in the street. An Indian scampered from the Shadley brothers' wagon, his arms full of plunder; but a bullet from the saloon dropped him like a stone. Nothing was heard from the two Shadleys; probably they were dead in their wagon.

The saloon was thick with powder-smoke; the air outside quivered to the whoops and jeers and threats. Would the store hold out? Hurrah! The boys in there were up and shouting, too. Shots spouted from the windows.

The first charge had passed on. Chief Quana re-formed his ranks, for another. Abode Walls, now rudely awakened, hastily prepared. There were the seven men in the Hanrahan saloon—a low, box-like affair, sitting by itself at one side of the store; there were Store-keeper Rath and his wife, and a couple of hunters, in the Rath house, on the other side of the

store; and in the long store itself there were twelve
or fourteen men.

Peeping out, dazed and bootless and coatless just
as they had sprung from their blankets, they saw a
wonderful sight. Fully six hundred Indians were
coming again, in a solid front.

The long feathered war-bonnets of the Comanches
and Cheyennes flared upon the breeze; the painted,
naked riders lashed and urged—"Yip! Yip! Yip!";
the ponies, of all colors, jostled and plunged, and their
hoof-beats drummed; above the tossing crests bare
arms upheld a fringe of shaking guns and bows and
lances. Unless he had been at Beecher's Island and
witnessed the charge of Roman Nose, not a man of
Adobe Walls ever had seen so terrible a spectacle as
this, under the pink sky of the fresh June morning.

On a hill to the right I-sa-tai the medicine-man stood,
all unclothed except for a bonnet of sage twigs. He
was making medicine.

The buffalo-hunters and the two or three freighters,
the clerks and roustabouts and Saloon-keeper Hanrahan and Store-keeper Rath jammed their guns
through every window and cranny fronting the charge,
and waited. It seemed as if the red cavalry surely
would ride right over the place and flatten it.

Four hundred yards, three hundred yards, two hundred yards—"Yip! Yip! Yip!" "Hi! Hi!"; the
hoof-beats were thunderous; it was an avalanche;
smoke puffed from the ponies' backs, bullets whined
and thudded—and the guns of saloon and store and
house burst into action.

They were crack shots, the most of those Adobe Walls men; had the best of rifles, and plenty of cartridges. Down lunged ponies, sending their riders sprawling; the white men's guns spoke rapidly, the noise of shot and shout and yell was deafening; the charging line broke, careering right and left and straight through. On scoured the shrieking squads, but leaving dead and wounded ponies and limping, scurrying warriors.

But this was not the end. Anybody might know that. The Adobe Walls men busied themselves; some stayed on watch, others enlarged their loop-holes or desperately knocked holes through the thick adobe, for better shooting. The windows were too few; the whole rear of the store itself was blank. The door had been battered, and now sacks of flour were piled against it, to strengthen it.

Indians, dismounted, skulked everywhere, taking pot-shots at the loop-holes, and forcing the men to keep close under cover.

Some seventy-five yards behind the store was a large stack of buffalo-hides. From the saloon Scout Billy Dixon saw an Indian pony standing beside it, and might just glimpse a Comanche head-dress, around the corner of the stack.

He aimed at the head-dress and fired. The head-dress disappeared, but the Indian must have dodged to the other corner, for Rath's house opened fire on him, and he dodged back again. Scout Dixon met him with another bullet. The Indian found himself in a hot place. His pony was killed. He had to stay or

321

run; so he stayed, and cowered out of sight, waiting for a chance to shoot or to escape.

But that would not do. He was a danger to the premises, and should be routed. Scout Dixon guessed at his location, behind the hides; drew quick bead, and let drive. The heavy ball from the Sharp's buffalo-gun—a fifty-caliber bullet, on top of one hundred and twenty grains of powder—tore clear through the stack. Out dived the Comanche, jumping like a jackrabbit and yelping like a coyote at every leap, and gained cover in a bunch of grass.

"Bet I scorched him," Billy Dixon chuckled.

Other guns were still cracking, trying to clear the skulkers and to hold off the main body. The warriors were concealed behind buffalo-hide stacks, in sheds, and lying flat upon the prairie. The firing never slackened; there were rushes and retreats. The scene, here on the dry plains of northern Texas, reminded one of the sieges of settlers' forts in Kentucky and West Virginia one hundred years ago. The Indians were outside, the frontiersmen were inside, and no help near.

The sun rose. By this time the Indians hiding close in had been disposed of, in one way or another. They were shooting from two hundred yards—but that was a dead range for the white men's guns. The buffalo-hunters asked nothing better.

Their rifles were sighted to a hair. The hunters were accustomed to lie all day, on the buffalo range, and from their "stand" to leeward plant bullet after bullet of their Sharp's .50-120, Ballard .45-90, and

Winchester .44-40 behind the buffalo's shoulders. A circle eight inches in diameter was the fatal spot—and from two hundred yards they rarely varied in their aim.

An Indian who exposed himself two hundred or three hundred yards away stood a poor show of escape.

The Chief Quana men soon learned this. They already knew it, from other fights, upon the buffalo range itself. They had grown to respect a buffalo-hunter at bay.

Now they withdrew, by squads, to six hundred, seven hundred, eight hundred yards; and firing wildly they sought to cover the retreat of their wounded and their warriors afoot. The Indians between the main party and the fort would spring up, run a few steps, and drop again before a bullet caught them.

Thus the fight lasted until the middle of the afternoon. The hunters inside the walls had no rest, but they ventured to move about a little. The men in the saloon bolted out, and ran into the store. From here Scout Dixon, scanning the country, saw a moving object at the base of the hill, eight hundred yards distant. The Indians now were mostly out of sight, beyond. He commenced shooting at the tiny mark, correcting his aim by the dust thrown up when the bullets landed. The old single-shot Sharp's, either fifty caliber or the forty-four sharp-shooter Creedmore pattern fitted with special sights, was the favorite gun of the buffalo-hunters. Scout Dixon kept elevating his rear sight, and pumping away. Finally he thought that he had hit the mark; it did not move. After the battle and siege he rode over there, to see. He had shot an Indian through the breast, with a fifty-caliber ball at eight hundred yards.

Toward evening the Indians stopped fighting. I-sa-tai's medicine had proved weak, for the hunters' guns seemed to be as bad as ever. But the battle was .not yet ended, as Adobe Walls found out, the next morning. There were charges again; guns grew hot, the smoke thickened, the Indians were everywhere around, determined to force the doors and windows. The hearts and hands of the twenty-five able-bodied men never faltered.

On the evening of the third day the siege was lifted; for with the fourth morning no Indians were to be seen. All about, on the grassy plain between the town and the hills, dead ponies were scattered; the walls of the buildings were furrrowed by bullets; rude loopholes gaped; and in the little street the dust was dyed red.

The two Shadley brothers had been killed, in their wagon; William Tyler, a camp hand, had been killed before he reached shelter. But the twenty-five others, and the brave woman, had stood off the flower of the allied Comanche, Kiowa, Arapaho, Apache and Southern Cheyenne nations.

How many Indians had been killed nobody knew. Nine were found among the buildings and within one hundred yards; four more were discovered, at longer range; in the hills the signs showed that the loss had been at least thirty or thirty-five.

Early in the morning, while Adobe Walls was busy

looking about, a lone buffalo-hunter ambled in. He was George Bellman, a German whose camp lay only eight miles up the Canadian; here he lived alone—he had not heard the shooting nor seen a single Indian, and the ponies strewn over the prairie much astonished him.

"Vat kind a disease iss der matter mit de hosses, hey?" he asked, curiously.

"Died of lead poison," answered Cranky McCabe.

The heads of twelve of the Indians were cut off and stuck up on the pickets and posts of the corral; were left there, to dry in the sun, for a hideous warning. But the buffalo-hunters decided to hunt no more, this season. The Pan-handle country was getting "unhealthy!"

So much had Chief Quana and his brother chiefs and warriors achieved. They had spoiled the buffalo hunting. After a short time many of the Arapahos and Kiowas and Apaches hurried back to their reservation in Indian Territory. The Cheyennes and others raided north, through western Kansas and eastern Colorado. The Chief Quana Comanches went south, to their own range. He and his Kwahadis or Antelope Eaters stayed out on their Staked Plain for two years; they were the last to quit. Then he accepted peace; he saw that it was no use to fight longer. Moreover, he became one of the best, most civilized Indians in all the West.

For his Comanches he chose lands at the base of the Wichita Mountains near Fort Sill in southwestern Oklahoma. He built himself a large two-story house, well painted and furnished; he lived like a rich rancher, and owned thousands of acres of farm and thousands of cattle; he wore the finest of white-man's clothes, or the finest of chief's clothes as suited him; he was still living there, in 1910, and no man was more highly respected. He rode in the parade at Washington when Theodore Roosevelt was inaugurated President. President Roosevelt paid him a return visit, for a wolf hunt.

But the old-time buffalo-hunters who were in Adobe Walls on June 24, 1874, never have forgotten that charge by the Quana Parker fierce cavalry.

CHAPTER XXI

WHITE MEN AT BAY AGAIN (1874)
THE "FIGHT OF THE PRIVATES".

WHEN the news of the attack upon Adobe Walls had gone forth, and reports of other raids followed thick and fast, the army in Texas, Kansas and Indian Territory were ordered out. Plainly enough, there was a great Indian uprising. The reservation peace had been broken.

Colonel Nelson A. Miles of the Fifth United States Infantry was directed to march from Fort Dodge on the Arkansas River just below Dodge City in southwestern Kansas, and strike the Indians in Texas. He took eight troops of the Sixth Cavalry, four companies of the Fifth Infantry, a section of artillery, twenty-five white scouts and a party of Delaware Indian scouts who were led by their gray-haired old chief, Fall Leaf.

Three other army columns, one from Texas in the south, one from New Mexico in the southwest, one from Indian Territory in the northeast, also were starting from the same place: the Staked Plain region of western and northwestern Texas.

Colonel Miles refitted at Camp Supply, one hundred miles south of Fort Dodge, and pushed on toward Adobe Walls.

His advance of scouts and one troop of cavalry were just in time to help save Adobe Walls from yet another attack by Comanches and Kiowas. But the little garrison of buffalo-hunters were still full of fight, and the heads of the twelve Indians still grinned down from the pickets of the corral.

The Indians fled southwest, for the Staked Plain. Colonel Miles pursued and had a brush or two. The marches were long and hard, through a very hot, dry country where the only water was bad. Soldiers suffered so from thirst that some of them opened veins in their own arms and sucked the blood.

The Staked Plain country is a desert except after the rains or where irrigated by ditches. It forms a high flat table-land whose edges drop sharply off in curiously pillared cliffs. Therefore the early Spanish called it El Llano Estacado—the Palisaded Plain; but the Americans believed that the name was given because the only trails across it were marked by stakes.

In later days it proved to be a vast range for cattle and horses; in the older days it was the stronghold of the Comanches, who knew every water-hole and every cave.

Drawing near to the Staked Plain, southwest of Adobe Walls, Colonel Miles decided that he must have more supplies. The trains were far in the rear, and may have been cut off. On the afternoon of September 10 he directed that dispatches be sent back, for the trains or else for Camp Supply on the North Canadian River in northwestern Oklahoma which at that time was Indian Territory.

The men selected were Sergeant Z. T. Woodall of I troop, Sixth Cavalry; Private John Harrington of H troop, Private Peter Roth of A troop, Private George W. Smith of M troop; and Citizen Scouts Amos Chapman and Billy Dixon—the same Billy Dixon of Adobe Walls. After the Quana Parker fight he had joined the army service. Scout Chapman had been stationed at Fort Sill, on the reservation in Indian Territory.

The four soldiers wore the regulation summer campaign uniform of Plains days. Their shirts were dark blue flannel. The light blue cavalry trousers were reinforced at the seats with white canvas. Upon their heads were high-crowned black felt hats. Upon their feet were the high cavalry boots. Scouts Chapman and Dixon wore buckskin trousers edged with long fringes, Indian style. Their blue flannel shirts had rolling sailor collars. Upon their heads were white wool hats. Upon their feet were moccasins.

Those were the army and scout uniforms in 1874.

They were armed with the stubby Springfield carbines, caliber forty-five, and Colt's six-shooter revolvers taking the same cartridge. In their belts were hunting-knives and two hundred rounds, each, of ammunition. They rode light—their only extra covering was their coats tied behind their saddles. They did not take blankets nor shelter-tents; for they had more than a hundred miles to go, every mile of it, to the North Canadian, through roving Indians, and might have to race for their lives.

Of course their horses were the best in the whole

column, and they themselves were accounted as among the bravest of the men. They well knew, like everybody else, that it would be nip and tuck to get through; but they felt that they had been honored by the orders.

So they rode out, in the evening of September 10. They trotted for the northeast, this night made a short camp, set on at daylight, covered fifty more miles before night, camped again, and at sunrise the next morning were approaching the Wichita River in what then was northern Texas but now is southwestern Oklahoma. From a prairie swell Amos Chapman pointed ahead.

"We're in luck, boys. There's the advance guard of the wagon train."

That was cheering news. They had done famously. The supplies were coming and possibly their dangerous trip had ended. They rode on, to meet the cavalry guard of the train. Scout Dixon suddenly spoke:

"Those aren't white soldiers! They're Injuns! They've seen us, too. We've got to run or fight."

"Yep; Injuns and heap Injuns," rapped Scout Chapman. "But we can't run. They'd catch us in a hurry and there's no timber to stand 'em off from. We'll have to face 'em and do the best we can."

When first sighted, the horsemen had been a mile distant, slowly riding among the grassy billows, and appearing and disappearing. They had dipped into a draw, had come out less than a half a mile away; a second, much larger party had galloped into view; all were spreading into a broad front and were tear-

330

ing forward. The sun shone on their red blankets, their painted feathers and their tufted lances.

"Look to your guns and cinches, boys," ordered Sergeant Woodall, his weathered face grimly set. "We're good for 'em. We've seen their kind before. Shall we make a running fight, Chapman?"

"No. There's too much cover for 'em. They'd lie in this grass like snakes and cut us off. Head into that first ravine, yonder. Maybe we can stand 'em off from there till help comes."

They six had only a moment for tightening their girths and unbuttoning their holster flaps.

"For'd! Gallop!" barked the sergeant. They galloped. They and the foremost Indians reached the ravine, on opposite sides, at the same time. They plunged in, could go no farther. It was the work of only an instant to vault from the saddles, leave the six horses to be held by Private Smith, and level their carbines from the brush of the rim.

The Indians volleyed from the ravine edge.

"They've got me," Private Smith called. He came running and dodging, his right arm dangling and bloody. "I had to leave the horses—couldn't hold 'em."

A moment more, and twenty-five of the Indians charged straight through the ravine, below, and up again; they were waving their blankets and yelling, and took five of the horses with them. It was done in a jiffy. Lead rained in, searching the ravine slope where the six white men were lying.

"This is no place," panted Scout Chapman. "We'll

all be dead, without a chance. The open is better, where we can see around. Come on, everybody."

"As skirmishers, men. Keep together and keep low," Sergeant Woodall ordered.

Out they lunged, into the very face of the enemy. The Indians gave way before but closed in behind.

"Fall back, fall back! Steady, now. Hold your intervals," Sergeant Woodall warned. "We'll try for shelter beyond. Mebbe we can make Gageby Creek. Don't waste a shot, but shoot to kill."

The sixth horse had followed them. Good old Baldy! An Indian dashed for him—Sergeant Woodall took quick aim and the pony scoured off, its saddle-pad empty. But Baldy whirled and was lost.

The short, thin line—four soldiers, two scouts—knelt, fired, ducked and ran a few steps, knelt and fired again. The Indians (there were one hundred and fifty) formed their circle; skimming around and around, shooting and whooping. Wherever the squad looked, they saw Indians. And they saw never a token of shelter: all the vast prairie was a sea of grass, unbroken by a tree. In spots the grass grew saddle high, but that was covert for the enemy too. When the squad halted, to rest, the Indians dismounted and commenced to crawl closer, through the grass. Then the six men had to jump up, and run on, shouting and firing. The Indians before leaped upon their horses again, and opened out; the Indians behind were afraid to shoot, for fear of killing their comrades opposite; but the Indians on either side pelted with bullets and arrows.

"None of us ever expected to get out alive," says Private Harrington. "We all determined to die hard and make the best fight possible."

The circling Indians charged to within twenty-five yards. Hanging almost under their ponies' bellies they shot from there, while those farther out daringly stood erect upon their saddles like circus riders and also fired at full speed; then racing in closer they swung low and fired again. Wherever the six men faced, before, behind, right, left, there the scurrying riders were.

They were Comanches and Kiowas. The Comanches were noted as the most skillful horsemen of the plains. They all were having fun. A medicine-man appeared to be their leader. He wore a head-dress of buffalo-horns and an eagle-feather trail streaming to his pony's tail. Time after time he charged to within twenty-five yards, at the head of his warriors, firing with a pistol and urging the braves to ride over the white men.

"Never mind him," Scout Chapman said. "He's harmless; he can't hit anything. Tend to the others."

The fight had begun at six in the morning. The long, long day slipped slowly by; the sun had changed from east to west, and the hour was four o'clock. By this time the six men were pretty well worn out. Private Smith's right arm was useless, but he shot left-handed with his revolver. Of the two hundred cartridges apiece, only a few were left. The Indians knew; they were growing even bolder. They all had dismounted, except the medicine-man, and were skulking through

333

the grass. They had no fear that the white men could get away.

The medicine-man rode up once more, this time to within twenty yards. As he passed he taunted and fired his pistol. That was his last challenge, for Scout Dixon answered with a sudden bullet. Reeling, the medicine-man galloped away and they never saw *him* again.

But the end seemed near. No help had signaled. The Colonel Miles column was thirty-six hours' distant. Something had to be done before dark.

"You see that little knoll yonder?" gasped Amos Chapman. "We've got to make it. If we're caught here in this grass we're dead before morning. Now, all together, and don't stop. There we'll stay."

They advanced by steady rushes. The Indians knew. One by one they vaulted upon their ponies and dashed across the route. The six shot briskly and carefully, to clear the way. Fully twenty of the saddle-pads were emptied by the time the riders had reached a patch of tall grass which commanded the trail to the knoll. The ponies raced on and were rounded up by the squaws who followed the fight.

That was good shooting, and seemed to discourage the other Indians from trying for the grass, but they pressed hard behind, driving the white men on. Rear as well as front had to be protected, and an hour was consumed in approaching the knoll.

Then, with the knoll almost within grasp, up from the tall grass leaped the twenty or more Indians supposed to be dead. From fifty yards they poured in a smashing volley. Down crumpled Private Smith, in a heap. Sergeant Woodall was shot through the side, John Harrington through the hip, Peter Roth through the shoulder. It had been an Indian trick. The warriors had purposely tumbled from their ponies, here; the warriors behind had purposely driven the white men within short range.

But the five gained the knoll; they had to leave Private Smith for dead.

On the top of the knoll there was an old buffalo wallow—a shallow cup like a small circus ring. The cup was only a foot or two deep, but the grassy rim helped. The Indians veered from the black muzzles resting upon the ring, and drew off, to wait and jeer, and form another circle.

"We mustn't show we're wounded, boys," Sergeant Woodall ordered, sick with his own pain. "Move about, act lively; we'll lick 'em yet. And save your lead for close quarters."

"Smith's not dead! I see him stirring!" cried somebody. "There he is! But he can't make in."

"They'll get him after dark, then," groaned Private Roth. "That's tough, fellows. I'd rather he was dead."

Amos Chapman laid down his carbine.

"They sha'n't get him. You boys keep those infernal redskins off me and I'll run down and pick him up and fetch him back before they can stop me."

Without waiting for answer, he dashed out, and down the little slope. He and Scout Dixon were the only two not disabled.

George Smith was lying seventy or seventy-five yards out. It was a long way to go, and a longer way back under a load. But Amos reached him, before the Indians knew what was up. Then—

"He wasn't a large man, one hundred and sixty or seventy pounds," said Scout Amos, afterward, "but I declare he seemed to weigh a ton. Finally I lay down and got his chest across my back, and his arms around my neck, and then got up with him. It was as much as I could do to stagger under him, for he couldn't help himself a bit. By the time I'd made twenty or thirty yards, about fifteen Indians came for me at full speed on their ponies. They all knew me [he had been on their reservation], and yelled, 'Amos! Amos! We got you now, Amos!' I pulled my pistol, but I couldn't hold Smith on my back with one hand, so I let him drop. The boys in the buffalo wallow opened up just at the right time, and I opened too, with my pistol. There was a tumbling of ponies and a scattering of Indians, and in a minute they were gone. I got Smith again and made my best time in, but before I could reach the wallow another gang came for me. I had only one or two ca'tridges left in my pistol, so I didn't stop to fight, but ran for it. When I was in about twenty yards of the wallow a little old scoundrel that I'd fed fifty times rode almost on to me and fired. I fell, with Smith on top of me; thought I'd stepped into a hole. The Indians didn't stay around there a minute; the boys kept it red-hot; so I jumped up, picked up Smith, and got safe into the wallow."

There—

"You're hurt, Amos! You're hurt bad, man!"

That was Billy Dixon.

"No, I'm not. Why?" panted Amos.

"You aren't? Why, look at your leg!"

Sure enough! One leg was shot in two at the ankle joint, and Scout Chapman had run twenty yards, with Private Smith pick-a-back—dragging his loosened foot and stepping at every stride on the end of the leg-bone!

"I never knew it," he said. And strange to add, from that day onward he never felt any pain.

The six were together again. Private Smith was conscious, but couldn't handle himself. He was fatally wounded. That didn't daunt his courage.

"Prop me sitting, boys," he begged. "Put me up where I'll do some good. You can shoot from behind me and I'll stop a few bullets, anyway."

"We'll not use you like a dead horse."

But he insisted on sitting with a pistol in his lap. He would have sat on top of the wallow, if they had let him. Amos Chapman tried to conceal his broken ankle; not a man there gave out a sign of wounds, to the enemy. While Billy Dixon dug with his knife and tin cup, the four others hastened hither-thither, serving the carbines. The Indians circled closer, swerving in and out, firing. It looked like a combat to the death. But the earth had been dug out and piled up, and just before sunset the Indians suddenly wheeled and raced away.

Pretty soon distant shooting was heard. Troops were coming? Rescue was due! No; for the darkness

337

gathered, and although the Indians did not appear, no soldiers appeared, either.

This night a cold rain drenched the wallow and all the country around. The six had no food; their rations had been in the saddle-pockets of the horses. They would have had no water, except for the rain. They drank and washed in the puddles that collected; but they all, save Billy Dixon, were wounded, and the puddles colored red.

They did their best for George, who lay dying. For the rest there was nothing but watching and waiting, and wondering what would happen in the morning. They had scarcely two dozen cartridges.

At last the day dawned, lowering and dark and wet. No Indians were in sight; nothing was in sight but the sodden grass and the equally cheerless sky. George was dead; four out of their remaining five were so sore and stiffened that they could barely move.

"I'm going to leave you, boys," spoke Billy Dixon. "I'm not hurt yet, and it's up to me to take the back trail and find Miles. If I get through I'll find him within thirty-six hours. If you don't hear from him with relief soon after that, you'll know I didn't get through. But there's a chance."

They agreed. Scout Dixon refused to take more than four cartridges. That gave them five or six apiece, for the defence of the wallow. As he explained, if once he was surrounded fifty cartridges would be the same as four. He could shoot only one at a time, and the Indians would kill him.

So he strode bravely away, in a drizzle, and presently vanished. Sergeant Woodall, shot in the side; Private Harrington, shot in the hip; Private Roth, shot in the shoulder; and Scout Chapman, his ankle shot off, peered and listened and waited.

They had waited about an hour when through the mist they saw an Indian cautiously riding in. He was reconnoitering the wallow. Their hearts sank. They kept quiet until he was within point-blank range—they could see his red blanket, rolled beneath his saddle.

"I'll get him," Sergeant Woodall uttered; took good, long aim, and fired. But he was shaky, the light was poor, and he killed only the horse.

"No matter. An Injun afoot is an Injun out of business and needs another Injun to give him a lift," Scout Chapman consoled.

Listen! Scarcely had the crashing report of the carbine rolled across the prairie and the horse fallen kicking, when from the spot where the rider had been pitched there welled the clear notes of a cavalry trumpet: "Officers' Call!"

What? Private Roth scrambled to his feet.

"That man was no Indian, sergeant! He's a trumpeter—he's a cavalry trumpeter—he's signaling us! Thank God you didn't hit him."

"I see others," Amos cried, craning and squinting. "Yonder; out beyond. Coming at a trot—one man ahead—another man holding his stirrups. It's Billy Dixon! Billy's back, with a troop of cavalry, and they sent that trumpeter on before to find us."

"Give 'em a round in the air, boys, and a cheer, to let 'em know we're all right," ordered Sergeant Woodall. "I can hear the bridles jingle. All together, make ready, fire!"

"Bang-g-g-g! Hooray! Hooray! Hooray!"

The trumpet gaily pealed. Answering the cheer, three troops of the Eighth Cavalry led by Major W. H. Price and the puffing Billy Dixon surged in.

The "Fight of the Privates," or "Twenty-five to One," as it is known in army annals, had gloriously ended.

CHAPTER XXII

BUFFALO BILL AND YELLOW HAND (1876)

A PLAINS-DAY DUEL

THE war parties of Kiowas, Comanches and Southern Cheyennes from the Indian Territory reservation rode about for a year, plundering settlers, fighting the soldiers, and trying to drive the buffalo-hunters off the range. Colonel Miles had charge of the campaign against them, which extended through the summer of 1874, and the winter, and well into the spring of 1875. Many brave deeds were done.

The Southern Cheyennes surrendered first, in March. Then the Kiowas and Comanches began to appear at Fort Sill, Indian Territory, and give themselves up. Chief Quana's Antelope Eaters were the last. They surrendered in June.

So the Military Department of the Missouri seemed a little more quiet; a few bands of outlaw Indians still roved in southwestern Kansas, southern Colorado, New Mexico and northern Texas, but the buffalo-hunters again established their camps as they pleased. General Sheridan, the commander of the whole western country to the Rocky Mountains, had said that the only way to bring real peace was to kill off the buffalo; then the Indians would have to stay on the reservations, or starve.

341

Trouble now thickened in the north, especially in the Department of Dakota and in Wyoming of the Department of the Platte. Forts had been planned in Chief Red Cloud's Powder River country of Wyoming, and miners were entering the Sioux and Northern Cheyennes' hunting reserve of the famous Black Hills of South Dakota. Another railroad, the Northern Pacific, was about to cross the northern buffalo range.

On their reservations in South Dakota the Sioux and Cheyennes were getting restless. Chief Crazy Horse and Sitting Bull the medicine worker stayed far outside, to hunt and fight as free men. They refused to lead their bands in, and warriors on the Dakota reservations kept slipping away, to join them.

In the spring of 1876 General George Crook, the Gray Fox, commanding the Department of the Platte, at Omaha, and General Alfred H. Terry, commanding the Department of Dakota, at St. Paul, started out to round up the Crazy Horse and Sitting Bull bands, in the Powder River and Big Horn Valley country of northern Wyoming and southeastern Montana. General John Gibbon was to close in, with another column, from Fort Ellis, Montana, on the west.[1]

Among the troops ordered to unite with General Crook's main column on the march, were the fighting Fifth Cavalry, with headquarters at Fort Hays, Hays City, Kansas, on the Kansas Pacific Railway half way between Fort Leavenworth and Denver. Their commander was Lieutenant-Colonel (brevet Major-General) Eugene A. Carr.

[1] For the story of Sitting Bull, see "Boys' Book of Indian Warriors."

The Fifth were glad to go. They already had made a great record on the plains, protecting the Union Pacific and the Kansas Pacific railroads; were just back from scouting against the Apaches in Arizona; and now they eagerly unpacked their campaign kits for another round. "Buffalo Bill" Cody, their old chief-of-scouts, was sent for, in the East where he had been acting on the stage with Texas Jack. He came in a hurry, and was given three cheers.

The Fifth Cavalry were to rendezvous at Cheyenne. The four companies at Fort Hays went by railroad, first to Denver and then north to Cheyenne. On the seventh of June there they were. They marched north to old Fort Laramie. Here the regiment was ordered to guard the great Sioux and Cheyenne trail that crossed country from the South Dakota reservations to the hostile Powder River and Big Horn villages.

There were several skirmishes, but the traveling Indians got away. On July 1 the new colonel joined the regiment. He was Brevet Major-General Wesley Merritt, from General Sheridan's staff at Chicago division headquarters. As he was a full colonel, he outranked Lieutenant-Colonel Carr, and became commander.

On July 6 terrible word was received from Fort Laramie. Buffalo Bill first announced it, as he came out of General Merritt's tent.

"Custer and five companies of the Seventh have been wiped out of existence, on the Little Big Horn, by the Sioux. It's no rumor; General Merritt's got the official dispatch."

343

"What! When?"

"June 25. It's awful, boys."

Sunday, of last week! Twelve days ago, and they only just now heard! And while they had been longing for Indians, and envying other columns that might be having fights,—even a little jealous of the dashing Custer's rival Seventh, who were hunting Indians instead of watching a trail—this same Seventh had been battling for their lives.

Of course, reinforcements would be rushed in at once. The Fifth would have their chance. And sure enough, the order came for the Fifth Cavalry to march north in earnest and find the General Crook column in the Big Horn country.

The route lay from southeastern Wyoming northwest through Fort Laramie and Fort Fetterman (which was farther up the North Platte River), and on to the Big Horn. But suddenly the march was stopped. A dispatch from the Red Cloud agency of the Sioux and Cheyenne reservation said that eight hundred Cheyennes had prepared to leave on the next day, Sunday, July 16, to join Crazy Horse and Sitting Bull.

There was only one thing for General Merritt to do: throw his troops across the war-trail between the reservation and the wagon-road of the white settlers to the Black Hills, and turn the runaways back. War Bonnet Creek of extreme southwestern South Dakota, west of the Red Cloud reservation, was the place where the red trail struck the white trail; Chief-of-Scouts Buffalo Bill knew it well. The troops must be there by Sunday night. It now was Saturday noon; the

BUFFALO BILL

(From the painting by Rosa Bonheur)

distance, by round-about route, was eighty-five miles; the Cheyennes had only twenty-eight to come. General Merritt resolved to get there first.

So he did. With his seven companies of cavalry, about four hundred men, he swung back, leaving his wagon-train and a small escort to follow after. From one o'clock noon until ten o'clock at night he rode; at the end of thirty-five miles camped until three o'clock in the morning; led again by Buffalo Bill rode all day Sunday, and at nine o'clock unsaddled. in the starlight, at the war-trail crossing of War Bonnet Creek, twenty-eight miles from the reservation. The seven companies had traveled their eighty-five miles over hill and plain in thirty-one hours, and had won the race. The Cheyennes had not yet passed here.

This night Lieutenant Charles King of K troop was in charge of the outposts stationed toward the southeast, and covering the trail from the reservation. At dawn he moved his posts farther on, to a steep little hill, from which the view was better. Much farther, two miles in the south and southeast, there was a high ridge, breaking the trail from the reservation. The Cheyennes would cross it. In the southwest, or to the right from the outpost hill, there was the Black Hills wagon-road, from which the cavalry had ridden to the War Bonnet here.

Lieutenant King and Corporal Wilkinson of the guard lay upon the hill slope, watching the morning brighten upon the war-trail ridge. It was nearing five o'clock, of July 17. The Cheyennes would be coming soon.

"Look, lieutenant! There they are! The Indians!"

Yes, at last! Five or six mounted figures had appeared atop the distant ridge. The number increased rapidly. But they did not come on. They galloped wildly back and forth, dodging the slopes that opened to the west, and seeming to care not at all that they might be seen from the north.

Evidently they knew nothing of the cavalry camp. It was concealed from them, by the outpost hill and by the bluffs along the War Bonnet. Then why didn't they hasten on, if they were in a hurry to join Crazy Horse and Sitting Bull, and share in the plunder to be gained from the fights?

At five o'clock they dotted the ridge on a front of three miles. They were fascinated by something in the west. What? Colonel Merritt and Lieutenant-Colonel Carr had been notified. They arrived at the hill, and they also scanned with their field-glasses. And still—

"What ails the rascals?" That was the question.

It took half an hour of waiting and wondering, to solve the problem. Then—the wagon train! The wagon train under Lieutenant and Quartermaster William P. Hall had trundled into sight, coming in to camp by the Black Hills road toward the right, in the southwest, opposite the ridge.

There it was, a white-topped line, apparently guarded by only a few cavalry troopers; but two hundred infantry were with it and Lieutenant Hall had stowed them *in the wagons*. The Cheyennes were waiting, their mouths watering; it looked like a rich plum; they could not see inside the wagons; they would meet a double surprise—one from the cavalry gathered at the War Bonnet, the other from the infantry riding in the wagons.

"Have the men had their coffee?" General Merritt asked, not a whit excited.

"Yes, sir," replied Lieutenant and Adjutant William Forbush.

"Then let them saddle up and close in mass under the bluffs."

Buffalo Bill Cody had arrived on the hill, with two other scouts: Tait, and "Chips" whose real name was Charley White. "Chips" imitated Buffalo Bill in every way; seemed to think that Bill made the world. He was Buffalo Bill's understudy.

Scout Cody did not wear buckskin, to-day. He wore one of his stage costumes—a Mexican suit of short black velvet jacket trimmed with silver buttons and silver lace, and black velvet trousers also with silver buttons down the sides, and slashed from the knee down with bright red. His brown hair was long and curling.

"What in thunder are those vagabonds down yonder fooling about?" he growled, on a sudden.

What, indeed? Something new had cropped out. From the ridge in the southeast a long ravine ran down, crossed in front of the hill and met the wagon-road trail at the right of the hill. It and the road formed a V; the two arms of the V were separated by a stretch of high ground, and the hill was at the point of the V.

Where the ravine headed at the base of the ridge a mile and a half southeast, thirty or forty Indians had collected, all ready to dash on. But why? Ah, see! Lieutenant Hall had sent two cavalry couriers forward, with dispatches for General Merritt. Two miles distant they were galloping hard, up the road, bent upon reaching the War Bonnet. The Indians knew. The warriors in the ravine were about to follow it down to the trail and kill the couriers.

The couriers could not see the Indians, on account of the high ground between. The Indians could not now see the couriers, for the same reason. But the Lieutenant King party on the hill could see everything, on both sides. The couriers, unconscious of their danger, could not possibly escape. They were far ahead of the wagon train, they were loping steadily on—were now within a mile of the War Bonnet camp, and as if at a signal the Indians in the ravine started, pellmell, to cut them off on their way.

The two parties, couriers and warriors, were converging for the west side of the hill. It might have been a pretty race to watch, had life not been the stake. But what to do? The couriers should not be sacrificed, of course; yet to send the cavalry forward now would spoil the bigger game.

Buffalo Bill exclaimed, his eyes bright, his face aglow.

"General! Now's our chance! Why not let our party mount here out of sight, and we'll tend to those fellows, ourselves!"

"Good! Up with you, then. King, you stay here

and watch until they're close under the hill; then give the word. Come down, every other man of you, where you won't be seen."

Besides the general and Lieutenant King, the party on the hill numbered Adjutant Forbush, Lieutenant Pardee, old Sergeant Schreiber, Corporal Wilkinson, the four privates of the picket, the general's orderly private, Scouts Buffalo Bill, Tait and "Chips": twelve in all. They will charge the thirty Cheyennes; or some of them will.

Alone, Lieutenant King watched, careful to lie flat and poke only his head over the brow of the hill. Much depended upon him. If he signaled too soon, the Cheyennes would wheel and escape. If he signaled too late, they would have passed in front of the hill and attacked the two couriers.

He waited. On the farther side of the slope Buffalo Bill, Scouts Tait and "Chips" and the five privates were mounted and set for a charge. Eight, to turn the Cheyennes! Just behind Lieutenant King were the general and the two lieutenants of his staff, crouching, ready to repeat the signal. And behind them were Sergeant Schrieber and Corporal Wilkinson, on hands and knees, to pass the signal back to Buffalo Bill, at the base of the hill, and then join the fight or their company.

The Cheyennes swiftly approached, swerving through the winding ravine, intent upon striking their unconscious prey. Their feathers, their pennoned lances, their rifles, their trailing war bonnets, their brass and silver armlets, their beaded leggins, were

349

plain to Lieutenant King's field-glasses. He might read the legend painted on the leader's shield. He let them come.

They were within five hundred yards; they were within three hundred yards; they were within two hundred yards. He did not need his glasses, now. He might see them slinging their rifles and poising their lances. It was to be lance work; they did not wish to alarm the wagon train with gun-shots. One hundred yards! Half a minute more and they would be rounding the point where the ravine bordered the hill slope, and would be upon the two couriers.

Ninety yards—

"Ready, general!"

"All right. When you say."

"Now! Into 'em!"

"Now, men!"

It occurred in an instant. With cheer and thud and scramble Buffalo Bill's little detachment had spurred from the covert of the hill. The carbines spoke in a volley. General Merritt is first to the top of the hill, to gaze; Corporal Wilkinson bounds beside him, takes quick aim and fires at the Cheyenne leader in the cloud of dust below. The leader (he is a young chief) had reined his pony in a circle sharply out and to the left; he notes the group on the hill—he notes everything; he ducks to the far side of his horse and still at full speed shoots back from under his mount's neck. The bullet almost grazes General Merritt's cheek!

Down in front there was lively work for a few minutes, as Buffalo Bill's little command charged in.

The Cheyennes scattered, astonished; they turned for their main body.

"Look!" Lieutenant Forbush cried. "Look to the ridge!"

Pouring down the ridge, all the Cheyennes were coming, to the rescue and the attack.

"Send in the first company," General Merritt ordered; and with his adjutant galloped away. The real fight was about to begin.

Out upon the plain the Buffalo Bill men were chasing the Indians, knowing that the cavalry would soon follow. At a short distance the Cheyennes made another stand. Their young chief cantered out in front of them, his hand raised. He called clearly to Buffalo Bill.

"I know you, Pa-he-haska (Long Hair). If you want to fight, come and fight me."

He rode boldly up and down along his line, waiting. Buffalo Bill galloped forward alone.

"Stand back," he ordered, of the men. "Fair play."

The young chief saw him coming, and with a shout gladly hammered to the meeting. They had started one hundred and thirty yards apart. They each rode at top speed for fifty yards, when from thirty yards, as they swerved, they fired. Down plunged Buffalo Bill's horse; he had only stepped in a badger-hole. Down also plunged the chief's pony; but he was dead and the bullet that had killed him had passed through the chief's leg, first.

They sprang to their feet. They were now twenty

yards apart. The young chief tottered—they fired together, again; they had to act very quickly. The chief missed; Buffalo Bill had shot true. He leaped forward, as the chief reeled, and sank his knife to the hilt. All was over in a moment.

A great howl of rage arose from the Cheyennes. They charged, for revenge. They were a fraction of a minute too late; the cavalry were coming. As Troop K, Lieutenant King's company, tore past, Buffalo Bill waved his captured war bonnet.

"First scalp for Custer!" he shouted. Custer and the Seventh Cavalry were to be avenged.

Seeing troop after troop of blue-shirts spurring over the divide and down, the Cheyennes, every one of their eighteen hundred, turned in flight. Away they went, the cheering troopers hard after, back up the trail for the reservation. The pursuit was so hot that they threw aside their blankets, rations, whatever they might drop. They lost several ponies and two warriors besides the young chief, but they won the race and were in their reservation by noon!

Here they hid their guns and their ammunition, washed off their paint; and when at seven o'clock that evening General Merritt's tired column filed in, they were strolling about, in their fresh blankets, perfectly peaceful.

Nevertheless, they and all the other Indians on the reservation were keen to see Pa-he-haska, the white man who had killed the skillful young chief Yellow Hand in single combat. They followed Buffalo Bill about, admiringly. Yellow Hand's father, old Cut

Nose, a head chief, offered four mules in exchange for Yellow Hand's war bonnet, shield and arms; but that was not to be. Buffalo Bill saved them, and used them on the stage.

CHAPTER XXIII

THE "SIBLEY SCOUT" (1876)

A FAMOUS ARMY TALE

MEANWHILE General Crook and his main column were in camp upon Goose Creek at the head-waters of the Tongue River, at the east base of the Big Horn Mountains and Cloud Peak, northern Wyoming. They had come here from Fort Fetterman, in the southeast, and were impatiently waiting for their wagon-train and for General Merritt.

The Gray Fox's northward march to meet General Terry had been stopped by the Sioux in the Battle of the Rosebud, fought June 17. The Chief Crazy Horse warriors had proved very strong. General Crook rather believed that he did not have a force large enough to break through to find the principal villages of Sitting Bull and Crazy Horse, or to join General Terry, in the Rosebud country south of the Yellowstone River; so with his wounded he had fallen back from southern Montana into northern Wyoming. Here he waited for supplies and reinforcements.

Up to July 10 he did not know that General Custer and almost half the Seventh Cavalry had been killed, to a man; but he felt that, with the Sioux so bold, something was happening.

His column was composed of five troops of the

Second Cavalry, ten troops of the Third Cavalry, two companies of the Fourth Infantry, and three companies of the Ninth Infantry: about one thousand soldiers. The Sioux had attacked him; they were more than he expected; things did not look good to the Gray Fox.

This waiting was vexatious as well as tiresome. General Crook was a fighter; he never quit a trail and he liked to travel fast and light, and strike the enemy. He knew that while he waited, the Sioux were gaining strength and choosing positions. Finally, on the night of July 5, he determined to send out a scouting detachment, and see if he could not locate the whereabouts of the nearest Sioux village.

Young Second Lieutenant Frederick William Sibley, born in Texas and appointed to West Point from Georgia, was selected to command the detachment. He was under twenty-five, had graduated from the Military Academy in 1874 and been assigned to the Second Cavalry. But although of only two years' service, he was no longer a "shave-tail"; he had the name of being a fine, thorough officer and soldier. Everybody liked Lieutenant Frederick Sibley, Troop E, Second Cavalry; many of the older officers remembered his father, General C. C. Sibley, who after thirty-six years in the uniform had died two years ago.

Lieutenant Sibley was directed to take twenty-five picked men, from his regiment, and two scouts; reconnoiter northwestward along the base of the Big Horn Mountains, and find the Sioux village if he could. General Crook was exceedingly anxious to know where

Chief Crazy Horse lived when at home. The Battle of the Rosebud had been an unpleasant surprise.

The two scouts were Frank Gruard and Baptiste Pourier. Scout Gruard had been born in the Sandwich Islands. He had ridden pony express in Montana. Chief Crazy Horse's Sioux had captured him, and had thought, by reason of his dark skin and straight black hair, that he was a Sioux, himself. So instead of abusing him, they rejoiced, and kept him, in order that he might learn the Sioux language again.

He stayed with Chief Crazy Horse, until a chance of escape came. Then he got away, and for a number of years he was one of the most valuable scouts in the army. He knew Wyoming and Montana like a book, and could read sign and weather as well as any Indian. And he was brave.

Baptiste Pourier was half French, half Sioux. He was called "Big Bat," to separate him from another Baptiste guide and trailer—"Little Bat," a half-Sioux boy at Fort Fetterman. "Little Bat" was now with General Merritt's Fifth Cavalry.

Packer John Becker of the pack-mule outfit, a frontiersman who had been a guide in the country, was added to the scouts. At the last moment John F. Finerty, a plucky newspaper man who was reporting the campaign for the Chicago *Times,* asked permission to go, also.

He had not heard about the proposed trip until that morning, July 6; but he did not wish to miss any excitement, and therefore he applied at once to General Crook. The general hesitated a minute. He well

356

knew that it was likely to be a dangerous scout, and that the Sioux were no joke. At last he said shortly:

"All right, sir. But I warn you that you're liable to get into more trouble than you bargain for."

That did not daunt the alert John Finerty. He already had fought side by side with the troopers, and was looked upon as a soldier although not in uniform. No man in the column was more popular. He hastened to tell Lieutenant Sibley, his friend. Lieutenant Sibley was glad. Other officers asked him what kind of an obituary they should write for him. Captain E. R. Wells, of Troop E—the Sibley troop—only remarked, without a smile:

"Orderly, bring Mr. Finerty a hundred rounds of Troop E ammunition."

This sounded like business, to Reporter Finerty.

They all rode out at noon; made thirteen miles and camped to rest the horses for a night march. Scout Gruard thought that they would not have to go far to find Indians. Two or three nights before he and Big Bat had reconnoitered forward twenty miles and had seen several parties of Sioux, only that distance from the main camp. Evidently General Crook was being watched.

At sunset the little detachment started on. In the dusk Big Bat imagined that he caught sight of a mounted Indian spy surveying them from a shallow ravine. Frank Gruard dashed for the place; but the object disappeared and he discovered nothing.

"Might have been an Indian, but we think maybe only an elk," he said.

Anyway, the mystery was not very comforting. The column were forbidden to talk; they rode on, northward, through the long grass of the rich bottoms; the two scouts led, Scout Gruard every now and again halting, to scan about from the high points.

The full moon rose at eight o'clock, and the lonely land of sage and grass and willows and pines and rocks stretched silvery; on the west the snowy tips of the Big Horn Mountains glistened.

Nothing happened. About two o'clock in the morning Lieutenant Sibley ordered camp. They were forty miles from General Crook, and near ahead, over the next divide, lay the upper end of the Valley of the Little Big Horn in the Rosebud country.

"We will find the Sioux villages in there, all right," promised Frank Gruard. "And," he added again, "we won't have far to go, either."

Yes, that had been the place; but General Custer and his Seventh Cavalry already had found the villages, and the Sioux were on the outlook to keep back other soldiers while the villages moved elsewhere. Young Lieutenant Sibley and his thirty men were advancing into a hornets' nest.

They had camped at the Montana line. With dawn they proceeded on very cautiously, through a broken country. They were approaching the stronghold of the Sioux. By sunrise they were about to strike the Little Big Horn, where it issues from the rough foothills bordering the north end of the Big Horn Range. Any moment, now, they might discover the Sioux, or, worse, the Sioux might discover them.

Scout Gruard motioned to Lieutenant Sibley to halt the column; he himself rode up a rocky outcrop, left his horse, and climbed afoot to the top; he lay flat, and crawled, and just peeking over he leveled his field-glasses upon the country beyond.

The little column watched him keenly. What would he see? He certainly saw something of great interest, for with his hand behind him he beckoned to Baptiste, below. Baptiste hastened, and crawled to Frank's side. They both gazed, through their glasses, between the boulders. They turned; ran, crouching, for their horses; mounted, and back they came at a tearing gallop.

"Be quick!" Scout Gruard rapped. "Follow me for your lives."

Everybody heard. Not another word was spoken. The soldiers who had been easing their horses vaulted into the saddle. Away they all raced, following Baptiste westward through the foothills. The route was rough, but he fled straight across red sandstone ledges, some dropping six and seven feet, in the arroyos and draws, until he rounded to behind a bare bluff.

He, Baptiste and the lieutenant immediately left the men and horses and climbed for a look at the back trail. Reporter Finerty soon overtook them, to find out what was the matter—although he had no doubts about it.

To this time only Frank and Baptiste knew, apparently. But when they four had reached a viewpoint, and had their glasses out, the lieutenant calmly asked:

"What did you see, Frank?"

"Only Sitting Bull's war-party! I could have told they'd be here around the Little Big Horn, without our coming."

Sitting Bull's war-party! That meant Sioux, with a vengeance. Lieutenant Sibley said nothing. Reporter Finerty caught his breath. They focused their glasses upon their back trail, and upon the country north.

They had no need of glasses. There they were— the Sioux, riding up the valley. Little bunches of warriors appeared: advance scouts mounting the high ground here and yonder, surveying before. Their figures, in full war costume, were outlined against the sky. Down they rode, and the others followed, until the low hills and the draws seemed to be covered as the wide front cantered forward in a half circle extending from the north into the east.

"Haven't seen us, I think," Scout Gruard remarked. "Don't act like it. If they don't strike our trail, we may be all right."

The four among the boulders could only wait. The Sioux were closing in. It was scarcely possible that they would miss the fresh trail of the thirty-one horses. The advance warriors riding southward were almost at the spot where the trail had turned in flight for the foothills. Reporter Finerty heard his heart beat furiously. They all stiffened. A few moments would tell the tale.

Aha! An Indian in a red blanket had reined his pony short, and was staring at the ground. Now he began to trot in a small circle. A signal! The Indians on right and left of him hastened in.

"Here's where we'd better look out," Scout Gruard sharply warned. "That fellow has found our trail, and they'll be after us in five minutes."

"What's the best thing to do, then?" coolly asked Lieutenant Sibley. The scouts knew the country, and in a pinch their advice was good.

"Well, we've just one chance of escape. That is, to make into the mountains and try to cross them. But we'll have to prepare for the worst."

There was no escape into the open; the Sioux blocked the way. They had the detachment pocketed against the mountains, fifty miles from help. To attempt a running fight, or a stand, would result in a surround, with the enemy pouring in a fire from every rise or else cutting off the water supply.

"Very well," the lieutenant agreed.

They went down to where the troopers and Packer John Becker were waiting and wondering.

Lieutenant Sibley spoke briefly. They had read bad news in his grave young face.

"Men, the Indians have discovered us. We'll have to do some fighting. If we can make an honorable escape, all together, we'll do it. But if that proves impossible, let no man surrender. Die in your tracks, for these Indians will show no mercy."

The bronzed countenances of a few of the men paled a trifle; but as soldiers they were ready to do their best, obey orders and trust in their leaders.

"All right, sir." That was all they said.

"Mount."

Away they trotted at a smart pace, Scout Gruard guiding, west by north, directly for the nearest slope of the first range. Carbines thumped, bridles jingled, leather squeaked, the horses' hoofs clattered on the sandstone ledges. They emerged from the last of the reddish defiles and proceeded to climb—up, up, up into the pines. The going was steep, and the horses puffed and groaned.

Gazing back, they might see the Sioux a mile behind, and below, bunched in council, and looking and gesturing. They appeared uncertain whether to pursue.

Soon Frank turned into an old, narrow pony trail, pointing still westward as if to cross the first range.

"This is an old Sioux hunting trail," he called, over his shoulder, to the lieutenant and Reporter Finerty. "It leads clear to the snowy range. If we can get there our chances are pretty fair."

The trail was good. They pushed on at a trot, never sparing the horses. They began to feel more hopeful. The Sioux were out of sight; there were no sounds of pursuit; was it possible that they had been let off? As everybody knew, the Plains Indians rarely ventured far into the mountains, except on quick forays against enemies who did not expect them.

After five miles more, Scouts Gruard and Big Bat stopped. The column had climbed almost to the top of the first range.

"Do you want to rest the horses, lieutenant?"

"Yes, if it's safe. What do you think?"

"Bat and I've about decided that those fellows have quit. We've given them the slip. They're not likely to risk attacking us in the high country. So you can take a breathing spell. We've a hard trip ahead."

"Dismount," Lieutenant Sibley ordered.

The word was welcome. The horses were badly winded, and the men were hungry and thirsty, for they had had an early breakfast and the sun beat down hotly.

Noon camp was made here in a little park, where amidst the surrounding trees the grass grew long and the flowers nodded. The sweaty horses were unsaddled and picketed short, to graze; coffee was set upon small fires, to boil; sentries had been posted, and the other men were permitted to stretch out, in the shade.

Everything seemed very peaceful, but—!

At any rate, they all might talk and laugh and sip their coffee and doze, and believe that they had outwitted the Sioux. In about an hour and a half they saddled up and rode on, still heading from the Sioux and into the mountains.

Where they were going, nobody knew save Scouts Gruard and Big Bat. Frank led, with Big Bat close behind him. Then came the lieutenant, and Reporter Finerty, and in long single file the troopers, with Packer John Becker closing the rear.

It was a splendid country, of clustered pines, scattered rocks and huge ledges, sunny, flowery parks, cold streams in the valleys, and tremendous, long slopes rising, before, to the white crest of the snowy main range of the Big Horn Mountains.

In mid-afternoon they were leisurely winding through a park lying between the front range and the main range. There was timber on the left, or southwest; rocks and timber on the right; and timber before, with the snow caps towering above.

Not a sound had been heard, to signal danger—when suddenly John Becker spurred up along the file, from the rear.

"The Indians, lieutenant! Here they are!"

What! Yes! War bonnets were moving rapidly through the trees and high rocks, quartering behind on the right. The troopers quickened, to close their intervals—for the column had strung out. Every hand dropped to its carbine butt.

"Keep well to the left, against that timber," shouted Scout Gruard.

"Bang-g-g!" He had been answered by a volley. There were Indians among the rocks and trees, on the right, within two hundred yards. The bullets whined and stung; wounded horses reared and plunged—Reporter Finerty's mount stumbled to its knees.

"To the left, men! Quick!"

Half wheeling, they dashed for the edge of the timber, there; gained it safely; under cover of the branches sprang to earth and faced about, guns ready. Lieutenant Sibley took command.

"Give them a few shots, sergeant, till we can tie our horses."

At the carbine reports the Indians in sight, out in the park, dived for shelter.

"Now tie your horses short, to the trees, men."

That was done.

"As skirmishers. Take intervals right and left. Keep under cover. Fire carefully, only when you see a mark. Don't waste ammunition."

The skirmish line ran in a semi-circle, from southeast to northwest, through the edge of the timber. There were many fallen trees, as if a storm or a forest fire had swept through; that closed the way to the horses, but furnished good breastworks.

The battle had opened in a hurry. The bullets from the Indians pattered like hail, sending the bark flying, and drumming upon the bare trunks of the breastworks. The heavy carbines stanchly replied. Horses reared again, and screamed and fell, kicking. The Indians were making certain of the cavalry mounts. That was the first job—to put the enemy afoot.

The attackers were Sioux and Cheyennes both. How they had come in so cunningly, was a mystery. Gruard thought it was an accident; they were not the same Indians who had been sighted, below. But that cut no figure.

The head chief wore white buckskin and an imposing war bonnet. He might be glimpsed, now and then, as he darted about, placing his warriors.

"White Antelope, that," asserted Gruard. "Eh, Bat?"

"Think so," Big Bat nodded.

"And he's a good one; among the best of the Cheyennes. Pass the word to get him, when we can."

After that, every carbine sought for White Ante-

lope. His time came when he led a charge. The
bullets seemed to mow him down, together with his
warriors. Whether he had been killed or not, was a
question; but he did not appear again.

The Indians tried no more charges across the park.
However, they were growing in strength. They were
extending their line; the bullets and yells arrived from
east, north and west. The line had crossed the head
of the park and the foot, and was closing in on three
sides. The detachment were being out-flanked.

More than half the horses were down. The rifle
fire never slackened. Matters looked very serious.
An Indian called to Gruard.

"Hello, Standing Bear! You are all dead. Do you
think there are no men but yours in this country?"

Civilian Finerty had many thoughts while he aimed,
fired, and loaded. He remembered the warning by
General Crook. He rather wished that he had stayed
safe in the big camp. He almost wished that he had
never left Chicago. How far away Chicago seemed!
There, people were walking about the streets—the
Times presses were thundering out first editions—
and here, in the Big Horn Mountains of Montana he
and half a company of United States soldiers were
fighting for their lives.

He did not so much mind meeting death, in a charge,
or in the excitement of open battle; but to be hemmed
in, and helpless—to be disabled, and captured, by
Indians—!

"No surrender!"

That was the word being passed now.

366

"Every man save one shot for himself."

They grimly buckled to the task of holding out as long as they could. By the volume of yells and the storms of bullets the force of the Sioux and Cheyennes certainly had increased. One big charge from the three sides, and the end would come.

Reporter Finerty held a hand upon his shoulder. It was that of Private Rufus, who had been his skirmish-line neighbor, and who had stolen to him.

"The rest are retiring, sir. Lieutenant Sibley says for us to do the same."

That was so. The line, except for half a dozen troopers, was cautiously creeping back through the trees and logs. Lieutenant Sibley, his lips set firmly, was still in position, to be the last.

"Take all your ammunition from your saddle-bags," he said quickly. "We're going to abandon what horses we have left. The Indians are getting all around us; our only chance, Gruard thinks, is to make back through the timber while we can, on foot."

Scout Gruard and his partner, Big Bat, were waiting impatiently.

"If the grass wasn't wet from that last thunder storm the Indians would have smoked us out long ago. It's drying fast. We can't hold our position; even if we got a man through to Crook, he couldn't bring help in time. There's nothing to gain by staying. Sibley hates to retreat, but if he doesn't go now not a man can escape. As for horses, those fellows have seized every pass on three sides, and they'll soon have the fourth side. That's where they're working to. So, knowing Indians and knowing the country, we put it up to him, for yes or no. He's agreed.''

It was planned to have the rear guard keep firing, until the horses had been stripped of ammunition. One by one the men dodged back, among the trees and rocks. The last man, and the lieutenant, came breathless; the single file followed Gruard and Big Bat at a trot, afoot, and only the few horses were left, as a blind. The horses were doomed, but there was no other way.

The file had hastened for a mile, through the fallen timber, through an icy cold stream, up a steep slope slippery with boulders and pine needles, and had paused, to catch breath, when they heard, below and behind, a series of brisk volleys and a chorus of wild yells; then, spattering shots, and silence.

The Indians had charged. Escape had been made by not more than fifteen minutes of grace! That had been a close call; Gruard and Big Bat had known what they were talking about. No one could help but shiver at the thought of having stayed down there, with the horses.

''They'll search a while. That means we're safe for a bit,'' panted Frank. ''Now come on. We'd better lose no time in putting more rocks between them and us.''

Even in the hurry some of the men chuckled over the game that had been played on the enemy. The Sioux and the Cheyennes would be sorely disappointed in their hope of scalps. They had made a water haul; had killed the horses, and gained nothing.

It was a tough climb in a country where white man apparently had never been before. Gruard and Big Bat did not slacken. The mountains opposed with timber and rock and precipices. All the file gasped; the air was heavy with thunderstorms; overcoats, blouses, everything was thrown aside, except the rifles and the ammunition. The Indians might follow, and might not; but distance was the only safety.

The two scouts led without another stop until midnight; then the little company camped amidst the rocks on the very top of a peak. A terrific storm of wind and hail swept over them, so that the falling trees sounded like the crashes of artillery. The temperature almost reached freezing; yet this was no time for complaining. They might have been lying, colder still, among the horses.

At first daylight they stumbled on. Gruard and Big Bat saw no rest until within touch of General Crook. The course turned southward, along the crests of the mighty range. They arrived at a canyon so steep that the tired troopers could not clamber down into it. Frank found a sort of a trail by way of a valley, to a crossing of the river at the canyon's bottom; and they needs must hustle madly, to cross and get out before any Indians discovered them in the pocket.

The main camp was now twenty-five miles southeast, Gruard thought. The plains were in sight through the gaps; but there would likely be Indians down on those plains. Gruard and Big Bat guided up the opposite side of the canyon. They had to cling like squirrels, following a sheep trail not more than a foot wide, five hundred feet above the stream, and two hundred feet below the rim.

But they got out. Gruard swung more eastward, toward the foothills. Beyond the foothills lay the camp of the Crook column. Presently the men were gasping for water. Everybody was pinched with hunger, for there had been nothing to eat and nothing to drink, since they had retreated just in time from the net.

It was decided to venture into a valley of the foothills, and find water. They went slipping and sliding down the slope, carpeted with the dried pine needles, and treacherous with loose gravel, and drank in haste. But Frank was still suspicious. His senses were keen. He instantly led them back into the first belt of timber, above; and on a sudden, with a hiss of warning, he flung himself flat. Down they all sprawled.

Just below, wellnigh at the very spot they had left, there were more Indians: Sioux!

The Sioux were riding, arrayed for war, in open order, like scouts for a larger party behind. If they struck the trail to the water and back, that would mean another fight. It seemed horrible to be cut off, again, when so near help; the location of the General Crook camp was plain in view, off there twenty miles to the east.

But the brave soldiers had grown too desperate to care. They were tired out, and determined to sell their lives dearly. Lieutenant Sibley motioned.

He and the two scouts crawled to position on a little

knoll; the others followed, and took their posts. Reporter Finerty crept to his commander's side.

"We're in hard luck again," young Lieutenant Sibley whispered. "But we'll show those red scoundrels how white men can fight and die, if necessary. Men," he said, "we have a good place; let every shot count on an Indian."

Yes, the spot was a strong one, for defense. On one side there was a stream, bounded by a lofty cliff, over-hanging. On the other side there was an open slope, with no cover for the attackers. On the rear there were a mass of boulders, handy in case of retreat. In front the timber was very thin. And where the party lay, there were plenty of rocks and trees, and considerable down timber, but not enough to be dangerous from a fire.

The Sioux warriors kept on, riding slowly; on, and on, their eyes searching the country. Hurrah! They did not stop; they had passed outside the trail; they were on the flank of the main body; no warriors followed; the scouts and soldiers and Civilian Finerty let down their rifle hammers to half cock. There would be no fight.

It had been such a strain that now everybody except the two scouts went to sleep, while Frank and Big Bat stayed on watch. At dusk Lieutenant Sibley spoke with fresh energy:

"We'll strike out of the mountains and make a night march to the camp. Might as well do it first as last. We've got to have something to eat; but we can't hunt here, or we'd call in the Sioux by our shots."

They descended, through the gathering darkness; reached the plains, and forded Big Goose Creek where snow-water ran breast high. Sergeant Cornwell and Private Collins could not swim, would not try wading, and had to be left in the bushes. The lieutenant promised to send back for them. He dared not delay. Camp was still a dozen miles across the plains.

The next six miles required four hours, to travel. The men were very weak, and their boots were in tatters. At five o'clock in the morning they saw more Indians, and the Indians saw them.

"Let 'em come for us if they want us," the lieutenant growled. "We're going on to camp, and we'll fight."

But the Indians hesitated, and stayed at a distance.

At half-past six they sighted two cavalry horses, saddled and grazing. The horses belonged to troopers on a hunt, and foolishly bound for the north, into the same kind of country where the detachment had been! They very willingly changed their program and galloped for the camp, with the news, and to get more mounts and supplies. The Sibley men stopped short, to lie on the ground, and wait. They were about at the end of their trail.

At eight o'clock the horses and supplies arrived. Sergeant Cornwell and Private Collins were sent for. At ten o'clock on this Sunday morning, July 9, the third day since they had ridden so jauntily out to find the Sioux, they entered camp; but they were an entirely different looking set of men.

The oldest Indian fighters in the one thousand of

rank and file agreed that it had been the narrowest escape on record, and achieved only by the skill of Scouts Frank Gruard and Big Bat Pourier, the good sense of Lieutenant Sibley, and the obedience of the men.

General Crook was away, on a hunt. Lieutenant-Colonel William B. Royall of the Third Cavalry was temporarily in command. Lieutenant Sibley wearily went to him, to report.

"We reached our objective in the Little Big Horn country, sir," he said, "and found the Indians."

"Very good, sir," Colonel Royall approved. And he added, with a twinkle in his eyes: "It looks as though you did! Or else they found *you*."

Reporter Finerty went through the campaign with the Crook column; he had many other adventures; but whatever they were, as long as he lived his hair bristled when he gazed back, with a shudder, upon the most perilous adventure of all: the "Sibley Scout."

THE END